Praise for *Ask, Measure, Learn*

Big data will soon become one of the most important assets of most companies. Using big data will be an integral part of many business models. Right now, though, the vast majority of companies simply sit on a heap of dark data, without strategy, uncertain how to interrogate them and unable to interpret the signals they might receive. In *Ask, Measure, Learn*, Lutz and Soumitra give companies key pointers to understanding the big data challenge, and for asking the right questions when it comes to tackling it.

—TIM WEBER, SVP EDELMAN, FORMER BUSINESS AND TECHNOLOGY EDITOR, BBC NEWS INTERACTIVE

Big data is an opportunity that individuals and enterprises alike are grappling to comprehend and leverage in its entirety. The book skillfully takes readers on a journey from understanding the concept of big data to deriving value from it.

—N. R. NARAYANA MURTHY, COFOUNDER, INFOSYS

Big data is a mystery, with too many answers to see the real one that you need. This book may change that. And it is fun to read as well.

—BEN VERWAAYEN, FORMER CEO, ALCATEL-LUCENT

This is an essential read for anyone who has to introduce big data into their company; it gives a balanced and complete view of the problem, and is written by people who not only have their finger on the pulse but are also able to see the changing coming through their extensive, worldwide network of connections.

—ALEX (SANDY) PENTLAND, PROFESSOR, MIT

Big data is perhaps the newest concept that everyone is talking about, but few really understand. *Ask, Measure, Learn* will go a long way in helping us grasp big data but also learn how to use it.

—J. FRANK BROWN, MANAGING DIRECTOR AND COO, GENERAL ATLANTIC PARTNERS

Insights, insights, insights...this is the most essential component of any kind of analytics. No matter whether it is in social media or on big data. Business leaders need insights and this book shows how to get there. *Ask, Measure, Learn* is a very helpful framework and a great collection of case studies. Use it and you will avoid any "paralysis by analysis."

—LOIC LE MEUR, CEO, LEWEB CONFERENCE

This book blows away all the myths around big data and is an excellent guide on how to use big data to create true business value. A must read for all companies facing the challenge to incorporate big data in their business strategy.

—ANNET ARIS, ADJUNCT PROFESSOR OF STRATEGY, INSEAD

I think this is the right book at the right time. The data revolution has just started. Every company that is dealing with big data or trying to become a data-driven business is searching for the V—value—in the massively growing amount of data available to them. I found very useful information in *Ask Measure Learn* and strongly recommend this book for anyone looking to define their data-driven strategies.

—UWE WEISS, CEO, BLUEYONDER

A great framework and a must read for every organization. Too often, business intelligence shoots off with data and graphs, forgetting that essentially, we are looking for insights. *Ask, Measure, Learn* helps put the business value back in the driving seat. Using very practical case studies, the authors show how easy and fun data science can be.

—STEPHAN ROPPEL, DIRECTOR OF E-COMMERCE, TCHIBO

This book helps with great examples to go from pure data to actionable Insights. A must read for everyone talking about social media or big data analytics. The concepts put forward by Lutz and Soumitra show how important it is to get the question (ask) right in order to successfully learn from the data.

—BJÖRN OGNIBENI, CEO, BUZZRANK

Recent breakthroughs in technology and the massive adoption of social media give access to unseen amounts of data. The problem: we suffer from a sensory overload and are incapable of capturing the business value of this data to effectively augment our decision making. *Ask, Measure, Learn* tackles that problem and helps business leaders to leverage this untapped opportunity to drive business value.

—BJÖRN HERMANN, CEO, COMPASS.CO

Ask, Measure, Learn

Using Social Media Analytics to Understand and Influence Customer Behavior

Lutz Finger and Soumitra Dutta

O'REILLY® Beijing · Cambridge · Farnham · Köln · Sebastopol · Tokyo

ASK, MEASURE, LEARN

by Lutz Finger and Soumitra Dutta

Printed in the United States of America.

Published by O'Reilly Media, Inc., 1005 Gravenstein Highway North, Sebastopol, CA 95472.

O'Reilly books may be purchased for educational, business, or sales promotional use. Online editions are also available for most titles (*http://my.safaribooksonline.com*). For more information, contact our corporate/institutional sales department: 800-998-9938 or *corporate@oreilly.com*.

Editors: Mary Treseler and Ann Spencer
Production Editor: Melanie Yarbrough
Copyeditor: Amanda Kersey
Proofreader: Eliahu Sussman
Indexer: Lucie Haskins
Cover Designer: Randy Comer
Interior Designer: Monica Kamsvaag
Illustrator: Rebecca Demarest

January 2014: First Edition

Revision History for the First Edition:

2014-01-22: First release

See *http://oreilly.com/catalog/errata.csp?isbn=9781449336752* for release details.

ISBN: 978-1-449-33675-2
[LSI]

To my loved Isabelle, who supported me in every line in this book.Lutz Finger

To Lourdes and Sara, whose love and support have made my life complete.Soumitra Dutta

Contents

Introduction | vii

Acknowledgments | xxv

PART I | Media Measurement by Function

1 | Marketing 3

2 | Sales 41

3 | Public Relations 67

4 | Customer Care 109

5 | Social CRM: Market Research 137

6 | Gaming the System 155

7 | Predictions 187

PART II | Build Your Own Ask-Measure-Learn System

8 | Ask the Right Question 217

9 | Use the Right Data 233

10 | Define the Right Measurement 261

PART III | Appendix

A | All Names 281

Index 293

Introduction

In April 2011, United States Special Forces descended on the hideout of Osama bin Laden, leader of the terrorist group al-Qaida. The ensuing raid killed bin Laden after over a decade of living in hiding and directing attacks by his followers. So who knew where he was located?

The answer may surprise you: *we all* did.

According to Kalev Leetaru, a researcher at the University of Illinois at Urbana-Champaign, an analysis of public news articles[1] about bin Laden pinpointed his location within 200 kilometers in diameter. In a very real sense, one of the world's most secretive hiding places may have ultimately revealed itself from the mosaic of individual data points. Each journalist had an opinion about the location, and all opinions together formed a true answer. The catch here: no survey was conducted, and no journalist was actually asked. They revealed their views about bin Laden's whereabouts through their articles. It is the power of public and unstructured data. The outcome is depicted in Figure I-1.

Figure I-1. Geocoded social media articles describe the location of Osama bin Laden. (Courtesy of Kalev Leetaru.)

1. Kalev Leetaru, "Supercomputer predicts revolution," BBC Technology, September 2011, *http://bbc.in/1kmj8VE.*

Most likely the US forces did not rely on crowdsourced wisdom like this. We know today that US governement agencies like the NSA are tapping into all kinds of different data sources, from spying on the phones of top-level politicians to tapping into everyone's communication from email providers. However, the principle is the same: actionable intelligence was derived from an aggregation of individual, and in this case, seemingly random, data points.

Herein lies the promise of what we call *big data*. It has become one of the trendiest digital buzzwords of the new millenium. It involves gathering business intelligence from the heretofore forbidden territory of data sets that are too large to curate or maintain as databases, often encompassing terabytes or even petabytes of information. One of its most compelling forms today is the use of social media data, a mirror that reveals what each and every one of us wants, needs, and prefers. This data, enriched with our clicks in the Internet, our mobile phone usage, and our location data, will create amazing insights about us and our future.

We, the authors, have for more than half a century been helping governments and NGOs draw conclusions out of big data, especially social media data. We built a company called Fisheye Analytics that offers a software as a service that analyzes media data around the world. We analyze about 70 TB of textual data monthly for our clients. But we have learned as well that it is not the *size* that matters, but rather the right *question* and the right *data*.

In this book we want to serve you as well and show you on a case-by-case basis how to gain insights out of data. It is not about data as such. It is not about size as such. It is about the value that data can bring.

The Fourth "V" of Data

Data has always had strategic value, but with the magnitude of data available today and our capability to process it has become a new form of asset class. In a very real sense, data is now the new equivalent of oil or gold. And today we are seeing a data boom rivaling the Texas oil boom of the 20th century or the San Francisco gold rush of the 1800s. It has spawned an entire industry, and has attracted a great deal of business press in recent years.

This new asset class of *big data* is commonly described by what we call "three V's."[2] Big data is anything that is high volume and high velocity and includes a high *variety* of information. Next to those traditional three "V's," we add would like to add a fourth "V," value. This is what everyone is looking for, and this is why big

2. Diya Soubra, "The 3Vs that define Big Data," Data Science Central, July 2012, *http://bit.ly/KoNxlM*.

data today gets so much attention. *Big data* can take the form of structured data, such as financial transactions, or unstructured data such as photographs or blog posts. It can be crowdsourced, as in the case of Osama bin Laden, or individually gathered like any insurance company has done for a long time. Paradoxically this value of big data is normally represented in *small data*. Such as "Yes/No" on the question, "Shall I buy this company or not?" or on a geolocation code for the whereabouts of Osama bin Laden. The quest for value is the quest to reduce *big* data so that it becomes "valuable" data.

Big data has also been fueled by one of the biggest trends of the 21st century: social media. Our collective discussions, comments, likes, dislikes, and networks of social connections are now all data, and their scale is massive. If all Facebook users were a country, it would be one of the largest in the world with over a billion active users, while Twitter users send millions of tweets per month as of early 2013. It is now the first time that we can study human interaction and human discussions in such depth. Each tweep (Twitter user) or each user in Sina Weibo[3] leaves a trail of publicly accessible data behind. But also our private communication on Facebook or Qzone[4] can create great insights: What did we search for? What did we read? Where did we go? Who do we associate with? What do we eat? What do we purchase? In short, *any* imaginable human interaction can be found and studied on the social networks. If we can data mine all that information, the results seem to be limitless. It seems even possible that we can find where Osama bin Laden may be hiding. Thus social media data will kill every secret.

At the same time, like every other trend in technology in our lifetime, there is a great deal of *hype* surrounding big data and social media. At the onset of social media analytics, people believed that social media could be used to convince anyone of anything if it was just analyzed correctly. That is obviously wrong. Even the best predictive analytics cannot save the wrong product. In other instances, social media were seen as the magic weapon for marketers to create the same "viral"[5] hype around their products as there was around social media itself. We will see later in this book why this has not come true. The run on predictive analytics and social media measurement today is similar to that of the run on websites, when those who felt that having a website was a guaranteed ticket to success back in 1996.

3. The Chinese Twitter equivalent.

4. The Chinese Facebook and messenger platform, respectively.

5. The word "viral" is actually misleading. We rather like to use the term "contagious," as we will explain later in "Virality versus Contagiousness" on page 98.

Meanwhile, the basics of big data and social media analytics will become enabling technologies for many of us, just like the telephone and the World Wide Web.

Big data has arrived. It is changing our lives and changing the way we do business. But succeeding with big data will require more than just data. Just as the US troops needed to decide whether to use crowdsourced social media data or internal data, businesses will need to decide what data to use. The data each business owns might be as different as the businesses themselves, from log files, to GPS data, to customer or machine to machine data, and each one will need to select its data source. Moreover, it will require the right way of dissecting and then in turn analyzing the data with the right analytics. It will require knowing how to separate valuable information from hype. That is the purpose of this book: to teach you the basic principles of what research has actually shown to work, and to help you become one of the businesses that will use big data to succeed.

The world of data is vast, and each business will need to look at its own data set. Throughout this book, we will use many examples of social media metrics, not because we believe that social media is the most promising data set to use for predictive analytics. Actually, with regards to social media, the opposite is true. Social media provide the most difficult data sets, as we will learn later. However, social media data is easily accessible to nearly everyone; and the principles, data structures, and lessons learned in this book can be easily transportable to your own personal data needs and availability. First, let's explore how the promise of big data can impact your business.

The Promise

> *The philosophy of the day is data-ism.*
>
> **—DAVID BROOKS (@NYTDAVIDBROOKS)**

Data analytics proponents are promising a bright future that will change our lives. They promise that we can predict things we never knew before, from price points to military intelligence. And they are right. For example, in Santa Cruz, California, a software application predicts what locations and times of day are the most likely settings for crimes to occur.[6] Recently, police caught two women who were peering into cars, had outstanding warrants, and were carrying drugs. They had no idea that

6. Erica Goode, "Sending the Police Before There's a Crime," *New York Times*, Aug. 2011, *http://nyti.ms/KtmNR6*.

they were done in by a big-data application, which in turn has helped preempt several crimes. While predictive data has in fact been used for many years in police work, this is an example of it being used in real time.

Of course, predictive policing is just one example, and one of the more exotic ones, of how we can use the power of large data sets. Today we see data being used more and more in our world:

- Google uses data to predict the next wave of influenza.
- IBM uses data to optimize traffic flow in the city of Stockholm and to get the best possible air quality.
- Zafu, 2Style4You, and others use self-collected body data to suggest clothes that will fit you best.
- Dr. Jeffrey Brenner, a physician in New Jersey, uses medical billing data to map out hot spots where you can find his city's most complex and costly healthcare cases, as part of a program to lower heathcare costs.
- The National Center for Academic Transformation is using data mining to help understand which college students are more likely to succeed in which courses.
- Insurance companies offer lower rates on car insurance if you place a GPS device voluntarily in your car. They use the data to predict whether you are going to have a car accident soon and then adjust your insurance policy accordingly.
- Many retailers use data for product recommendations and targeted advertisements to the point that they know that you might be pregnant.

We are now living in a world where anything and everything can be measured. "Data" seems to be a new ideology. We are just at a beginning of a long journey where we will measure and analyze more and more information about everyone and everything in order to drive our businesses and our decisions.

This world has also become a source of concern. The consequences of this data on privacy and other areas of society are not yet known, and there are prominent critics such as Jaron Lanier, who asks people to not readily believe any result created by the "wisdom of the crowd." Moreover, applications of data in policing or military intelligence have created a growing concern for privacy. At a time where US agencies even tap into the mobile phones of their closest allies to gather information, many users feel that governments as well as companies have crossed the line of what is acceptable. We will touch on some of those aspects throughout the book and will recommend that transparency as well as open data will be the main way to counter those worries.

Despite those warnings and concerns, for many of us, "data driven" is the new management philosophy. *The Economist* Intelligence Unit[7] released survey data showing how people feel big data will help decision makers and employees alike, as shown in Figure I-2. Roughly two-thirds feel it will help us find new market opportunities and make better decisions, nearly half feel it will help us compete better, and more than a third believe it will boost financial performance and exploit more opportunities.

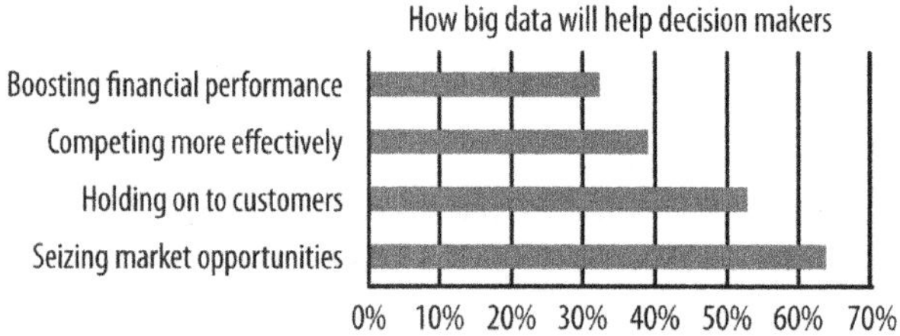

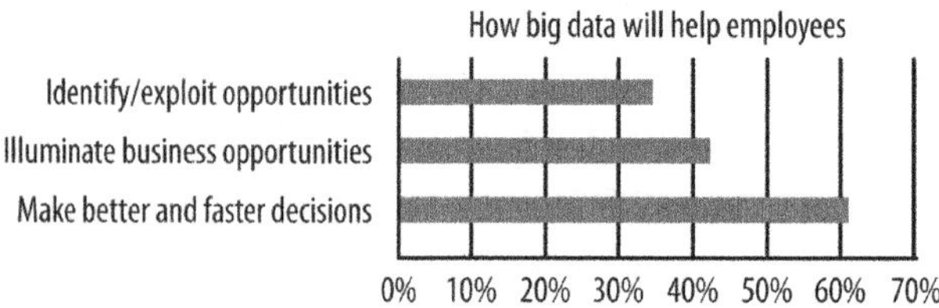

Figure I-2. How big data will affect business[8]

But the promises are sometimes too much. Like any nascent technology, big data is being sold around a lot of 'hype. If you were to believe it, the problems of the world—and your business—could be solved by simply increasing the size of your data set or surveying the latest tweets. It's to the point that Chris Anderson (@chrisa), at that time editor-in-chief of *Wired Magazine*, made the bold claim that we will reach "The End of Theory" if we just have enough data: "Google's founding

7. *Economist Business Unit*, "In search of insight and foresight Getting more out of big data," 2013, *http://bit.ly/1e5hFQA*.

8. *Economist Business Unit*, "In search of insight and foresight Getting more out of big data," 2013, *http://bit.ly/1e5hFQA*.

philosophy is that we don't know why this page is better than that one: if the statistics of incoming links say it is, that's good enough."[9] The future is bright indeed, but it will never be *that* bright. In Chapter 9, we will discuss the differences between correation and causation and why it is and always be difficult to measure causation.

This book is designed to sift through the challenges and hype of big data. It will help you realize the fourth "V" of big data, *value*. Not the wisdom of the crowd nor "more data" by itself is the value. To find value in big data, one has to have right, well-formulated questions, the right methods, and the right data. Only then you will get the desired competitive advantage.

The Data Focus

> *Data really powers everything that we do.*
>
> **—JEFF WEINER[10] (@JEFFWEINER), LINKEDIN**

You might argue that you always wanted to be results oriented. As results are measurable, you had to also be data driven. Right? Also, *predictive analytics* does not seem to be anything particularily new, given that insurance companies have been using it for a long time. Thus why this sudden run on data and predictions? There are two main reasons for this increased focus:

1. There is more data publicly available.
2. The technology is there to process large amounts of data.

Let's look at both of these factors.

MORE DATA

Today, more and more, data has become the center of many discussions. It used to be that data was something hidden. Your insurance company would use data to calculate your policy by comparing your data with those of many peer groups, but this was highly confidential. Today Twitter gives out some parts of its 140 million tweets. StackOverflow regularly allows anyone to download complete answers to its

9. Chris Anderson, "The End of Theory: The Data Deluge Makes the Scientific Method Obsolete," *Wired Magazine*, June 2008, *http://bit.ly/1dLKMEE*.

10. *Adam Lashinsky*(*@adamlashinsky*) , "Where LinkedIn is headed next", CNN Money, June 2012, *http://bit.ly/1fjJBNP*.

programming questions. In addition to those companies, there are data markets and governments that offer access to census data and other data types.

The volume of this data also continues to grow, in some cases exponentially. As of 2011, the Library of Congress was collecting over 200 terabytes a month of information; and in its best months, over half a billion tweets are sent on Twitter.

Where Does the Term "Big Data" Come From?

Steve Lohr (@SteveLohr) has best explained the origins of the term "Big Data" in the *New York Times* blog.

> *In 1989, Erik Larson, later the author of bestsellers including "The Devil in the White City" and "In The Garden of Beasts," wrote a piece for* Harper's Magazine, *which was reprinted in* The Washington Post. *The article begins with the author wondering how all that junk mail arrives in his mailbox and moves on to the direct-marketing industry. The article includes these two sentences: "The keepers of big data say they do it for the consumer's benefit. But data have a way of being used for purposes other than originally intended."*[11]

In a sense, "big" in big data refers here to the first "V," volume, the idea of lots of data. However, "big" in big data sometimes refers to high-velocity data, where fast decisions need to be made by taking in data within a few milliseconds or even microseconds. For example, with real-time bidding engines, the system has less than 25 milliseconds to react to a request from the ad server. The ad server gives data points such as, "We can show your ad to a person on that site from this IP range. How much are you willing to pay?" Thus the ad agency needs to crunch its own big data set in a few milliseconds to be able to answer. Another example of high-velocity data are the computers that trade stocks within a fraction of a millisecond. A new real-time world of data has emerged.

Sometimes the term big data is also used when structured and unstructured data are combined. It used to be that data scientists only looked at structured data. We will understand in Chapter 9 why this kind of data is much easier to deal with

11. *Steve Lohr*, "The Origins of 'Big Data': An Etymological Detective Story," *New York Times*, February 2013, *http://nyti.ms/1f6YWk3*.

and build models around. Today, however, data often come in a variety of different fomats. We will learn throughout this book when and how unstructured data, such as the media data used to predict bin Laden's location, is helpful. For example, one could crunch millions of unstructured tweets to figure out whether the weather in New York is nice. However, it is probably easier to just take a single data point from a weather website: sunny or not? In all this discussion on data, the fourth "V" is the forgotten one, but that is the reason we do data at all. Therefore in this book will focus on finding "value" in data.

BETTER TECHNOLOGY

The second reason for the hopes connected to predictive analytics is that today the technology exists to deal quickly (velocity) with large quantities (volume) of decentralized data in different formats (variety). In the past, predictive analytics worked by "loading" highly structured data into a big data warehouse and processing all of the data. This approach became more and more difficult and expensive. Today companies start to to deal with an unknown quantity of data that can be stored anywhere, in any quality and in any structure.

The technology underlying this is called Hadoop. Apache Hadoop, represented throught the logo of a yellow elephant, can be described as an open source ecosystem. Within this ecosystem one can query very large, distributed, and loosely structured data sets. With Hadoop you can do the following:

- Instead of keeping all data in one database, you can work with distributed databases.
- Instead of processing all data on one server, you can distribute the server processing to many systems, creating a much more powerful system.
- Instead of using only structured content, you can also work with unstructured content.
- Instead of "hindsight" results, businesses get nearly real-time results.

While symbolic of the big data movement, Hadoop is one of many tools now available for working with large distributed data sets, in addition to a veritable army of startup and consulting firms designed to help you make sense of big data from social media and other sources. These tools, and this data connectivity, are in turn creating a revolution.

This is not a technical book, and we will touch on technologies only to the extent that it is needed to understand the *value* of the data. Thus you will not learn the details of plumbing tools such as Hadoop or NoSQL. There are already good resources for these technologies, and once you understand your goal and aim for using big data, you can turn to these excellent books on plumbing:

- *Hadoop: The Definitive Guide*, Third Edition, by Tom White (O'Reilly)
- *Programming Pig* by Alan Gates (O'Reilly)
- *Getting Started with NoSQL* by Gaurav Vaish (O'Reilly)

Analytics Focus

> *Gold requires mining and processing before it finds its way into our jewelry, electronics, and even the Fort Knox vault. Oil requires extraction and refinement before it becomes the gasoline that fuels our vehicles. Likewise, data requires collection, mining and, finally, analysis before we can realize its true value for businesses, governments, and individuals alike.*
>
> **—WORLD ECONOMIC FORUM**

We have the data and we have the technology, so what is stopping all of us from getting to the fourth "V," the value? What is stopping us from creating great algorithms that in turn will yield great data products or services? This book is all about the three major challenges we face in doing this and the way around them:

Ask the right question.
: Do you want to increase revenue? Then "how to get the most hits on YouTube" may be the wrong question to ask—these viewers may not be buyers. Good questions are measurable, actionable, and informed by domain knowledge. Asking the right question is the most important part of data analytics and an issue we will refer to frequently throughout this book.

Use the right data.
: Big data is called big data for a reason: you cannot always analyze it all directly. This means that choosing the right data (preferably structured and quantifiable data) together with the right sampling techniques is a critical factor in extracting knowledge from this data.

Creating the right measure.

How do you turn data into predicted levels of purchasing intent—or the love of your life on a dating service? Metrics are the quantifiable drivers of your analysis, particularly with structured data, and data analytics pivots around them.

And of course, and equally important fourth step is to *learn* and take the right actions from these results.

Let's start understanding these challenges by using two of the greatest successes in business use of big data as of this writing: the growth of *Amazon.com* as a marketplace, and the dominance of Google as a search engine of choice. The former built its success around a system of predictive recommendations, while the latter developed a data metric—Google's PageRank algorithm—that made its search results much more relevant to the user. We discuss both of these cases in more detail later in this book.

Both of these successes are examples of asking the *right* question. Amazon has more products then any other retailer. No customer would find them easily. Thus Amazon's question was, "Which product would fit which person?" Google's challenge was similar: it tried to find the page you were looking for based on a few hints it got not only from your search but also from your location and more.

Helping you find the right question is a central aim of this book. However, please note that there is no defined and absolute way of finding the right question or if you have the question, finding the right metric. This very much depends on your business and your data. Short of a bulletproof, five step approach, we are using practical examples. We will show you how to formulate the specific question for typical parts of your business.

The book gives you a short introduction into the world of data, and more importantly, an introduction to the fourth "V," the value. You will learn how to create your competitive edge. With practical examples, the book shows you the most common pitfalls and how to avoid them.

Finally, a common thread throughout each chapter is to *learn* from what data can teach you. Not just in the obvious sense of drawing conclusions from the information it contains, but also in the more subtle sense of knowing the limits of your data. Sometimes social media data can give you insight that you will find nowhere else, as it aggregates the digital footprints of a large crowd of people. Sometimes it may lack critical information, or even mislead you. For example, a YouTube view count may or may not correlate with purchasing intent, and a Twitter stream may measure the loudest partisan voices rather than the wisdom of the crowd. And sometimes this data will frankly lie to you to suit the agendas of others, a topic we will cover at length later in the book. Learning from data *and* from the nature of the data is a critical skill we hope to teach you.

Each and every organizational unit has its own unique questions, metrics, and data requirements. Sales worries about the top line, marketing would like to create reach for a brand message, and product development wants to know how to improve the product. Chapter by chapter, we look at different parts of an organization to show you how analysis of internal and external data can improve your business: just jump to your section, as the following section explains, for real-world examples.

What This Book Covers

> *Predictive analytics can figure out how to land on Mars, but not who will buy a Mars bar You should expect Big Data to have big impact... but if you're counting on it to make people much more predictable, you're expecting too much.*
>
> **—GREGORY PIATETSKY-SHAPIRO (@KDNUGGETS)**

This book has a clear purpose: to help you ask the right questions, measure the right data and the right content, and learn from the insights to uncover the fourth "V" of big data.

The book is particularly designed to give you the big picture that you need to leverage the wide range of tools out there—tools that will continue to evolve beyond the scope of this book.

Be aware that not every problem we are discussing in this book will be a big data problem; quite the opposite is the case. The problems will involve data and the measurement of the data. But will you need NoSQL or millisecond processing to address them? No. Our goal is to teach you where data can lead you first, before you scale data problems upward. We will use a lot of examples from social media analytics. Ultimately, we want to teach you how to work with a large and increasingly socially linked network of data to improve your business.

You do not necessarily have to read this book from Chapter 1 through the end to benefit from it. Depending on your level of expertise, there are a few ways you could navigate through this book, depending on how you'd describe yourself. Are you:

A manager?

This is a book for you. You are looking for managerial advice for your own department such as marketing or PR, so you can jump right to the correct chapter. Then continue with either the rest or Chapter 6, where we explain how any metric can be abused. If your function or department was not present, do not despair, because we offer in Part II a small guide to design your own ask-measure-learn system.

A data scientist?

The biggest issue within data science is the *learn* part. What does this data tell us? You have probably created dashboard after dashboard for your business partners but were wondering how to take this to the next level. Select the department that interests you most and start reading. This book contains many anecdotal stories and business cases on how to effectively learn by using data.

Someone with no time?

If you're somewhat in between the previous descriptions and don't have much time, go to Chapter 2. Sales has the advantage of being easily measurable. Thus the questions, concepts, and metrics of this book are perhaps best described here.

A first timer in data?

If you have not had a lot of exposure about statistical concepts and want to get some background, we urge you continue on to Part II. Here, we will go through a high-level overview through the main concepts of data analytics.

At the end of each chapter you will find some workbook questions. You can use those to discuss your discoveries with your colleagues, manager, or board. We also encourage you to share your own views and thoughts via Twitter (@askmeasurelearn) or on our LinkedIn or Facebook pages.

CHAPTER OUTLINE

Here are the specifics of what we will cover in each chapter.

Part I, Media Measurement by Function

Many companies focus on collecting data. But only once the data is reduced to a small insight will the fourth "V" of data be visible. The process to reduce big data to small data is always the same. First, *ask* the right question; second, *measure* the right things; and lastly, *learn* from the results. We have broken the chapters down by functions:

Chapter 1

In a marketing context, social media can be used to create reach, brand awareness, or purchasing intent—and each of these are very different things that often require different approaches and different measures. Using case studies and examples, this chapter examines how social media can be used to reach or target potential customers and what factors influence its effectiveness. Perhaps more importantly, it explores the myth of the "influencer" and the viral spread of information.

Chapter 2

What is the difference between reach and purchasing intent? For data-driven social commerce, purchasing intent is often driven by factors such as user-generated ratings and reviews, the capability to spread information about a product to a social network, and recommendations based on consumers' online behavior. This chapter looks at the mechanics and technology of the kinds of recommendation systems that underlie online selling.

Chapter 3

Public relations has two key functions: to distribute information and to warn people. Distributing information via social media offers the advantage of measurements to assess both individual networks and how central people are within their own network, while social media engagement metrics and network topology can help to anticipate critical situations beforehand. This chapter examines how PR has changed in an era of social media and big data.

Chapter 4

We now have the capability to connect with our customers via social media and leverage their data footprint to derive everything from customer satisfaction levels to automated business intelligence. This chapter examines how customer care and CRM are evolving in the era of big data.

Chapter 5

Social media and CRM data are potentially rich sources of market research data. Capabilities such as Facebook Graph hold the potential to enable us to know more about targeted groups of people than ever before, and some companies are leveraging their CRM data to make customer retention even more predictive. But does social media add valuable insight or noise to this process? This chapter examines the potential future for social CRM in business research.

Chapter 6

You have a new friend. Is it a bot or not? This chapter looks at all the ways that fake results can impact your social media analytics in any of those functions, ranging from fake followers and tweets to "astroturfing," a movement or campaign using automated social media identities. It also examines how the nature of social media itself can be misused to create fake virality, influence, and intention.

Chapter 7

Can we predict whether you will succeed in college, who will win the next election, or what job is the best fit for you? This chapter examines the role of big data and social media in predictive analytics—the science of predicting future behavior from data. It is a summary providing a look at where the future of big data and social media analytics is taking us.

Part II, Build Your Own Ask-Measure-Learn System

Was your department not mentioned earlier? Was it mentioned, but your data problem is slightly different than what was discussed here? Or would you like to dig deeper into the mechanics of big data analytics? If yes, then this section is for you. Here, we will help you formulate your own ask-measure-learn system to dig into the data:

Chapter 8

Big data analytics starts with asking the right question up front. Getting millions of views on YouTube or thousands of followers on Twitter could be extremely valuable or mean nothing at all, depending on what it is that is of particular interest: Do you want to find new customers? Do you want to increase revenue? Or do you just want to create brand awareness? Likewise, data mining approaches could easily yield either wheat or chaff, depending on the question you are asking and the measurements/data you use to answer it. This chapter examines how to create measurable and actionable questions to drive your efforts to understand what social media can tell you through big data.

Chapter 9

You want to analyze data from tweets posted about an issue or use someone's social network for targeted marketing. Are you choosing accurate data? Is it from the right context? Does it align with your strategic objectives? Are you confusing causation with correlation? This chapter discusses working with structured versus unstructured data, selecting the right features, and integrating this with the right question.

Chapter 10
: What you measure determines, in large part, what benefit you will obtain from social media and big data analytics. For example, "likes" on Facebook may have very different meanings for your objectives versus survey data, a Net Promoter Score, or other measures. This chapter explores examples and risks of common social media metrics, as well as the "measurement paradox," where the act of measurement itself can affect what is being measured.

If we do our job well, you will begin looking at big data and social media analytics as a structured process that starts long before you put your finger to the keyboard, with clear business objectives for how you engage and leverage this data. Let's start by learning on how to use data for marketing purposes.

Safari® Books Online

Safari Books Online is an on-demand digital library that delivers expert content in both book and video form from the world's leading authors in technology and business.

Technology professionals, software developers, web designers, and business and creative professionals use Safari Books Online as their primary resource for research, problem solving, learning, and certification training.

Safari Books Online offers a range of product mixes and pricing programs for organizations, government agencies, and individuals. Subscribers have access to thousands of books, training videos, and prepublication manuscripts in one fully searchable database from publishers like O'Reilly Media, Prentice Hall Professional, Addison-Wesley Professional, Microsoft Press, Sams, Que, Peachpit Press, Focal Press, Cisco Press, John Wiley & Sons, Syngress, Morgan Kaufmann, IBM Redbooks, Packt, Adobe Press, FT Press, Apress, Manning, New Riders, McGraw-Hill, Jones & Bartlett, Course Technology, and dozens more. For more information about Safari Books Online, please visit us online.

How to Contact Us

Please address comments and questions concerning this book to the publisher:

O'Reilly Media, Inc.
1005 Gravenstein Highway North
Sebastopol, CA 95472
800-998-9938 (in the United States or Canada)
707-829-0515 (international or local)
707-829-0104 (fax)

We have a web page for this book, where we list errata, examples, and any additional information. You can access this page at *http://oreil.ly/ask-measure-learn.*

To comment or ask technical questions about this book, send email to *bookquestions@oreilly.com.*

For more information about our books, courses, conferences, and news, see our website at *http://www.oreilly.com.*

Find us on Facebook: *http://facebook.com/oreilly*

Follow us on Twitter: *http://twitter.com/oreillymedia*

Watch us on YouTube: *http://www.youtube.com/oreillymedia*

Acknowledgments

The more we know, the faster we know more.

—JOSÉ-MARIE GRIFFITHS[1]

We are creating data and knowledge at an incredible speed. The more we know, the faster we know more. The attempt to consolidate and condense knowledge into a book might at times seem like an uphill battle if we did not have support from people who encouraged us, helped us, and gave us interesting insights.

A big thanks to Ashwin Reddy, our cofounder at Fisheye Analytics. Together with a great team of engineers, we have built a social media data mining company. We focused on collecting and processing massive amounts of data. At the time of writing, all textual data stored in our storage systems amount to a whopping 37 TB. Additionally, 69 TB of textual data is downloaded from the Internet every month. On a typical day, our programs and databases handle over 100 million news articles and social media posts collectively. But our algorithms melt down those data amounts to a few kilobytes to answer the relevant question. With Ashwin, we learned to detect the fourth "V" of data. It was a rollercoaster ride, and we thank him for this journey.

Also we want to send a big thanks to Melvin Lee, a.k.a., "the commander," and Jasleen Dhingra. Both have lead the operational teams at Fisheye Analytics. Their data visualization skills helped more then once to detect insights we would have not seen otherwise.

The main aim of this book is to uncover the fourth "V" of data, the value. We explain why it is harder to create actionable insights out of data. The important part in any data discussion is the right business question. Thanks to numerous discussions with Sebastian Knief, Deepanshu Bagchee, John Timothee, and Lydia Ng, we learned how to query our client for the right questions and how to find this most important fourth "V."

1. José-Marie Griffiths, "Scholarly Communications Challenges for Research Universities," CRPGE Summer Forum, *https://www.aplu.org/document.doc?id=4048*

To guide the reader throughout and shape a good understanding of data measurements, the book is full of anecdotes and small stories we heard from others. Thanks to Bjoern Lasse Herrmann from Compass.co as well as Michel Rogero from 2Style4You. We are honored to advise both of those startups on data questions. Their fresh approach toward data has excited us and brough many new aspects into our thinking. Thank you as well to Björn Ognibeni, Luke Brynley-Jones, Lasse Clausen, Kasper Skou, and Michael Liebmann. All of them are inspiring entrepreneurs who have given us insights into data, measurement, or social media.

This book wouldn't exist without peer reviews. Thank you to Kord Davis, who has reviewed the book in detail. It was his idea to add workbook questions at the end. Thank you as well to Frederik Fischer and to Uwe Weiss for their long and in-depth review. Both have helped to "de-buzz" some of the concepts. Thank you to Abdi Scheybani and Thomas Stoeckle for their reviews and input.

Our final thank goes to Ann Spencer and Melanie Yarbrough from the incredible O'Reilly team and to Magdalena Sołowianiuk, who created all of the comic strips throughout the book.

Thanks to all of you!

PART I

Media Measurement by Function

Marketing

Wikipedia, itself a product of crowdsourcing, defines *marketing* as the process of communicating the value of a product or service to (potential) customers for the purpose of selling that product or service.[1] Like a shiny new sports car in a dealership full of sedans, marketing has always been the sexiest and most visible application of big data and social media analytics, and also its greatest source of hype; tap in to the Twitterverse or make your latest video "go viral," so they say, and your product or service will hit the revenue jackpot.

Marketing was not the first place where data analytics was put to use. That honor goes to the finance industry, which invested heavily in big data analytics methods for high-speed trading over stock performance. Through the onset of online commerce and social media, however, big data ultimately entered the marketing area, sometimes with stunning success, but only sometimes. It comes as no surprise that social media outreach or social media listening is one of the top strategies to optimize marketing.[2] Today there is a certain degree of hype about using social media within marketing. You may be reading this book for that very reason. There is an implicit promise with social media that it will help people succeed in marketing their products and services. But how to measure its impact? Moreover, with social media marketing, we have created more data and more measurements. Can we find here the fourth "V" of data?

> *Disentangling the effects of selection and influence is one of social sciences greatest unsolved puzzles*[3]
>
> **—KEVIN LEWIS**

1. Wikipedia contributors, "Marketing," *http://bit.ly/1dcOa97*. Accessed 7 November 2013.
2. *http://adobe.ly/IPJ5LJ*
3. Kevin Lewis et.al., "Social selection and peer influence in an online social network", PNAS, Jan 2012, *http://bit.ly/1coTups*.

The short answer to this is that appropriate metrics are the key to using big data and social media effectively in marketing. This chapter will explore various measurements in social media marketing. Using these metrics, we will uncover a few of the myths surrounding social media marketing on one hand, and hopefully sharpen your eyes in looking for the right metrics for your business on the other.

Marketing and Social Media: The Promise and the Reality

This promise of social media and social media analytics often lies in viral success stories about products or services. One such example is a case reported by McKinsey & Company: months before the US launch of its Fiesta subcompact, Ford Motor Company lent early models of these cars to 100 people recognized as social media "influencers" and asked them to share their observations online. YouTube videos related to this campaign generated over 6.5 million views, Ford received more than 50,000 requests for information, and when the car was finally released in the US, 10,000 were sold in the first six days alone.[4]

Scenarios like this play out all over the business world today. For example, at a recent conference discussing small business success, one participant after another took to the podium to describe how their businesses grew through social media, viral videos, an online community, and, well, you get the picture. And of course, you want to become one of these success stories. So, how do you use social media to succeed at marketing?

The good news is that for the right products, and at the right moment, social media data can drive both awareness and intent. In the case of the Ford Fiesta, for example, the awareness generated led to a successful launch. It was not only the outreach to social media influences that created this success, but also factors such as our natural attraction to automobiles, the existing brand recognition of Ford Motors manufacturer, and above all, a unique and captivating new product. However, as we will discuss later more in depth in "Testing for Correlation" on page 241, it will be difficult to bring proof that those initial car sales can be attributed to the social marketing buzz.

The use of social media can bring unique benefits to marketing campaigns. At the same time, the idealized view that many of its success stories present is not accurate. Thus, what can we measure realistically? This chapter explores three key aspects of social media in marketing:

4. Roxane Divol, David Edelman, and Hugo Sarrazin, "Demystifying social media," McKinsey Quarterly, April 2012, *http://bit.ly/1coTups*.

- How social media can build brand awareness through measurable quantities such as reach, click-through rates, and consumer engagement levels.
- Which approaches to using social media can determine the intent to buy, leading to behavioral and social targeting.
- Whether or not influencers—people who determine our actions and choices—exist, and if so, where to find them.

Brand awareness and intention to buy are the main two aspects of marketing. Said differently, marketing wants to create a desire for a product (make it known) and have customers act on it. Social media can drive both of those aspects effectively. Social media enables you to engage your consumers at a level beyond that of other traditional marketing channels, including giving you permission to connect with their own social media environment. Social media can also be the final trigger to buy.

An equally important focus of this chapter, however, is understanding and avoiding the hype that surrounds the use of social media in marketing. Social media is not as inexpensive or viral for most people as the war stories would have you believe. It is not a single, monolithic marketing channel, even though many people speak of it that way. And studies have shown that the concept of influencers who spread your brand message far and wide is often a myth. To succeed using social media, understanding its misconceptions is just as important as knowing its advantages.

Social media is still a young area that has undergone extremely rapid growth. For example, Facebook and the microblogging service Twitter date back only to 2004 and 2006, respectively, but as of 2013 boast 1.1 billion and 500 million users, respectively. The result is nothing short of a revolution in society that has unleashed a wealth of unstructured data and that, in turn, has drawn massive interest from data scientists. Our hope is to show you how to use social media in ways that are most likely to be effective in the real world of marketing. Is it worth the effort? How do you measure it? When and where should it be used?

The cartoon in Figure 1-1 shows the core conundrum of social media data in marketing: the often tenuous link between this data (such as this dearly departed person's 2,000 Facebook friends), brand awareness (who paid attention to this person), and intent (in the form of attending his funeral). This chapter will explore both the possibilities and pitfalls of using this data to influence purchasing behavior. Let's start by exploring some of the common myths behind the use of social media.

Figure 1-1. The useless metric "number of friends." (Courtesy of Dan Piraro.)

Three Myths about Social Media

Social media seems like an ideal place to create awareness by brand advocacy, and many anecdotal success stories seem to serve as proof of this. The level of hype in many of these stories can be compared to the US gold rush in the mid-1800s, when claims of easy riches led many people to seek their fortunes in the American West. Most would-be miners ended up disappointed, and yet this movement ultimately spawned trade, commerce, and infrastructure, as well as a legitimate gold industry.

Today's modern social media gold rush takes the form of people believing that they can become rich through viral videos, messages retweeted far and wide, and thousands of followers on Facebook. While few succeed in getting rich quick, they are all part of a legitimate social media infrastructure that is changing marketing for good. Before we look at how to leverage this infrastructure to build brand awareness and assess sales intent, it is important to understand the myths that still pervade social media. Here we will discuss three of the most misleading and prevailing ones encountered in marketing today.

SOCIAL MEDIA IS CHEAP

The first myth about social media is that it is cheap. Please do not get fooled: it is not cheap anymore. Danny Brown (@DannyBrown), CEO of Bonsai Interactive, estimated in 2011 that the cost of a social media campaign is about $210,000 per year. That is not as expensive as a full traditional media campaign, but much more than the prevailing myth that social media provides free advertising.

We saw this kind of myth before at the dawn of television. Did you know that a TV advertisement could be as cheap as nine dollars? Yes, that was the cost of the first TV ad in 1941: a 10-second spot of a black and white map of the United States shown in prime time before a baseball game. (See Figure 1-2.)

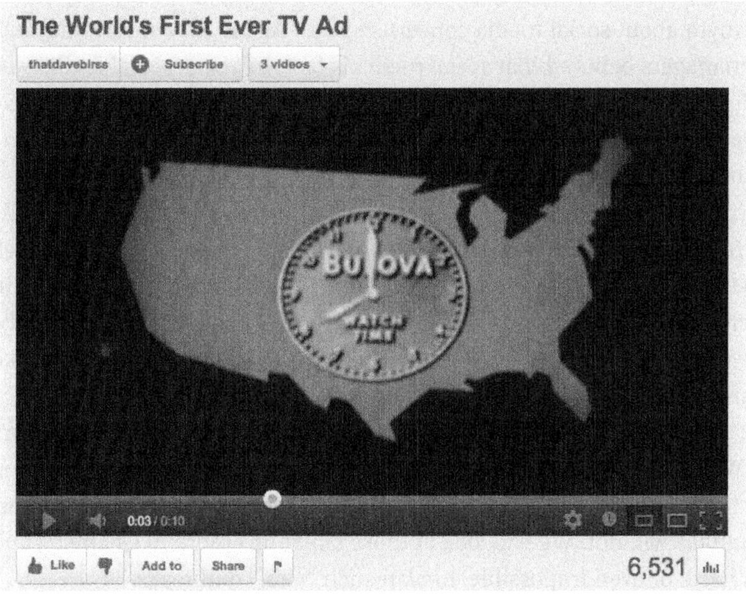

Figure 1-2. America runs on Bulova time. (Courtesy of Bulova and YouTube.)

In this ad, a voiceover simply says, "America Runs on Bulova Time." The descendants of Joseph Bulova paid only nine dollars. No one would have imagined that they had just entered an industry that is now supposed to reach $214 billion by 2014.[5] As inexpensive as TV advertisements appeared to be at the beginning, social media campaigns seem to be cheap today.

But similar to the steady rise of TV advertising costs, we are starting to see a rise in the cost of social media advertisements. For example. the advertising tool developer TBG Digital noted that the average cost of a Facebook ad has increased by 62% over the course of just half a year. Social media advertising is no longer inexpensive.

Another similarity is the discussion on the effectiveness of the new medium. Similar to TV back then, social media is often doubted to be effective. How often have you heard that the return on investment (ROI) in social media is unproven? Bulova simply tried TV out and became successful. Social media advertisers are in a similar spot today.

SOCIAL MEDIA IS FAST

The second myth about social media concerns speed. Again, driven by initial success, many managers believed that social media is fast. In 2004, social media was a new way to reach out to consumers, and the first marketeers to use it had the advantage that they only needed to put up a Facebook page and people would come to it almost by themselves.

Those times have changed. Today it is more and more clear that social media has value in the marketing mix; thus, more and more brands are using this channel. This means that it is harder than ever to be heard. Take Twitter as an example: in 2012, Twitter updates alone produced 8 billion words per day, more than twice the number of words[6] the *New York Times* produced during the last century. To make yourself heard in this space is now more often a slow process.

We say "more often" even though there are the shiny and sometimes scary exceptions. Within a few hours, issues, news, or ideas might spread like lightning within social media networks. They might, but they do not have to, and in most cases they actually will not. We will look at those situations more in Chapter 3 and see that it is hard, or even impossible, to plan such "viral" outbreaks.

5. Stuart Kemp, "Global TV Ad Market To Grow By $60 Billion By 2017, Report Says," Hollywood Reporter, Dec 2011, *http://bit.ly/18UOX37*.

6. Kalev Leetaru, "#bdw12 Introduction," Big Data Week, *http://bit.ly/1kA7rW8*.

SOCIAL MEDIA IS JUST ANOTHER CHANNEL

The third myth is how people talk about social media as if it were one channel, just like television is one channel and print is another. However, this will lead to confusion once you try to design measurements for this so-called social media. A tweet using 140 characters to broadcast generic information has completely different goals and mechanics than, for example, a forum discussion or a YouTube video.

Social media is not one type of media, but rather a *class* of media with different mechanics and goals, and thus it needs very different kinds of measurements. Social media enables users to create, to engage, to share, or to play games; and for these purposes, many different technologies are used. For a business this means that it will not deal with one platform and five different measurements, but perhaps 10 different platforms and 70 different measurements that may appear similar but are hard to compare.

As a class of media, social media can be broken down into three distinct types:

Earned

This is content about the brand shared or created by consumers themselves. In the early days, social media was only earned. A good example of this is product reviews on sites such as *Amazon.com*. For example, the first book in the Harry Potter series (*The Sorcerer's Stone*) received close to 6,000 reviews by 2012. Why would someone bother to write the 6,001st post? Because customers want to share their excitement and tell it to the world. To share positive and negative moments is a human trait and often core to the existence of earned media.

Paid

Most traditional marketing channels, such as television advertisements, are paid. While Amazon does not allow reviews to be bought, other social media channels allow so-called promoted articles. For example, Twitter offers promoted tweets; Facebook displays your status updates only to a limited percentage of your fans except when you pay additional fees for advertisements or so called featured stories; Stumble-Upon promotes your link with a so-called paid discovery, and so on. These are all effectively paid advertisements.

Owned

Brand owners and companies can start their own blogs or fan pages and thus create "owned" content and accounts that they control, like their own YouTube channel, web page, or Twitter account. In this way, brands became publishing houses by themselves.

It is not always easy to see the differences between an owned and an earned Facebook page. While most brand pages on Facebook are owned pages, the most well-known exception to this is the Coca-Cola Facebook page. It was started by two enthusiasts, and Coca-Cola did not claim the page but gave the two founders a nice treat of a visit to Atlanta. Coca-Cola actively promoted this story through a video that went around the world.

In addition to these three types of social media, we can add a fourth dimension: sharing. How and whether data is shared creates a new dimension. Sharing is different across social media platforms, however. Sharing has one common trait: it is easy to do. There's no need for long explanations or owned content. It should be as easy as the click of a mouse. However, no matter which of those four dimensions we analyze, not a single social media channel is the same; they follow different rules, and you will use different metrics to measure success. A good classification of social media is given by Kaplan and Haenlein,[7] who have described social media in terms of the following different platform categories:

- Collaborative projects such as Wikipedia or Github
- Content in blogs or microblogs such as Facebook, Qzone status updates, and Twitter and Seina Weibo Messages
- Content communities such as YouTube and Tudou[8]
- Social networking sites such as LinkedIn and Facebook
- Virtual game worlds such as FarmVille and World of Warcraft
- Virtual social worlds such as Second Life and SMEET

We would also include content curating (such as Digg, Pinterest, Scoop.it, and many more) as an additional category, as we believe that since its initial publication in 2010, this has become an independent social media activity with its own dynamics and own measurements. Thus it is easy to see that social media is not just another channel, but at least seven different types of channels.

This means that depending on how it is used, social media carries with it the potential to earn an audience, attract an audience through owned publishing

7. Kaplan and Haenlein, "Users of the world, unite! The challenges and opportunities of Social Media," Business Horizon, 2010, *http://bit.ly/18UPUs1*.

8. Tudou is the video-sharing website in China.

activities, or serve as a channel of paid advertising. Each has different objectives and measurements, which interact with the inherent attraction of your products, your services, your marketing activities, and the reach of the platforms themselves to produce results we can measure.

Branding

Social media is often employed to create awareness and boost branding. How is this done? There is no one single answer.

The content and the medium need to be the "right" ones. Coca Cola, for example, suggests that its content should be "liquid and connected."[9] For the Coca-Cola company, advertisements need to not only advertise but also to inform, amuse, and engage, along with many other objectives. However, what works for one company does not necessarily work for another. Very often the same marketing logic cannot be replicated for another product or target group. That is an issue from the data perspective. It is hard to learn from those cases as it is difficult to abstract from a given context. Thus in the near future we will not have the algorithm that tells us the right marketing message to write. Branding will always needs a high level of creativity together with the notion of finding the right tone to inspire your customers.

Thus content is still king and not the media channel as such. However, those who seek to use social media to make their messages "viral" are on a quest similar to that faced by the motion picture industry. Within the movie industry, any measurement that could help to improve or to better predict the performance of a film is worth millions of dollars. However, despite lots of focus groups, detailed studies, and the like, the bullet-proof formula for film production still fails to exist. Arthur S. De Vany describes this in his book *Hollywood Economics: How Extreme Uncertainty Shapes the Film Industry* (Routledge):

> *There is no formula. Outcomes cannot be predicted. There is no reason for management to get in the way of the creative process. Character, creativity and good story-telling trump everything else.*

Despite an entire industry devoted to the viral use of social media, similar principles apply. There is *no guarantee* of virality,[10] nor does the ability exist to design for this using a smart metric. While a good branding message depends on creativity,

9. Coca-Cola Content 2020, *http://youtu.be/LerdMmWjU_E*

10. We will later explain that the term "virality" is wrong and it should rather be called "contagiousness."

and there are ways to measure when a branding effort has worked, the market ultimately decides what messages are worth spreading, just like with a hit movie.

Such measures need to answer the simple question: "How many can recall the brand?" It is important to remember that there is more than one type of social media, and not every social media type can measure this. As we discussed earlier, this is a broad and diverse class of media where each type will measure reach slightly differently, often requiring separate benchmarks. From there, the question remains of how to translate *reach* to *awareness*, and beyond to *purchase intent*, as we will explore.

SOCIAL MEDIA: A NEW CLASS OF METRICS

Within each type of social media there are several underlying platforms offering different metrics. For example, let's examine Twitter to show how difficult it can be to have a mutual understanding of reach.

Table 1-1 shows a selection of some metrics from different social media measurement companies on Tim O'Reilly's Twitter account (@timoreilly).

Table 1-1. Tim's measurement overview (as of May 2012)

Company	Metric Name	Value
Twinangulate	Combined Reach	120,310,807
Klout	True Reach	56,000
Twitter Grader	Rank	2,987 out of 10,997,926
How Sociable	Magnitude	4.4 out of 10
Fisheye Analytics	Influence	High
Peer Index	Audience	94
Twitanalyzer	Effective Reach	1,630,000
Twitanalyzer	Potential Reach	3,060,000

This table shows several different measures that can be summarized under "reach"; for example, his rank in the Twitterverse, his effective reach (i.e., his more than a million and a half followers), and his potential reach, as well as numerous quantitative measures of influence. Metrics such as these serve as examples of how you can quantify a social media footprint. However, it also shows that there is a whole range of metrics that all try to describe something similar. Thus, while numbers do not lie, each of these numbers tells at least a slightly different story.

Moreover, this example looks only at Twitter. Other media types such as Facebook or YouTube add a whole new list of reach metrics of their own. These may range from number of page views or video views to frequency of comments or "likes."

REACH DOES NOT EQUAL AWARENESS

While there are many different metrics for reach per social media type, none of them are well set to measure awareness by itself. While it is easy to reach many potential consumers with a sufficiently big media budget, it can be hard to make them remember the brand. Direct marketeers often try to build such awareness by employing a so-called trigger that will make the audience react, such as a phone number to call or a question to answer. Those actions will make the audience remember the brand more easily.

Social media now offers a bigger range of technical possibilities to trigger a reaction. The Ford example from the introduction to this chapter is already a highly elaborated one. More simple ones can be as easy as just clicking "like" or "retweet." With one mouse click, consumers can much more easily react or engage with these channels versus traditional media, and their reactions can be measured. Here are some examples:

- How many people clicked something? The biggest example here is click-through rate (CTR), which is well known from web analytics.
- How many people redistributed a given article? This could mean that they tweeted, scooped, pinned, liked, or shared the article in any other form.
- How many people engaged with a given article—replied, discussed, or reacted in any form?
- How many people copied content or took the main idea from an article?

All of those actions can be classified as *earned* media. It is the customers who conduct them according to their free will and without control by the advertiser. *Engagement* is thus a very important metric for any marketeer, as there is a good correlation between the engagement and the created awareness.

Of course, there is a deeper issue beyond the connection between reach and awareness: awareness is not sales intent. While branding looks mainly to create awareness, an essential step is still missing. What constitutes the right purchase trigger? How can you make a person buy? We will look at this later in this chapter, when we discuss the issue of sales intent.

The next section looks at a successful example where social media was used in a branding campaign. It effectively uses all four dimensions of social media (earned, paid, and owned channels, across multiple platforms), and in the process merges social and traditional media around a common focus. Finally, it produces measurable results consistent with branding objectives. Let's take a look at how this campaign was created and executed.

CASE: VIRGIN ATLANTIC AIRWAYS

Social media offer a wide range of different engagement metrics, and it makes sense to combine those measurements in any awareness campaign. A brilliantly executed campaign in this respect was the case of Virgin Atlantic Airways' "Where is Linda?" promotion.

Where is Linda?

In early 2011, Virgin Atlantic launched a $9.7 million global campaign starting with a fast-sequenced and flashy TV commercial.[11] The combination of the surreal pictures with good-looking people reminded one more of a promotion for a new James Bond film than of an airline advertisement, with the underlying song "Feeling Good" by Muse playing during most of the commercial. A the very end of the commercial, in the last five seconds, one of the flight attendants pointing at a girl in the sky asked in a colloquial tone, "Is that Linda?" This abruptly broke the overall atmosphere of the commercial and left the audience wondering, "Who is Linda?"

This hint in this video advertisement formed the start of a new Facebook campaign. It was a well-placed *trigger* for consumers to start their search for Linda. At a dedicated Facebook page from Linda, consumers could guess and find out where this imaginary flight attendant just flew to and win flights if they were correct.

This sweepstakes campaign was well received, and even years later Linda still gets friends on Facebook and receives comments on her wall. This campaign is a great example of awareness marketing done right. It used a combination of many media types, including social media and television, to create an overall awareness for the brand. Through the use of a dedicated Facebook page and a sweepstakes, Virgin Atlantic created a combination of *owned*, *earned*, and *paid* content, as discussed previously.

But was it a success? The answer is yes if its goal was to create brand awareness for Virgin among potential air travelers. An easy way to estimate brand awareness

11. Virgin Atlantic ad, Guardian, RKCR, October 2010, *http://bit.ly/1gpMGiD*.

is to measure the engagement created. Wildfire Interactive, the company that helped create the campaign, later reported the following results:

> *By the end of the promotion period, the airline had received 15,449 sweepstakes entries and gained 8,282 "Likes" on its Facebook page! Additionally, Linda helped engage consumers in a new way: she gained over 1,900 friends during the promotion's lifetime.*
>
> **—PRESS RELEASE FROM WILDFIRE INTERACTIVE**

Return on Investment: Was Linda Worth It?

For that time, those numbers of likes and friends made the campaign unquestionably successful, at least when one looks only at the interactions on Facebook. However, what about the ROI? The question is whether the campaign ultimately led to sales of more airline tickets on Virgin Atlantic Airways. Linking the cost of $9.7 million of the campaign to the number of engagements, you'd have a hard time calling this a success. A good measurement should not only look at the direct link to awareness and intent. A good measurement would need to look at incremental ticket sales compared to a time before the actual advertisement or compared to the previous year at the same time. Additionally, a good measurement would try to measure the longterm impact that an awareness campaign is intended to build.

The question of return on investment (ROI) often comes up in conjunction with branding campaigns. As awareness by itself does not lead to a sales action, it can be difficult to calculate a ROI that is directly correlated with measurements such as number of sweepstakes entries or television viewers reached.

A link to a financial figure such as ROI can only be established if the branding campaign can be assumed to have caused a type of action. An action in the case of marketing this will be most likely sales related, such as sales conversions, which, in turn, will have a direct financial impact. But is that the case with "Linda"?

Compare the following three tweets on Twitter as an example. The main differences between these tweets are in their action orientation and in their measurability:

> Buy the book *Ask, Measure, Learn* today. Get a 10% discount with this tweet before the 15th of this month. *tiny.url/buynow*.

> *Ask, Measure, Learn* shows how influencers are often overrated and how this may lead to poor decisions.
>
> *Ask, Measure, Learn*, the reference guide on how to measure and apply social media in business, is out in bookstores now. Go get your copy.

One tweet, for example, may contain an action that you can measure, such as a link to a book where you can measure how many people clicked, how many of these people actually bought the book, and at which margin. The second tweet does not contain any action at all, and the third one contains an action that cannot be directly measured.

At the same time, the capability to track and link an action back to a financial number does not in and of itself determine a `causal` relationship. For example, the first tweet might have good conversion rates because it was tweeted at a time where someone spoke about the book on national TV. In such a case, it would be wrong to attribute the book's sales success to this single tweet and neglect the bigger impact of the interview. In data science, we call those variables that have an impact but weren't taken into consideration by mistake "lurking variables." We will discuss them more in detail in Chapter 9.

Nevertheless, most of you will agree that the first tweet is probably the best one to use, as it helps us tracking the success of our marketing actions, as well as triggering an action through a promotion. Thus we see that Twitter, especially, is often used for the distribution of promotions leading to worse customer lifetime values (CLV) compared to other media channels. A recent study by Custora found that US customers acquired on twitter were 23% below the normalized average.[12]

The missing part to include, as well as the longterm effects on a ROI for Virgin, is the question of how can you convert these contacts on Facebook into sales later; in other words, how can we move from awareness to an intent or to a purchase?

There is no automatic process saying that because you "liked" Virgin on Facebook, you will fly Virgin next time. Thus, these contacts become like an email address in a distribution list, and their value very much depends on what Virgin does with these Facebook contacts over their lifetime. For example, the airline can offer

12. CUSTORA E-Commerce Customer Acquisition Snapshot, 2013, *http://bit.ly/1e5VUQF*.

them promotions; it can ask them for customer feedback to improve their service, and it can use them to spread its brand in word-of-mouth campaigns.

Thus to understand the value of *the fans,* one needs to analyze the following questions. Please note that one could phrase the same questions for Twitter or any other social media community tool instead of for Facebook by replacing *the fans* with *the followers* or other appropriate nomenclature:

- How often, on average, can one reach out to *the fans* without losing them?
- What is the average conversion rate on offers sent to *the fans*?
- How many new fans will *the current fans* engage and thus grow the fan page?

The value of the branding campaign can only be answered if we say what we are going to do in the future with those contacts. Often, however, that is not yet clear because the tools and the medium are relatively new. With traditional email addresses, many marketing managers have a good feeling about what a *good* address should yield. But with a *friend* on Facebook, this value often is yet to be determined.

Companies usually first build a fan base on any social network so that the value of the fan base can be tested later once it is set up. Such testing is a highly relevant and important step. Often the expectations between what the company believes they want to do with the *friends* and what the customers expect from the company can be very different.

A 2011 study[13] by Carolyn Heller Baird (@cjhbaird) and Gautam Parasnis, for example, revealed that there are often differences between what consumers expect from interacting with a brand through a social network versus what companies hope they will gain from them. For consumers, the foremost reason to connect to a brand-centric social media site was to get a discount or to be able make a purchase. Meanwhile, business leaders thought the main reason for them to set up such a site was to educate the consumers about new products or give them general information. The ability to give a discount ranked last under all possible reasons (see Figure 1-3) for most businesses. This research shows very clearly an expectation gap that is independent of the actual platform used; therefore, it will be an issue no matter whether brands are using Facebook, Twitter, Quora, or any other community building platform. In building a brand-centric community within a social

13. Carolyn Heller Baird et. al., "From social media to Social CRM: What customers want," IBM Institute for Business Value, 2011, *http://ibm.co/1aVPHPu.*

network, businesses will need to proceed in small steps and will need to test their assumptions through data over and over again.

Figure 1-3. Expectation gap in social media. (Courtesy of IBM Institute for Business Value.)

So, was the "Linda" campaign ultimately a successful use of social media data? Yes, in the sense that it yielded tens of thousands of new connections, which in turn could be leveraged for marketing purposes. It accomplished the stated objectives of making Virgin Atlantic known to more people, building its brand image, engaging customers, and building a user base. However, it is not clear whether it was a success in sales and whether the marketing investment has returned a profit. This is mainly due to the fact that we do not know if a consumer who "liked" something on Facebook developed into a customer who "spent" money. In the next section, we will turn our attention to the more complex issue of finding and measuring this sales intent.

Purchase Intent

The Linda campaign, while successful, points to a dilemma for any business using social media for marketing. The holy grail for any brand campaign is to link its marketing actions to a solid financial return. The missing link here between brand awareness and the sales is the intention to purchase. There are two possible questions to be asked with regards to purchase intent:

1. How do you find customers with the right purchase intent, i.e., how do you focus sales resources at the right moment to create the greatest likelihood of sales?
2. How do you create purchase intent out of awareness? Social media has been seen for a long time as a tool to accomplish this, particularly in terms of the idea that word of mouth, combined with some kind of influencer, will create such purchase intent.

Let's look at both questions in the following sections.

HOW TO FIND PURCHASE INTENT

The easiest way to spot purchase intent is if the customer tells us that he or she intends to buy. We all know this from the traditional sales floor. As soon as a customer tells a sales representative that he or she would like to buy a certain product, the sales person knows that he has a potential lead.

In the online world, the best parallel is the *search term* the user is using. If you query your favorite search engine for "cheap flights to Florida," it is likely that you have a purchase intent to buy those flights. Online advertising became the major success story for search engines such as Google. The question for data scientists was which search strings will create the highest close rate. While this is not a simple question, there are many ways to model this problem.

The more complex question, however, is how much you should pay for a given keyword. For a long time, online search advertisers have mixed up cause and correlation. If a search advertisement would cause the consumer to buy, then a big part of the marketing budget should be focused on online search. However, in reality the user may have seen an offline advertisement such as a television spot, he might have heard about the brand via friends, he may have read articles about the brand, and so forth. Thus, he might have gone through many interactions before finally typing in his search term.

The CEO of a media company we supported once complained: "When we publish an article on how good olive oil is for your overall health, our clients will go online and look for olive oils. They will most likely buy something we have recommended in our publication. However, the search engine will get the money, not us."

It is probably safe to say that search engine advertisement has very little to no causal effect on the intent to buy. The consumer had a predefined intent, and the search engine added no value to it except matching already existing purchase intent with the possibility to buy. For a long time, however, Google received all of the value attributed to the success of a sale. To compare this with an example in sports, this would be like attributing all the success of a game to the player who finally scored the winning goal, neglecting the team who helped to lay the foundation.

But what creates intent? What triggers people to buy? The paradox is that the more we move away from a clear formulation of an intent (for example, by querying a search engine), the more difficult it will be to actually understand intent. There are, however, clues to make intent visible:

Information intake
: Leads to behavioral targeting—for example, if I start actively reading about cars, I am more likely to have the intent to buy one.

Engagement
: Leads to social targeting—if I start talking to people about buying a new car, I might really do so soon.

While behavioral targeting has existed for a number of years, and we know that on average it is not as effective in predicting purchase intent, social media has created the dream that if you know all my friends and all my discussions with my friends, you would be able to actually predict when I am looking for an article *before* I query the search engine. This was the dream and the hope brought to you by the word "social."

Let's look at these promises in detail, from the vantage point of both behavioral targeting and social targeting.

BEHAVIORAL TARGETING

Behavioral targeting can be defined as trying to infer purchase intent based on a consumer's online behavior. For example, "browsing the Web" can be monitored. With every page the user calls up, a cookie can be placed to see what the user is reading. Cookies are effectively used to analyze what people look at and draw conclusions that people exhibiting similar reading behavior have a high chance of buying a certain product or reacting positively to a certain advertisement. Assuming actual intent based on historical behavior is called "behavioral targeting." Behavioral targeting has been a huge research area for many marketing companies. Today it is standard that every website places some kind of cookie on your computer to keep track of who you are and what you do. This kind of "spying" is often criticized, as consumers all over the world perceive this kind of "silent watching" as creepy.

The Creepy Factor

> *If you're not paying for something, you're not the customer; you're the product being sold.*
>
> **—ANDREW LEWIS (@ANDLEWIS)**

Everyone likes being greeted by name in their favorite restaurant: it is considered a courtesy. But how would you feel if you were greeted like this: "Welcome back, Mr. Smith. You have been here 35 times, mainly during the week. You usually spent about $43.50 on a main course and a dessert. You have only ordered an appetizer once, and you have never ordered any of our more expensive fish dishes. Here is a menu suited for your preferences, where we removed all other items. Oh, and please take a seat at the back of the room, because we know that when you sit closer to the window you will use your laptop after the meal to email people without purchasing any additional food.

This is an example of where knowledge and customer data can cross the line from helpful to creepy. Figure 1-4 researched by Krux,[14] provides an overview of American attitudes toward online tracking.[15] The lesson here? As we gain the ability to learn more about consumer preferences, never forget that privacy does matter.

Browsing, however, is often much less intentional then searching within a sales engine (such as Travelocity for airline tickets or *Amazon.com* for books). If I am reading an article about Florida, one can assume that I have an interest in Florida. However, this will not necessarily mean that I have the intention to buy a flight to Florida. I might just have a general interest in Florida and no plans to visit. And even if I do plan to visit Florida, it is by no means clear when I would like to purchase a ticket. Thus user interest online displays a higher "entropy"[16] and is less likely to relate to an *intent* than a search query.

However, to understand the moment of *intent* earlier would be highly valuable for many online companies. This is the quest of behavioral targeting. What does this mean? Behavior targeting tries to draw a conclusion of your behavior in order to know what you want before you voiced it. In short, you look at websites the average user has looked at *before* performing an action, then find users with a similar

14. This survey includes respondents who answered "yes" and "yes, with some visibility/control."

15. Krux, Krux Consumer Survey, Jan 2011, *http://bit.ly/1dqHar4*.

16. "Entropy" is used here as measure of disorder that resuts in a higher uncertainty.

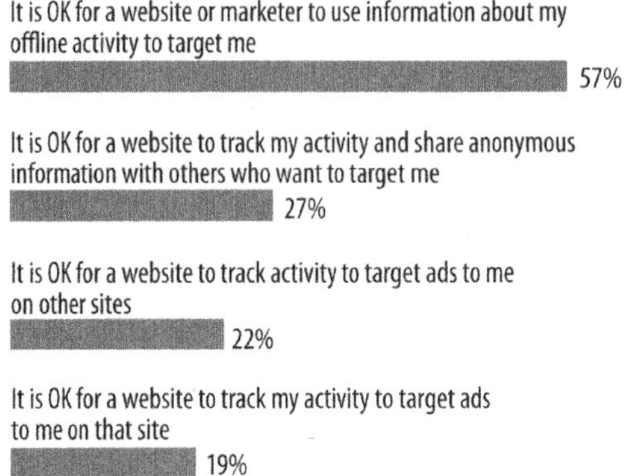
It is OK for a website or marketer to use information about my offline activity to target me
57%
It is OK for a website to track my activity and share anonymous information with others who want to target me
27%
It is OK for a website to track activity to target ads to me on other sites
22%
It is OK for a website to track my activity to target ads to me on that site
19%

Figure 1-4. Internet users attitudes toward online tracking. (Courtesy of Krux.)

behavior. Based on this pattern, we assume that you are about to want something specific and so we offer you a *trigger* to take an action before you go and ask a search engine.

Behavioral targeting started in the 1990s, and its models used to be highly manual. For example, a media agency would aim for a target group "sports car interest," and the technology partner for that agency would *translate* this into certain limits in its system, such as, "Display this online advertisements to users who have read three automotive articles this week and at least two articles about sports." The biggest shortcomings of such a system was this kind of manual work. Someone had to assume that "sports car interest" translates into a certain reading behavior. If this assumption were wrong, behavioral targeting would not be very effective.

Such guess work and linear rules were not a good approach to reduce the *entropy* of user behavior. However, the more information we collected about users, the more companies built *automated* models and dug into the long tail by applying machine-learning mechanisms. Today, companies like Rocket Fuel or group M build models to reduce this kind of "entropy" by analyzing the total consumption behavior of many users and comparing them to the one who in the end bought a flight to Florida. Patterns about the kind of articles or the kind of content that precedes a flight booking to Florida will emerge without manual assumptions. Companies like Semasio take it even a step further and create even more rich patterns by moving from category-based analytics to semantic analytics of each page (see "How does a machine-learning approach work within behavioral targeting?" on page 23).

How does a machine-learning approach work within behavioral targeting?

Within the traditional world of behavioral targeting, action settings are defined manually, and the classification is done half manually. Each website the reader visited is grouped into a specific category (such as "travel" or "automotive"). Those classifications are often manual, sometimes based on the domain name. However, not every article on an automotive website has to be really about automotive. Such errors can impact the validity of a predictive model as discussed in Chapter 9.

The company Semasio took the data approach one step further. It applied a semantic analysis on each article the user reads, creating a kind of word cloud on each article read, and subsequently for each individual user profile. Such a pattern contains more rich information about the user.[17]

While more data is not necessarily better data, this approach is definitely working for Kasper Skou and his team at Semasio. Their semantic analytics has reduced the amount of manual classification and manual rules setting to a minimum.

For a given task such as "generate online sign ups for a car test-drive," the algorithms look at the ones who have signed up for a test-drive. It then automatically searches for statistical "twins" in regards to their reading profile. "We don't know ex ante which information is going to be important in discriminating the action-takers form the non-action-takers," says Kasper Skou. "The target generation process will determine what are important classifications."

Not surprisingly, the best prediction for intention is if the consumer states an interest clearly, similar to what he or she would have done with a search query. If, for example, the user puts an item into his online shopping basket but never checks out, there is a high likelihood that he had an intent to buy such an item. This type of behavioral targeting is called "re-targeting." However, this does not necessarily clarify cause and effect. We do not know why the consumer put the item in his basket; all what we know is that he has an intent. We do not know where this intent came from.

17. Kasper Skou, "Making behavioral targeting work," March 2012, *http://bit.ly/18UWuPp*.

Despite recent advances in behavioral targeting, it still does not always work smoothly. In a recent post, Avinash Kaushik (@avinash), a knowledgeable expert in web analytics, complained about how bad targeted advertisements still are. Despite a long cookie history at ABC News, he still gets served ads badly fitting his needs.

> *There is nothing in my history or cookies to suggest I want botox or to lose weight or am interested in e-cigarettes (who the heck is!). [...] I don't know who the ad provider is. But there is no way these ads are going to save ABC News. And people blame the Internet for killing the news business.*[18]
>
> **—AVINASH KAUSHIK**

The underlying issue in this case is that the content providers—in this case, ABC News, which has a cookie history of Avinash, is most likely not sharing these insights with the advertiser. ABC News knows that owning information on Avinash can be a competitive advantage for them, and thus will probably not easily distribute this information to others.

The Limits of Behavioral Targeting

It is known that matching an ad to website content and increasing an ad's obtrusiveness independently increase purchasing actions. However, you often can find that these two strategies are ineffective. Ads that match both website content and are obtrusive do worse at increasing purchase intent than ads that do only one or the other. Therefore, overdoing it, particularly in a social media context, can be dangerous to your reputation, as well.

SOCIAL TARGETING

While behavioral targeting focuses on what an individual does online, social targeting uses consumers' behavior within their social graph online to predict purchase intent. Examples of this can range from Facebook ads served based around your activities on the site all the way to targeted marketing based on the demographics of the people you are connected with online. It's based on the old Assyrian proverb, "Tell me your friends, and I'll tell you who you are." Social

18. Avinash Kaushik, "Why I'm wary of Display Advertising," Google Plus, Jun 2012, *http://bit.ly/1dqlwSB*.

targeting represents a source of tremendous interest and promise for marketing. Social targeting can use, for example, the posts and comments you make to others, the pages you "like," your connections, and the activities of these connections. All that information contains "hints" that could be used to impute purchasing intent.

But it still seems to not work well yet. The apparent master of current social and behavioral targeting—Facebook—appears to still be worse off than the current best-in-class advertiser, Google. These two channels represent the difference between "searching the Web" (in Google's case) and "talking within social media" (in Facebook's case). So, for example, if you are trying to find the highest level of purchasing intent, should you advertise using Google AdWords (which streams your ad in Google based on user search terms) or Facebook?

According to a recent WordStream study, Google AdWords still offers 10 times higher click-through rates (CTR).[19]

There are probably three major ways by which marketeers hope to translate social signals like our social graph or a discussion with our friends into signals of intent which could trigger a purchase:

- You say it.
- You like it.
- Your friends do it.

More and more advertisers will use this kind of data to place their advertisements more effectively. But as we will see when we go through those three points one by one, none will be as effective in predicting your purchase desire as the data of a formulated search goal like the one Google records.

You Say It...

The best situation is that you actually casually announce that you would like to do something. However, these situations are rare, as we are not always stating our intent out loud to our friends in public. Moreover, any marketeer realizes that what people say does not always translate to what they want or do. Nevertheless, some companies are actively using social media conversations for marketing purposes, often through the efforts of a "community manager" to engage people and try to

19. WordStream, "New Research Compares Facebook Advertising to Google Display Network: Who Comes Out on Top?" May 2012, *http://bit.ly/1iXBuvi*.

trigger an action. For example, when I (Lutz) once shared my frustration by tweeting, "Spent an hour solving conflicts with PayPal," it did not take long for the community manager from Paytoo, an up-and-coming competitor, to react, "Try Paytoo.com! We take pride in our customer service!" (see Figure 1-5).

Figure 1-5. One-on-one engagement via a community manager

Surely one can also "trigger" a situation where "you say it" to "influence" your friends. However, since direct statements of interest are rare, particularly in a publicly watched social network, a more subtle form of marketing often needs to be used.

You Like It...

To "like" something, in a social media sense, is similar to "saying" that you "like" it, but with two fundamental differences:

- The action creates structured data, and is thus easier to understand, while to "say" that you like something is unstructured data and requires some analytical understanding first.
- To "like" is easier than to say that you like something. It is a click versus a few words, which means more people will do it, and it becomes easier to measure.

Note

This phenomenon is part of a broader trend: the evolution of least effort in the Internet, where interactions have become smaller and smaller. While initially one had to write a blog post to share desires and ideas, it has now become as easy as the click of a mouse: select *like* and a statement is made. These likes overall will build up a personalized track record of what you are interested in, which in turn could be used to better send you a trigger for your interests.

The idea is that marketeers can predict the right *intent* trigger if they know what you generally have "liked." Many likes together might create a stronger signal for interpretation than, for example, behavior targeting information. If you know that your customer has read certain stories on a newspaper, it still does not tell you anything about his feelings, position, or consent toward those stories. However, so far there has not been any major study on this subject, especially since the most "likes" are owned by one social media company. Moreover, this phenomenon is still in its early days: perhaps if you have hundreds of billion of likes, you may be able to map out something as diverse as the human interest effectively.

Nevertheless, many companies try to build a business on this. Circle Me is, for example, a young Italian startup founded by Giuseppe D'Antonio. Their major business model is to collect likes from all different sources, of which Facebook could be only one. As we will see in the next chapters, neither likes nor friends truly reveal our intentions, so to have a collection of likes will be mainly useful for brand awareness purposes, as described previously.

Your Friends Like It...

Tell me with whom thou art found, and I will tell thee who thou art.

—JOHANN WOLFGANG VON GOETHE[20]

So far, the area we know most about is the behavior of you and your friends, in such a way as to "marry" behavioral targeting with social network information. The underlying assumption is that your friends' behaviors are a good proxy of your own behavior. The buzzwords here are "word of mouth" and "influencer." But how effective is this in reality?

20. This proverb seems to have many origins. There are similar Assyrian, Russian, English, German, and Dutch proverbs. A similar quote has also been attributed to Miguel de Cervantes.

We all know word of mouth from our own anecdotal experience. We ask friends for advice. Did you recently move to a new town? You probably asked your friends which neighborhood to move to, which school to send your kids to, and the like. If you did this online via a social network, then perhaps this is a way to see *intention* in the making? Or better yet, do social networks play a pivotal role in influencing peoples' decisions?

The traditional view is that only a few people will have a big impact over us. Malcolm Gladwell called it 2,000 in his book *The Tipping Point* (Back Bay Books) the "law of few."[21] However the idea that a few people determine what we like, think, and do has been around for a while. Katz and Lazarsfeld called them opinion leaders back in 1955,[22] followed by Merton who called them "influentials" (1968),[23] up to Gladwell and the PR agency Burson Marsteller, who now calls them e-fluentials. Those influencers tell us what to do, as depicted in Figure 1-6, and we all have anecdotal evidence where someone helped us make a decision. If we move to a new town, most of us will contact friends who are familiar with that town to ask about schools or doctors to use. As human interaction moved now partly online, the hopes are that those influencers are also online in social networks.

21. Gladwell, Malcolm, *The Tipping Point: How Little Things Can Make a Big Difference*, New York: Back Bay Books, 2002.

22. Katz, Lazarsfeld, "Personal Influence: The Part Played by People in the Flow of Mass Communications," 1955

23. Robert Merton, "Patterns of influence Local and cosmopolitan influentials," Social Theory and Social Structure, 1868

Figure 1-6. The last of the few: A few tell us what we should do. Is that really true?

There are many success stories that social media referrals have an influence. Henry Blodget (@hblodget) from Business Insider provides a few examples:

- Rent the Runway has 200% higher conversions from social referrals from fashion magazines than from paid search.
- ShoeDazzle says that Facebook-connected users are 50% more likely to make monthly repeat purchases.
- Friends referred by friends at One Kings Lane have twice the lifetime value of customers from other channels.
- When a Facebook user clicks on a Ticketmaster purchase shared by a friend, it is worth between $6 and $8 in new ticket sales.
- Each viewed video on YouTube creates a 3% chance that someone will click on the "buy" link at the end.

Many more anecdotal examples exist of the influence of social connections on purchasing behavior. You can also infer purchasing intent from the nature of an online community and/or its past behavior. For example, a network of people who own Ford Mustang automobiles—a highly committed consumer group that often spends money to customize these vehicles in the aftermarket—may have a stronger correlation with purchasing intent versus people who discuss, say, bowling, but are not necessarily in the market for more bowling balls.

Given the impact of influencers, we as marketeers only need to spot and target them with the correct marketing message to multiply their influence. Sounds exciting, right? Or as Rand wrote in 2004, "Influencers have become the 'holy grail' for today's marketeers."[24] But can we deduce from examples such as these—of which there are many in print—that social marketing is "the next big thing" in social advertising? Do those *influencers* even exist?

The answer, once again, is yes and no. Those "few" influencers as Gladwell described them do not exist. We are fortunately not the kind of lemmings depicted in Figure 1-6. However, surely the process of influencing exists. It is only way more complex then many social media tools make us believe. When we move from anecdotes to formal literature, we will understand the role of influence between peers. In the next sections, we will describe how:

- Influence is overrated; it is more often *homophily*, or the tendency of individuals to bond or join with those who are similar.
- Your social connections are not a the factor with the highest influence and thus not the best predictor of your behavior.

HOMOPHILY VERSUS INFLUENCE

So how do we differentiate real influence that spreads from social connections from homophily, where people flock by affiliation? As one example, Kevin Lewis from Harvard tried to analyze how taste spreads.[25] Who is influencing the taste of whom? Over the course of four years, he interviewed college students and monitored their Facebook friends, and his conclusion on how taste spreads is that "it depends" on the topic. For example, he found that students do influence one another's taste in classical or jazz music. However, indie music acts anti-correlated. So if I have

24. Paul M. Rand, " Identifying and Reaching Influencers," *American Marketing Association Journal, http://us.prolog.biz/resource1.html.*

25. Kevin Lewis et al., "Social selection and peer influence in an online social network," PNAS, Jan 2012, *http://bit.ly/1coTups.*

someone within my network who likes a certain indie direction, it seems that I am less likely to like on this same direction. This might be because listeners of the indie music want to be more "independent."

Moreover, Kevin Lewis et al. found that we overestimate influence. In many of his samples he could not find statistical relevant proof that one person was influencing the other. Nevertheless students with similar taste form communities more often than those without this similar taste. This is not due to influence, but a phenomenon known as "homophily" (literally translated as "love of the same"): people become friends in the first place because of common, shared interests that already exist. In other words, your friends like things because you do. We tend to hang out with people who share the same visions, like the same sports, or have similar opinions as we do. Thus the more friends you have in one special interest group, the more likely it is that you fall into the same interest group.

Our friends can be a good predictor of our interests, and in turn may serve as a good proxy to make us receptive to branding advertisments. But at present, they do not seem to be a good predictor of our intentions or our actions.

SOCIAL CONNECTIONS VERSUS BEHAVIOR

Even if there is no influencer, can the selection of our friends, even when we had selected them out of homophily, help advertisers to target our needs better? One of the key questions of social targeting is whether it can be superior to behavioral targeting or even analysis of search terms. In other words, does studying the behavior of your social connections add value to assessing your potential purchasing behavior as compared to simply studying *you*?

Kun Liu and Lei Tang from Yahoo! Labs did one of the most extensive studies to date on the influence of friends' behavior on behavioral targeting in an online network.[26] Using the resources of Yahoo, the authors examined the predictive impact of social data for more than 180 million users across 60 consumer domains, over a period of two and a half months.

The authors figured that users were more likely to click at a given online ad in a certain behavioral targeting (BT) category, if they had at least one of their friend in their network who clicked into the same category.

Can we conclude that users will have similar intent and follow similar actions if we know that their networks share similar interests? Not necessarily. Despite this

26. K Liu and L Tang, "Large-Scale Behavioral Targeting with a Social Twist", ACM International Conference on Information and Knowledge Management, October 2011, *http://labs.yahoo.com/node/597*

measured uplift, Liu et al. could not find that ad targeting based on social connections performed better than traditional behavioral targeting. The metrics to best use for comparing those different approaches is the area under the curve between click-through rate (CTR) and reach. Those two metrics influence each other. The more sure you are that a person will click, the fewer people you can address. On the other hand, the more you spread the advertisement to many viewers, the lower the probability will be that someone clicks. Liu et al. used several methods to calculate an uplift through the social community. Figure 1-7 compares the average of those attempts versus the traditional behavior targeting. As it turns out, behavior targeting—meaning we display ads based on the content what you have read—is more than twice as effective as any of the suggested social targeting approaches. The baseline in Figure 1-7 indicates that the ads are displayed at random without any further calculation.[27] The best results, however, were obtained by combining both sides, the social network information as well as the behavioral information.

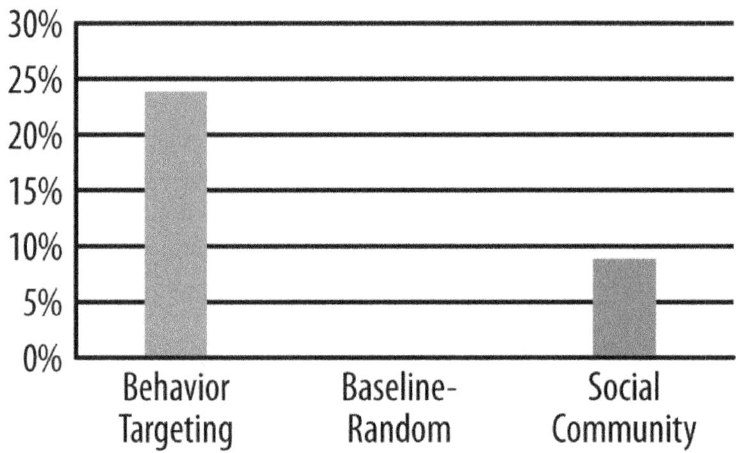

Figure 1-7. BT is outpacing social network information. (Courtesy of Liu et al.)

So far we have discussed the effectiveness of ad placement. Looking at different questions (Chapter 8) will alter the effectiveness of the social connections. Let's look at the adoption rate of a product. For example, a study from Bhatt et al.[28] analyzed the adoption rate from a PC to Phone product. Bhatt et al. did find

27. Data taken from the study conducted by Liu et al.

28. Rushi Bhatt et al., "Predicting Product Adoptions in Large Social Networks," 2010, *http://bit.ly/1iKyvW3*.

influence. However he did not find what Gladwell called[29] the "law of the few." An hypothesis that some few "external influencers" can influence our daily actions. But he found that the product adoption was more strongly influenced by direct peers as compared to external influencers. Thus not a few but many different individuals seem to influence our decisions. Other research has found similar type of influence. Especially for products with strong network externalities one often finds that the influence is growing strongly the more of your peers adopt a product. This is quite the opposite to the proposed "law of the few." Similar is true for certain situations, such as a purchase decision. Social media can clearly be influential here. The best example are reviews: 22% of users indicate that their purchase decision was influenced by a review (Figure 1-8). For electronic goods, this rate goes up to 33%.[30]

Figure 1-8. Rating and reviews are important

The conclusion? Social targeting appears to hold promise for creating awareness and branding, and one can see this in the previous example about Facebook's promoted stories. But it is just an incremental improvement. Social targeting will neither reduce the importance of search, which is still the best predictor for *intent*, nor the importance of behavioral targeting, which is still the second best

29. Gladwell M., *The Tipping Point: How Little Things Can Make a Big Difference*, Little, Brown, New York, 2002.

30. "Consumers now pay more attention to online reviews than word-of-mouth," accomplished, May 2012, *http://bit.ly/18mwNGN*.

predictor. However, social targeting does incrementally improve the predictions done by behavioral targeting as shown by Kun Liu.

THE INFLUENCER

But what is influence then? Whether you can be influenced or not depends on three different factors:

- You are *ready to be influenced*. This is the the case of reviews. Users want to be influenced. They are looking for an answer.
- The *topic is right*. As we saw in the last sections, there is a topic dependence for influence.
- The influencer needs to have contact to you. Thus some form of *reach* is necessary, but not a sufficient criterion for influence.

Very often the term "influence" within social networks is reduced to *reach*. Without reach, we will have difficulties influencing someone. However, even with reach, there is no certainty that we can. Bakshy from the University of Michigan found such results in 2011 by looking at the spreading of Twitter information, tracking 74 million events across 1.6 million Twitter users, and found that propagation via social networks is not predictable.[31] That means that we cannot predict whether a certain link, joke, or piece of information will spread only by looking at the reach someone can create. Hold on, you might think. We all know the stories about that one tweet that went around the world. What is with these situations? Well, we could call them luck, because if you try to build a deterministic model of when a tweet is going to spread and when it will not, you will fail. It remains hard, if not impossible, to quantify the phenomenon of influencers.

What we can say for sure is that information from well-connected people does spread better, and we will look at this in the next chapter on public relations (Chapter 3). However, these spreading effects can perhaps be more easily explained by either a pure broadcasting phenomenon (where the "spread" among social network users is analogous to each of them seeing, say, a television ad) or by homophily. Thus we still should discuss, at least briefly, typical measures of how reach within a network is measured.

31. Eytan Bakshy, "Everyone's an Influencer: Quantifying Influence on Twitter," 2011, *http://bit.ly/1kAqqjb*.

A key factor here is the concept of *centrality* within a network. This is a very important metric for information dissemination. If a person is quite central, we frame that person as being a broadcaster. Note that often influence could be happening at a micro level on the edges of a personal network, in those moments where you talk to new nodes that are not yet part of the network, and by doing so are *influencing* them to become a part of that network.

Others look at the reach of a message and how often others engage people with this message. Again, we would claim that this is not necessarily influence but a more PR-centric measure. We have also assumed that the actual metrics are easily available. There are many metrics available from many tools. Most of those tools analyze the influence of the person, including Klout, Kred, PeerIndex, and Traackr. Many other tools also have some form of "importance" measurement as part of their offering, such as Fisheye Analytics, Radian6, Sysomos, and others. Also you will find tools that restrict themselves to only one media type, such as Twitter. Twitter offers a nice structure, which enables assessing your network quite easily. Services like TweetLevel, TweetReach, Twitalyzer, and TwitterGrade are good ones to check out.

Influence Is Local

Influence depends on the topic and is local. This was shown quite nicely at Strata 2011 by Marcel Salathe (@marcelsalathe). He used the controversial topic of child vaccination as a good example on the results of active influence.

This topic often provokes strong reactions among both supporters and opponents. While the former note the medical benefits of not getting outbreaks of child illness, the latter view this data as part of the lobbying work of a too powerful pharma industry and warn about the side effects of vaccination.

It seems sensible that the rate of parents who object to vaccinations and exempt their kids would be relatively uniform throughout a state. However, if we look at district-level data within Washington state, for example, this is not the case. There are clear local extrema in which the acceptance rate is either quite high or quite low (see Figure 1-9).

It seems unlikely that such a variance is induced by a sort of homophily that is correlated by place, if we assume that immunization efforts are equally strong throughout any district. One potential explanation is that those local extrema have strong influencers supporting or objecting strongly to immunization.

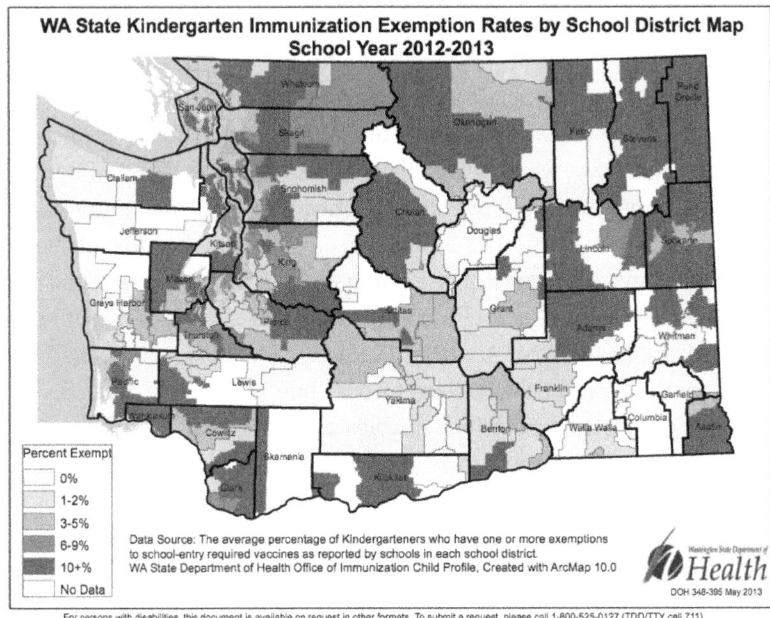

Figure 1-9. Local areas where vaccination acceptance rate is low. (Courtesy of Washington State Department of Health.)[32]

32. http://1.usa.gov/1gpXxc7

Summary

Social media has created a whole new discipline in marketing. It is different from traditional methods of marketing, and thus measurements are very important in guiding our efforts. What has an effect and what does not? In order to find this out, you need to first understand why social media is different and should not be measured with the same tools you have used before. Despite these different measurements, you somewhere need to bring all measures back together to make efforts comparable.

The effect is different for each business, but in summary, one can say:

- Social media marketing has been overhyped, and solid metrics have not yet been applied.
- The effect of social media marketing is visible but not as pronounced as assumed.
- Social media channels are particularly good for the distribution of information or as a vehicle for *branding*.
- Since distribution of information—*reach*—is no guarantee for *purchase intent*, it is as hard to quantify ROI, as is the case with any other image campaign.[33]

The ultimate aim of social media marketing is to drive sales *intention* through *awareness*. We therefore break down the different levers of *intention* mainly into behavioral clues (behavioral marketing) or social clues (social marketing). Behavioral clues such as your search behavior will be the best data to answer the question about future behavior. Thus behavior clues are best to uncover the fourth "V" of data. But social clues such as what you or your friends say are becoming more and more an important metrics to predict intention.

Here there has been a lot of hope placed onto influencers: people to whom you are socially connected and who can drive up your intention. We know from anecdotal evidence that social media should have an effect on purchase decisions. But the assumed "law of few" means that the influencer effectively does not exist. Influence is more a function of a readiness to be influenced, and that depends very much on the topic as well as reach. For example, in the case discussed earlier of the

33. The ROI will be easier to calculate once we link social media with sales actions as described in Chapter 2.

adoption of the PC to a phone product, peer pressure played a role, and thus social media's ability to broadcast and connect with others multiplied the effect.

In closing, social media does have unique advantages as tools in marketing. For branding, social media can create a more sticky *reach* with greater consumer engagement, and in finding purchasing intent, it can add an incremental step to behavioral targeting. Will it spread brand awareness and increased sales of your product on a massive scale? In all likelihood, only for the lucky few. But for all of us, the right metric in social media marketing can mean the difference between success and failure.

WORKBOOK

How to measure social media and how to use social media in your own marketing depends very much on your business. To get you thinking, let's look at the following workbook questions. How does your company use social media? Social media is a broad and fuzzy category. Go back and look at the seven different categories that can be used to describe social media. Now let's dig into some descriptive measures of social media:

- What are the realistic costs to the organization?
- How would you define a branding impact of social media?
- Are the measurements your company set up really smart? (Please see further discussion on the right question in Chapter 8.)
- Looking at your marketing teams, are they measured by metrics that could lead to wrong measurement behavior? (Please see further discussion on misused metrics in Chapter 10.)
- ROI is a hot topic for any organization. Can you quanitfy it? How do you make sure not to have any lurking variables within your ROI calculation?

Since the ROI discussion is such an important one in the area of social enabled marketing, please share your approach. Solved or not? Silver bullet or not? Please explain your ROI measurement on our LinkedIn or Facebook page.

Further to the descriptive measures, let's look into predictive measures using the data from the social media campaigns you are using:

- What are levers of *purchase intent*? Where is the *value* to predict future consumer behavior in your data?
- Can you predict purchase intent using *social or behavioral clues*?
- What are the best features of your data set? Past purchases? Country? Age? Reading behavior? Published comments?
- Can you improve purchase intent by using social strings such as influencers or social peer pressure? By how much?

Sales

Introduction

The sales process has always been driven by knowledge and trust: knowledge from the sales person about what the customer really wants, knowledge from the customer about the existence of the product, and trust from the customer in the salesperson or company. Data analytics and social media play distinct roles in archiving knowledge and trust. However, social media and the data taken out of social media are often confused as one and the same. They are not.

On one hand, we can use social media to create knowledge about a product and trust into this product. On the other hand, data derived from social interactions or the shopping experience as such can be used to create knowledge about the customer and thus serve the customer better. In both cases, the social sales approach as well as the analytics of social data are aiming to support our sales efforts. But the actual work and skill sets are quite different. In this chapter we will look at both areas. In the first part, we will discuss social networks and how they can be used. In the second part of this chapter, we will look at data analytics derived either from social data or from customer purchase behavior.[1]

SOCIAL SALES

A social layer within an online sales process adds not only the possibility to create reach, as discussed in Chapter 1, but also knowledge and trust. Consider the following case:

- While shopping Walmart online, you find a product you like. You can discuss whether you should buy it, ask friends about its quality, or just comment on how it looks via Facebook, Twitter, or Pinterest directly. By providing the

1. It will come as no surprise that purchase behavior is structured and, consequently, for most applications, the better data set to work with.

opportunity to discuss this product, Walmart can not only offer a way for its customers to gain *trust* in the product, but it helps as well to create *reach* and spread the word.

This is an example of *social commerce*. The term social commerce was first coined by Yahoo! in 2005. It describes ecommerce transactions that are triggered or guided by social interactions or supported by social network data. Social commerce usually consists of one or more of the following elements:

- User-generated recommendations such as ratings and reviews
- The ability to spread information about a product to a social network
- Recommendations based on consumers' online behavior

Because the social media world is full of different tools, platforms, and functions, the social commerce world also has many names and faces: "T-commerce" stands for commerce via Twitter and "F-commerce" for sales via Facebook. We are sure there are many more terms to come. Social commerce seems to have become the "next big thing," and the numbers appear to justify this hype. There are over a billion users on Facebook, and more than 170 million active Twitter accounts. Let's assume we could sell each of them something for only $2—that would result in a revenue of $2.3 billion.

Social commerce is sometimes presented in terms that practically guarantee raining money, if you only implement "F-", "T-", or whatever-commerce. The reality, of course, is often different from this, and many merchants have lost money from "being social." Should we thus refrain from social commerce?

Let's be guided by lessons from history. For example, in the mid-1990s, people promoted the practice of having a page on the World Wide Web as a sure-fire way to sell products and services. A few years later, the crash of many dot-com startups taught us that the medium itself wasn't the ticket to sales success. Today, social commerce has had the same glow of youth and promise for boosting sales, ever since the term was first coined. In all likelihood, history will prove these tools to have a similar trajectory to the growth of the Web.

Of course, websites and ecommerce not only work as selling tools but have also created a billion-dollar industry. They are now ubiquitous for anyone in business today, much like having a telephone. However, their adoption took longer than anticipated, and online capabilities are only an additional tool for the sales process.

In much the same way, social commerce will develop. It is here to stay and will become a significant part of the online commerce world, but the adoption will take longer than expected. Social commerce is not the one-and-only savior; it is one additional tool to facilitate the sales process.

Using social commerce, we will also find an answer to the often-discussed question of ROI from social media. Sales are the ultimate link to ROI for efforts in social media. As discussed in Chapter 10, often it is hard to link effects from social media, such as an improved audience *reach* to an ROI. The "R," or the financial *return*, is often too undefined, or a causation is too hard to prove (see Chapter 9). This is different with social commerce. One can create a direct link between the investment into a social sales channel and the return in terms of additional margin dollars earned.[2]

DATA-DRIVEN SALES

Related to *social commerce* is the usage of data within the sales approach. But while the data might be taken from social interactions, this data is by no means the only source available to support sales activities. The second part of this chapter will touch on a few standard topics about the way data can be used to improve the sales experience. The underlying aim here is the same. Like with social commerce, we are using data to create one of the two major drivers in a sales process: *knowledge* and *trust*. Let's look at the following cases:

- You are about to choose a movie to download on Netflix, and the site recommends one that has already been seen by three of your friends. Netflix uses your social graph to motivate you to see this movie as well. You know your friends and you trust their taste, and this might motivate you to watch the movie.
- You search for a book on Amazon. In addition to showing you the book itself, Amazon lists its ratings from other customers, and suggests books other people have purchased. Some of these look interesting, and you add one or two of them to your order. Amazon is using the purchasing behavior of you and others to gain knowledge about you.

2. Please note that other channels might be cannibalized, prohibiting a 100% direct relationship between investment and return.

Those two cases are using the data available about you. In both cases, an algorithm combines data taken from your user behavior—meaning what you have bought and done before on the site—with information about your friends (in the Netflix example) or with information about what the general public (in the Amazon example) would do. The data is used to create knowledge about you. We commonly refer to this process as *recommendation engine*. The second part of this chapter will explain what recommendation engines are and the main challenges in setting them up.

Reach Versus Intention

Social commerce can be seen as having two distinct levels: creating brand awareness (*reach*) and stimulating a *purchasing intent* with subsequent sales. It is important to understand that they are not the same.

Reach describes how many people notice your product offering. Many of the social features of ecommerce sites offer a way to create reach (e.g., one can like a product so your friends see that you liked it). But commerce as such is only then generated if there is a *purchase intent*. Therefore, social commerce will be successful only if both components (*reach* and *intent*) are linked together.

There are many ways to create *reach* via social media to spread the news about your product and to find customers (buyers) online. For example:

- People can create their own "like lists" and offer them publicly. These can also be personalized and sent to specific friends.
- People can easily share ideas and fashions with others, both on general social networks like Facebook and specialized sites like Pinterest.
- People can be encouraged to share their interests through incentives ranging from attention to overt rewards. For example, eyeglass manufacturer Warby Parker ships prospective customers five pairs of frames and encourages them to post videos on YouTube of themselves modeling the glasses for friends to vote on. Still other companies reward sharing, like address book manager *evercontact.com*, which gives a free month of service to customers who tweet about the company.
- People can have songs they are listening to or news stories they are reading automatically posted to social networks such as Facebook.

All of these could build reach and, potentially, awareness. Also, each of them is easily done. This kind of ease of use is a necessary feature of socially created reach. To support the product and to spread knowledge of it should be as simple for consumers as a click. This is the geniality of the one-click "like" button from Facebook. You can find many similar examples, all of which pretty much make possible the spread of information by piggybacking on the social network connections of the customer.

But as we have noted previously, reach or awareness is not purchasing intent. Creating intention is much harder than creating reach. For example Compass.co,[3] a young startup founded by Bjoern Lasse Herrmann, found out that social media as a primary acquisition channel is two times more effective than traditional methods if the company offers "free" products (monetized indirectly). To get a "free" product onto the market, no high intent is needed. Thus reach or awareness are sufficient and can be created by social media. The picture is different if you look at paid products. Here, Compass.co found out that most companies naturally tend to focus on traditional methods such as direct sales and partnerships, as they are better in creating a purchasing intent in comparison to a pure social media outreach.

And how do you create intent? Any human salesperson will know that trust and knowledge are essential in creating purchase intent. For example, the sales rep at a brick-and-mortar fashion store might offer a customer a jacket based on her age and what she is wearing at that moment. The salesman's knowledge guides him, as he knows that this specific type of jacket sells best with people like her. He then will build *trust* through small talk. At the end, he will compliment the customer with, "This jacket looks fantastic on you" to entice her to buy it. Likewise, an insurance salesperson will often create a relationship of trust, which she then will leverage to explore the needs of a client and his family, and then fulfill those needs through her knowledge of insurance.

Trust and knowledge are not only needed in the offline world but also in the virtual world. In the following sections, we will see two ways in which social media can be used to create *purchasing intent*: via social confirmation and peer pressure. Later, we will see how the knowledge gained from a social group can be used to create recommendations and therefore purchasing intent.

3. Lutz Finger is an advisor to Compass.co.

SOCIAL CONFIRMATION CREATES TRUST

Social confirmation involves people online saying that a given product is good. It creates the trust that was missing so far in online interactions beyond big brand names. Examples of this include two forms of displaying actual purchasing intent.

User Ratings

User reviews can create a significant competitive advantage.[4] These display intent by enabling users or customers to give a numerical or "star" rating, often anonymously. Physician evaluation website HealthGrades.com, for example, enables patients to provide anonymous ratings from zero to five stars, without fear of reprisal from their doctors seeing the ratings. Similarly, RateMyProfessors.com enables students to provide ratings for their teachers on criteria such as easiness, helpfulness, and clarity, as well as a separate binary "hotness" rating if they are physically attractive. In both cases, rating results are displayed publicly.

It is important to note that social confirmation alone is not always a measure of quality. For example, a highly competent but gruff doctor may get poor ratings online, and the same could be true with a brilliant professor who is a tough grader. Ratings that reflect the feelings of someone who posts online are often no substitute for objective data such as medical or academic outcomes. However, *trust* is important, and personal opinions online often contribute to the process of building this *trust*.

User comments

Just as we normally select only restaurants where there are people happily eating at this very moment, we tend to buy things when there are positive user comments. Many of us will no longer book a hotel room or go to a restaurant without first visiting a site such as TripAdvisor.com, an independent source that enables people to post comments about their traveling experiences. The power of such user comments sites can be gauged by the fact that hotel booking sites like Hotels.com, which has its own rating and commenting systems, now also link to TripAdvisor's comments.

Please note that social confirmation can be utilized in any tool. It could be Facebook, Twitter, or anywhere else. In order to decide which kind of social media to use, you should ask yourself two questions:

4. Tim O'Reilly, "What is Web 2.0: Design Patterns and Business Models for the Next Generation of Software," Communications & Strategies, 2007, *http://ssrn.com/abstract=1008839*.

- Which tool can create the best *reach* into my customer base?
- Where will I be able to own the user comments so that I can use them for other purposes the way I want to?

PEER PRESSURE

A step up from social confirmation involves someone from a customer's own personal network confirming his *purchasing intent* for products and services. This is the ultimate social confirmation, because it is not just anyone recommending a product, but a friend whom the customer knows. Many sites facilitate this process by displaying pictures of people from an individual's network who bought something—or, more recently, as in the case of Facebook's Open Graph Search functionality, by creating the ability to mine data through one's social connections (for example, a list of books that are liked by journalists).

This aspect of social media is especially helpful if a service or product depends on network externalities. Take the adoption of a messenger service like Whatsapp or Skype. Both services would benefit highly from a tool that tells the user which of her friends are on it. Another example is the decision to purchase a ticket for a concert. If a person already knows that some of his friends are going, he will make sure that he is there as well, so as not to miss out.

This process leverages the network of an individual, and thus people with a bigger network can be used for more social confirmation than others. Are those people influencers? As we discussed in Chapter 1, the concept of an "influencer" is often overrated. The person with the biggest network might be used the most to create a social confirmation. But the network size does not say anything of its ability to create an intention. Intention might be created at a local level by only a few very specific personal contacts. A well-designed social commerce setup will need to learn this kind of network information that goes way beyond any network size description.

DO SOCIAL CONFIRMATION AND PEER PRESSURE WORK?

Most of us marketeers wish that social commerce would enable us to click a few buttons and suddenly we've created purchasing intent with our potential customers. We get this asked all the time: "What do I need to post so that my products sell more?" or "Which tool should I use so that my sales double?" Reality does not work this way, of course. Whether or not social commerce works depends on the customers and the product. We see, however, that some social commerce tools work better then others in most cases.

It also seems that average shoppers prefer structured data, such as ratings and reviews, as social confirmation. There is a demonstrable impact: one study by eccomplished found that the number of people using online ratings and reviews is about eight times higher than the number of people using only social media recommendations (see Figure 2-1). For us, this shows that the ordered format of an aggregated sum of online reviews is more successful in persuading someone to buy something than the relatively unstructured format of different blogs, tweets, and the like.

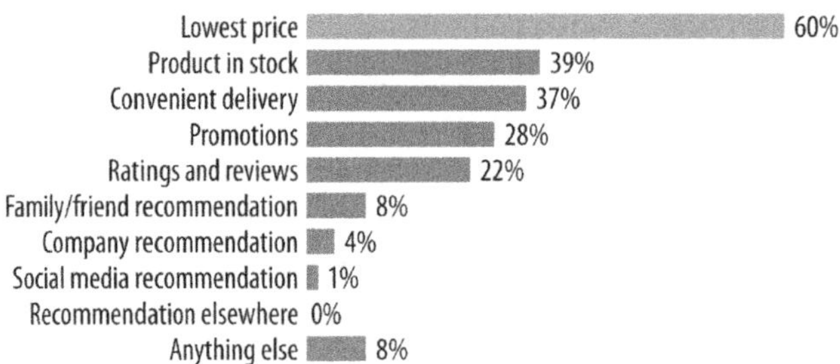

Figure 2-1. Reviews are more important than social media alone. (Courtesy of eccomplished.)

Unfortunately up to 38% of those reviews are actually fake or paid.[5] Those fraudulent reviews are an issue for all social networks. As soon as consumers realize they were tricked, they'll lose trust and the power of social endorsement and social confirmation will vanish. That is the reason why more companies offer what was specifically recommended by your connections. Those kinds of recommendations are so far not that common since there are often not enough reviews within one person's network to provide an effective customer experience. This will change as social networks become a bigger part of our daily shopping experience. Friends' recommendations will become some of the most effective ways to create *intention*. They can be easily transported into the world of social commerce even without the knowledge of social media tools or social graphs. For example, Leskovec and his

5. Arjun Mukherjee et al. "Spotting Fake Reviewer Groups in Consumer Reviews," International World Wide Web Conference (WWW-2012), April 2012, *http://bit.ly/1jSvvWH*.

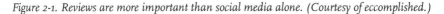

colleagues described the success of a sales attempt in which the first person to purchase an item recommended through an emailed referral link got a 10% discount, and the recommender received a 10% credit.[6]

Data such as these indicate that social confirmation and peer pressure do, in fact, influence our purchasing intent. This view is further validated by the large sums of money many large firms spend on mining and delivering such social confirmation. Though we feel that we are independent, and indeed we do not like being told what to do, the opinions of others often influence our own decision-making process.

WHAT—OR WHO—WOULD MAKE YOU BUY?

Reviews and recommendations can influence consumer decisions about what to buy and whether or not to buy something. But how can one manage these in order to have the most positive impact on purchasing intent? For instance:

- If there are many reviews, which one should we feature first?
- If there are many friends who liked a product, how should we rank them?
- If consumers' friends or people similar to them bought something, should we or should we not recommend this to them?

Those questions can be answered using recommendation engines or systems, the point where big data analytics and social media intersect. Recommendation systems select the product, review, or even site layout that is best for the consumer's given aim. Compared with pure review sites such as TripAdvisor.com, which does not rank comments from visitors, a recommendation system openly facilitates a purchasing decision by suggesting things a consumer is most likely, based on data, to want.

Even if, on the surface, there are no social features—and thus no comments, no ratings, and no Facebook friends—recommendation engines use a collaborative approach to recommend products that others "like you" have bought. Thus it is a social group feature, as the engine has put similar consumers into a group and then suggested something for them to buy. The work of those engines often occurs within milliseconds, in a way that is invisible to the normal user.

6. Jure Leskovec et al., "The Dynamics of Viral Marketing," ACM Transactions on Web, 2007, *http://bit.ly/1bymUAt*.

Recommendation systems are perhaps the most critical link between social data and purchasing intent. The next sections explore the function, technology, and development of these systems.

Recommendation Systems

Go to Amazon and look up one of your favorite books. It will show you information about the book, of course. But one of the most prominent things that will catch your eye on the same page is a section entitled "Customers Who Bought This Item Also Bought" with a list of other books.

Or go to Netflix, which recommends movies based on factors ranging from your social circle to box-office performance. You may not realize it, but these recommendations have as much to do with algorithms such as regression analysis and singular value decomposition as they do with what people rented last week.

These are examples of recommendations systems, and their purpose is to foster incremental purchasing intent. They have become extremely common, and these days, they are ubiquitous among ecommerce systems. They are also big for business. For example, roughly 60% of rentals from Netflix are based on personal recommendations, and their Netflix Prize competition awarded $1 million in 2008 to the first team to develop an algorithm that could improve the accuracy of its predicted movie ratings by 10%. For companies the size of Netflix, which generated a revenue of $3.2 billion in fiscal year 2011, better recommendations can have a tangible financial impact.

While recommendation systems are not always obvious to the end user, they are everywhere, and not only restricted to social commerce. For example, Google ranks search results for you personally, your favorite newspaper selects news articles on its web page to fit your taste, Last.fm suggests music to you based on your previous musical choices, and a social network like LinkedIn suggests people you might know and thus should connect to.

Recommendation systems try to take as much information as they can about consumers and calculate on the fly what to recommend. Recommendation engines are the best example of how to get value—our fourth "V"—from the data. Often to get this value, companies try to gather as much information as possible. For example, Google measures up to 25 signals about each consumer, and based on those signals, it will offer search results. These signals include:

- Whether the user is on a mobile device, a PC, or a Mac

- Location data, such as whether the user is signed in from the US, Europe, or India
- The user's search patterns, including whether or not the user has signed into Google and opted in to sharing data

Depending on these signals, different search users may see Mac applications versus PC ones, German versus English commentary, or articles about baseball batters versus cricket batters. More importantly, the context of previous unrelated searches may influence the results; one person may get travel articles about a country, while another may get political or economic articles.

Recommendation systems creating knowledge about a user and his purchasing behavior, together with user reviews and ratings creating trust and reach, form the backbone of what we call *social commerce.* Their underlying strategy is to make the customer feel special. They use a system that adapts the website to each consumer personally and decides what is best suited for the consumer in hopes of increasing his purchasing intent.

All of those systems used to create recommendations based on data. This data could be based either on consumers' past behavior, or it could be based on the content of the product itself. Thus, recommendation systems can be split into two areas: *collaborative* systems that leverage one's social data, or the collaborative wisdom of the crowd and *content-based* systems that rely exclusively on content.

COLLABORATIVE RECOMMENDATIONS

Most of the examples we discussed in this chapter are based on collaborative recommendation systems. Sometimes we refer to them as crowdsourced systems, as they use patterns from other users or user actions. As a very simple example: if Pete and Tom both purchase items 1 and 11, but Tom also purchases 2 and 4, then 2 and 4 are likely to be recommended (rightly or wrongly) to Pete. Tom is also sometimes called the "identical twin," as his behavior is similar to Pete's. In reality, those systems will look not only for Tom to recommend products to Pete but to many others as well.

The most famous example of a collaborative recommendation system is Amazon's listing of what people who bought the same book also purchased, as described previously. Amazon can take advantage of a database of millions of users to drive these recommendations.

Note that this collaborative approach is different from the content-based approach, which we will discuss next.

Recommendation Systems Can Guess Inaccurately

It is important to note that recommendation systems are more than capable of guessing incorrectly. Since they use the collaborative approach, they predict what is on average the normality. But the average might not always be correct (see Figure 5-1). For example, *New York Times* bestselling business author Carol Roth once complained in a blog that Google infers that she is a male over age 65, when in fact she is a woman decades younger.[7] Note that Google will gladly disclose its assumptions about your demographics at Google Ads.

If you are logged in to Google, it can save all your searches and deduce your demographic profile using this past search history. Huffington Post columnist Catharine Smith—another young woman typecast by Google as an older male—notes that you can also change these preferences within Google.

A fictional reference in a US television show, *The Mind of a Married Man*, underscores the skepticism people can have for such systems. One of its characters declares, "My TiVo thinks I'm gay" to his friends, complaining that because he asked his TiVo device (a video recording system) to save a couple of shows that are also favored by homosexuals, he now cannot stop it from recording shows such as *Queer as Folk*, even after he tries to force it to record traditional "man" fare in a vain attempt to reprogram it.[8]

In the case of Carol Roth, content-based recommendation systems do not fare much better. She notes that because of her frequent purchases of baby oil for use in the shower, the department store chain Target now believes that she is pregnant, even going so far as to send her a sample of infant formula from one of its suppliers. Her point? Be careful what you presume when you are targeting customers based on big data. On a broader scale, it means that human nature is more complex and less deterministic than even our best algorithms can deduce today, which means that while they do help marketeers, they are not a guaranteed solution in every case.

7. Carol Roth, " Big Data: Google Thinks That I'm a Dude and Target Thinks That I'm Pregnant," blog, May 2012, *http://bit.ly/1bZ6Bmy*.

8. *http://youtu.be/PoUJvAQg7KI*

You might think that these are random issues of accuracy that might go away over time. Yes, again, on *average*, you will be right. However, please also see that there is a more complex underlying issue if we trust too much on the "wisdom of the crowd." If we believe that the algorithm with millions of data lines knows more than we do, we are giving up on our own ability to judge and to stand up for ourselves. Jaron Lanier, who is a pioneer in virtual reality, criticizes this tendency. He coined the term digital Maoism, pointing out that it is wrong to readily trust the wisdom of the crowd: "If we start to believe the Internet itself is an entity that has something to say, we're devaluing those people and making ourselves into idiots."[9]

CONTENT-BASED RECOMMENDATIONS

Each of us has already touched a content-based recommendation engine. At a shopping site, for example, a system might pull up items that are similar to the ones you recently purchased. For example, if you selected a red shoe for checkout, suddenly there might be a lot of other red shoes on your screen. Those shoes might be placed via advertisements on banners or via your online store, directly in the "recommended" section. The algorithm selected the shoes because it realized that you are about to buy a red shoe. As we saw in Chapter 1's discussion of behavioral targeting, the chance of creating purchasing intent is greater the closer a consumer is to the point of sale. So if you already voiced the purchasing intent to buy a red shoe, why not have the system try to suggest other red shoes? This approach has nothing to do with the tastes of your friends or similar people. It has only to do with the content of the item selected, hence the name *content-based* recommendation engine.

Data for content-based recommendations often takes one of two forms: either data based on consumers' shopping, purchasing, or search history or a specific user profile that enables the consumer to define her preferences for easier shopping. For example, US shoe retailer Payless allows consumers to enter their gender and shopping preferences, and keeps track of their past ordering history. This data is used to customize in-store recommendations or mail advertising. It is purely based on the content consumers said they like and not based on the patterns of others.

Content-based systems have one disadvantage. To identify similar products, you need a specific description of any product. When looking at a product (clothes,

9. Jaron Lanier, "One Half A Manifesto," Edge, Mai 2005, *http://bit.ly/1j08hQr*.

ladies, evening wear), you can easily suggest an evening dress from the same category. However, these categories need to exist in the first place; if you have a product that falls into fewer categories (clothes, ladies), then the system might choose a pair of gym shorts to display next to the evening dress.

When customers do not have the ability to rate items, and companies do not have an infrastructure for evaluating the purchasing history of similar buyers, businesses are often left with content data as the only criteria for making purchasing recommendations. Such data is often less accurate than collaborative data and requires careful planning of data categories to avoid wildly inconsistent recommendations. At the same time, these content-based systems are often much easier to implement, particularly for applications with a smaller audience and/or limited access to social data.

Kickstarting Content-Based Recommendation Systems

Content-based recommendation systems need classifications for each item. Let's say you run an online store for clothing and shoes. Each of your items needs a tag describing the item. For example, one item could have the tags `class=shoe`, `sex=female`, or `type=high-heel`. Once a customer chooses an item with those tags, a content-based recommendation system would look for items that have the same kind of tagging.

What would you do if you do not have such a classification? One way to kickstart your system would be to tap into the unstructured knowledge of social media. For example, you could have your system read all tweets and user comments about a given product. That content in aggregate would create a tag cloud that classified the product. The more customers referred to this item as a "shoe," the higher the tag `shoe` would be ranked. This process is an unsupervised machine-learning effort, as there is no right or wrong way that can be used as training data.

To be successful, you should be quite targeted; in other words, the keyword search terms used to create the tagging algorithm should be very limited. As we see in Chapter 4 while talking about sentiment, the efforts needed to train a generic sentiment algorithm would exceed the potential gain from such a system. However, by only focusing on a specific category such as hotel rooms and searching discussions about stays at a hotel, you could successfully employ such a tagging system.

The beauty is that this would quickly enable you to create a content-based recommendation system with a good set of classifiers. All you need is historical social media data about your products. Those are available via offerings such as Gnip or Data Sift.

The Technology of Recommendation Systems

So what goes into a system that predicts whether a potential customer is going to like a specific item? Basically, the computer stores data for each customer. What did he buy? What did he look at? Which country is he in? At what time was he online? What is the weather like? (Yes, even the weather is a factor. If it is sunny, people are less likely to go online and buy things.)

Based on these data points, the recommendation machines are trained by situations in which people actually bought something. At a more abstract level, this is called positive reinforcement, meaning that the desired action was successfully completed. In the future, the algorithm should suggest the same thing in a similar setting in order to create another positive reinforcement. Because there is a *true* answer, as there is in our previous case to the question of whether the customer did or did not buy, the learning process is called *supervised*.

Supervised learning is a classical machine-learning problem. It has existed since 1959, when Arthur Samuel wrote a program that played the game of checkers against itself. Here was a possibility for the system to learn, because after each move, the computer would realize whether or not it had lost. In this way, the computer soon learned to play checkers better than Arthur himself. What has changed since 1959 is the amount of available data. Any supervised learning program needs the data in order to "learn." Thanks to billions of user transactions online, this data is now available.

It is beyond the scope of this book to look into the technology of machine learning, but to give a simple example, let's discuss regression analysis. Assume you are living just outside a big city and you have to commute each morning to work. Once rush hour kicks in, you know it will take a really long time, so you wonder when would be a good time to leave. You will determine this by using your "intuition": "If I leave after 8:15, it normally takes me much longer to get into the office." Machine learning, or regression analysis, in its most basic form, would formalize this process. You do not need to be a statistician to do this. If you plot the duration of your daily commute over the time you leave the house, you will soon have a nice graph that will help you to predict your commuting times. If you get a computer that could draw that curve for you, the program would be considered a machine-learning program (Figure 2-2).

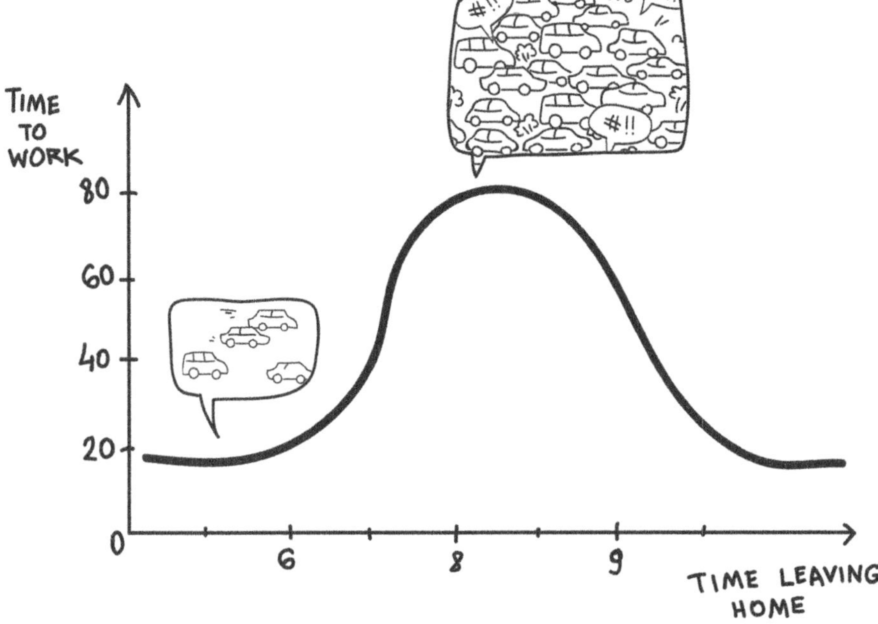

Figure 2-2. Regression algorithm to decide when you should leave home to minimize the commuting time

This is, of course, a simplified example, and in reality you would need to include variables such as weather conditions and school holidays. The more complex the problem becomes, the more difficult it will be to solve it. If you want to know more about support vector machines (SVMs), linear regression, logistic regression, naive Bayes, and other algorithms, there are excellent introductory texts, videos, and online courses. For the beginner, the Stanford class on YouTube by Andrew Ng is a good place to start.

Machine learning has reached such a maturity over the last half century that you can create a learning setup quite easily, simply by using a packaged solution of most statistical language programs such as R, SAS, or others. Those software packages already offer a wide selection of different algorithms. They all compete along two dimensions: speed and accuracy.

If you do not want to be too technical, you could even more easily use a prepackaged solution such as the Google Prediction API, which was launched in 2011.

This program enables users to build a recommendation engine on the fly. However, be aware that data is the competitive edge for your social commerce and that this power is shared via the API, meaning Google learns from your data as well.

Next, we will look at the typical issues you can face when starting a recommendation engine, beyond pure technical issues such as speed or scalability.

THE COLD-START PROBLEM

Collaborative recommendation systems are based on "supervised learning." In order to make recommendations based on what others have done or purchased, the program needs to analyze similar historical data. Therefore, at the beginning of a program, the computer doesn't know anything, and the likelihood is high that its recommendations will be wrong. Being wrong is a bad thing, because your early customers could lose trust in your ability to make recommendations. This is why sites such as Amazon had to wait until they were running for a while and had more data to work with before they could start making recommendations.

For example, FOUNDD is a young Berlin-based startup that has built a recommendation engine for the movie industry. Despite its brilliant algorithm, the cold-start issue is a serious problem. Without having a long purchase history, such as Netflix would have, the algorithm will not be able to recommend anything useful. Fully aware of it, the founder created a "hot or flop" page in the beginning. Each customer has to rate 10 movies before the system aims to recommend anything. "It has to be fun," said Lasse Clausen, one of the founders. "Otherwise the user won't do it, and we will not get up and running." In order to bypass the cold-start problem, Lasse and his team are are initially using a content-based approach by pre-clustering similar movies according to their genre or popularity.

Only after 5 to 10 movies are rated can the system start recommending. Are 10 movies enough? Most likely not for a superb recommendation, but the more the users rate the movies, the better the system will become at detecting each individual's preference.

The combination of pre-clustering and initial user input is the best way to avoid the cold-start issue as demonstrated by FOUNDD. Alternatively, if possible, initial "learning" data can be drawn from external sources and then improved upon over time with a company's own customer data.

NOT ENOUGH DATA

A much bigger issue than the cold-start issue has yet to be faced by FOUNDD, the startup we just discussed. They have focused on a set of movies, but when you have thousands of items in your store, it is difficult to figure out which ones are best to recommend.

This issue is often called *data sparsity*. It is similar to the cold-start issue but broken down in terms of each product. If a retailer has millions of items, it is hard to find good ways to suggest items from the "long tail," or the millions of items that are not best sellers but still get sold. To recommend products from this long tail, the algorithm needs to include a minimum number of purchases for each of these products.

According to one of the top five online retailers in Germany, the biggest sales come from a changing online assortment, thus the data for their long tail is quite small despite having the potential for many users and many purchases. As a result, the recommendation engine could only suggest its biggest non-changing sales item, which happens to be socks. Of course, recommending socks with each and every purchase did not drive increased incremental sales. The retailer eventually addressed this issue by having a student write manual recommendations for more appropriate goods instead of using a machine-learning approach.

The more complex the system is, and the more items there are to recommend, the more difficult it is to make a good recommendation due to the potential issue of *data sparsity*. For example, LinkedIn serves employment advertisers by recommending the right people for their posted job ads. For this functionality, LinkedIn needs a tremendous amount of data; such a service was not feasible even with 10 million users. But now that they have more than 100 million users with highly variable data points, it must be addressed as a big data problem. In the extreme, issues such as tastes in human style or matching specific body shapes to clothing choices can also require millions of matching data points in order for a machine to begin to make an accurate recommendation.

NO SURPRISES

Machines only learn based on popular choices. Thus, they are more likely to recommend the obvious popular choices that are safer to recommend.

Let's say you have just finished the fourth book of the seven books in the Harry Potter series. What will be a likely recommendation from a machine-learning algorithm? The correct answer: books one through three. But that is not useful, since you most likely have already read them. Similarly, recommending book five would not be helpful, as you probably already know that it exists. A good recommendation would be a book in the same genre or style or maybe based on one of the other attributes of the book that you appreciated the most.

A good bookseller will understand your needs quickly. A recommendation engine will, at least so far, only recommend what others have read. This is the reason Amazon cannot replace the recommendation of a human bookseller—at least not yet.

Who Filters Your Information?

Online recommendation systems are all around us. They get trained with the most popular choices, and they might take away the element of surprise from us, even without us noticing. Online political organizer Eli Pariser speaks about what he calls the "filter bubble," where online content providers start narrowing our worldview in a misguided effort to personalize.[10] Let's say you are interested in politics and you have a liberal opinion. A machine-learning algorithm will soon realize your personal choice as you seem to read more liberally toned articles than anything else. To improve your satisfaction and your own click rate, the machine will start to filter out conservative views. Those opinions will slowly disappear, and you will not see them anymore.

HOW TO BUILD A RECOMMENDATION SYSTEM: START SMALL

If you were to scratch the surface of the major recommendation engines, you could envision a set of complex analyses guarded by a top-secret formula. At the top of the online retailing spectrum, there is in fact some truth to this stereotype. But a more important point is that, for most people, recommendation systems revolve around making use of clear and observable data.

Let's look at the leaders in recommending emotional content, such as Amazon and Netflix. Both have great recommendation systems. Their sites suggest things to their users such as movies to watch or books to read, and the recommendations are very important to sales. At Netflix, 75% of all user choices are based on recommendations made for them by their own system. During the Strata 2012 conference, Xavier Amatriain (@xamat) from Netflix explained some of the inputs that are used by their recommendation system:

User ratings
: Plain user feedback on movies watched.

10. Eli Pariser, "Beware online 'filter bubbles'," TED Talks, March 2011, *http://bit.ly/IRt6N3*.

Context
Uses, for example, the time of the day or week as an indicator.

Popularity
General metric on what is popular among users overall.

Interest
What is the user normally interested in, and what kind of interests did she list in her profile?

Freshness
The aim to offer new and diverse ideas to the user.

Friends' recommendations via Facebook
What do the user's friends like?

Those are many variables, and there are surely more. But more importantly, each of those six areas are influenced by several indicators taken out of millions of data points from 23 million subscribers in 47 countries with over 5 billion recommendations. Mind-blowing? Probably not! If you look further into your own company, you will find similar amounts of data lying around. Most of it is probably not used; or even worse, it might not be easily accessible as it is within Netflix. However, you have a complexity of your own, and the question you must ask yourself is how to use the data.

Let's have a look at how Netflix has used the data. It did not start out with many different variables; it started out with just a simple method of recommendations. As discussed in Chapter 9, the strategy it used is highly suitable because it is:

Easy to measure
Netflix asks the users for their preferences directly.

Low on error
We can assume that people are rating those videos accurately or, at least, honestly.

High on correlation
The correlation between the users' tastes in the past and in the future is very clear.

The lesson learned from Netflix is to start simple. Only after the correlations were proven did Netflix start to expand the system step by step. It started by optimizing a few metrics where causation was highly predictable and then built from there. Even today, when according to Netflix, 75% of what people view is recommendation-based, it continues to refine features and algorithms using a simple baseline of viewer opinions. Looking at your own process of using recommendations, you could boil the process down into three key guidelines:[11]

- Start small and with only a few data points.
- Refine your effectiveness, and don't use all the data available because data without a sound approach is just noise.
- Reduce your variables based on accuracy, relevancy, and cost.

Trust, Personality, and Reason

As we discussed earlier, trust is a critical component of any kind of sales transaction. It has become particularly important in light of the issues discussed in the chapter on astroturfing and bots (Chapter 6), such as how people use social data to game the system. Things such as spam, fake followers, and astroturfing increase our suspicions, particularly when someone wants to sell us something. We see that there are two key ways to instill trust when it comes to online interactions:

- Trust in a product by the social confirmation of others.
- Trust in the algorithms to recommend the "right" item for our taste.

It is this social component of social commerce that instills trust. With trust, there will be a higher likelihood to buy, but please note that this is only one of many factors that could trigger purchasing intent. Moreover, the process of creating trust is, as we all know, not completely deterministic. Thus, while we may understand the overall logic and purpose of social recommendations, it is not 100% predictable how this process will work in any given moment or for any given product. In this way, the fuzzy logic of learning by machines can help. In time, we can create data that guides us in selecting, for example, which of several reviews might create the highest trust and with it the highest likelihood to lead someone to buy.

11. Xavier Amatriain, "Netflix Recommendations: Beyond the 5 stars," Netflix Tech Blog, April 6, 2012, *http://nflx.it/1bHzkKZ*.

Next to trust, there are two other factors that are supportive of the sales process: personal relationships and reason.

PERSONAL RELATIONSHIPS

"Hi Lutz, I am Brad your community manager. I wanted to check in with you to see how you like our product." Brad's Facebook picture smiles at the top of his email. It is a family photo of him at the beach. It is difficult to know whether Brad is a real person, a robot, or perhaps a human-guided robot, but this company clearly understands that personal relationships are an important part of the sales process, even if—or maybe especially when—someone shops online.

Netflix, as we mentioned earlier, benefits from the ability to tell customers which of their friends watched a movie and uses it as a trustworthy recommendation. However, not every company has products that are so commonly bought by many friends. If you are a bike retailer, you would need to be lucky to find some friends of your customers who just happened to have bought a similar bike and thus could be used as an endorsement to instill *purchasing intent*.

Therefore, in the future, we will see more and more attempts to create personal online connections between salespeople and customers in order to facilitate sales. The need for personal connection is not only needed for the sales process, but also for retention purposes. We will see in Chapter 4 how customer-care efforts in social media help to create a more personal face for a company and thus satisfy this human need for connection.

REASON

Research shows that users are highly sensitive to the reasons something is recommended to them. Providing an explanation seems to trigger an automated response pattern similar to the one observed by Robert Cialdini (see "Give Me a Reason" on page 63). The best recommendations are, of course, often those that can be linked to personal data, but this is not necessarily a requirement. Take Amazon, which analyzes our purchasing habits without knowing that our friends are, say, mountain bikers. Amazon's explanation of why these book recommendations are being made —because others liked them as well—is still much more powerful than just displaying the recommendations alone.

Give Me a Reason

An interesting experiment demonstrates the value of one of social psychologist Robert Cialdini's principles of influence.[12] Someone asks permission to cut ahead of people in line to use a photocopying machine, using one of three wordings, and then the number of people who agree is measured. The wordings are as follows:

"Excuse me. I have five pages. May I use the Xerox machine?"

"Excuse me. I have five pages. May I use the Xerox machine because I'm in a rush?"

"Excuse me. I have five pages. May I use the Xerox machine because I have to make some copies?"

The results were dramatically different when the person provided a reason for cutting in: 94% of people who gave the second statement were allowed to cut in, versus 60% of those giving the first statement. It is even more interesting that 93% of people using the third statement were allowed to cut in as well. With the second statement, a sound reason was given. With the third statement, a "placebo" reason was given—everyone waiting to use the machine had to make copies.

The difference is the use of the word "because," which triggered a reflex to treat the request as valid when *any* reason was given. This technique is known as *controlled responding*, in which results are governed by the language of the request rather than by the content of it.

Language has its limits. For example, in this study, placebo reasons were no more effective than no reason when the request was bigger. But it is clear that language—and testing—are potentially important factors in building trust for online purchasing intent.

Summary

A sales process relies on *knowledge* and *trust*. As noted in many other chapters, social media can be used in two distinct and very different ways. On one hand, social media supports sales operations: the tweets, the blogs, the reviews, and all the interactions with customers can create knowledge and trust in the products and hopefully increase sales. On the other hand, social media data by itself can create

12. Robert Cialdini, *Influence: The Psychology of Persuasion*, December 2006, *http://amzn.to/JiD9vO*.

insights that lead to knowledge about a potential consumer. Those methods of usage are very different and require very different skill sets. Do not ask the marketing agency for deep analytical insights. They will most likely fail in the same way the data scientist will fail to write a catchy marketing message for your Twitter account.

In the first part of this chapter, we discussed how to use social media during the sales process. Essentially the ideas are similar to the ones in Chapter 1. However, in comparison to the discussion there, we can link our action closer to sales success. Thus, we do not need so many descriptive variables. Revenue or closed sales are sufficient metrics. Social media, like no other area, has a feasible and impactful ROI metric.

In the second part of this chapter, we discussed the social media data. This data contains clues about our consumer. What do they think? What do they need? Those clues can help predict what the customer might want to do next. Unlike other areas in a company, predictive modeling comes into play. The binary form of sales process is helpful. Did he buy or not? Using machine learning we can build recommendation systems. We went over the different types and challenges of recommendation engines.

Ultimately, using social data to increase sales leverages human nature and human psychology. We want to trust what we buy, and in the process, we want to feel connected to others. Therefore, if we use smart algorithms to predict behavior, we need to be very careful how we communicate this knowledge.

There is still no magic bullet that will make people buy something, and there likely never will be; however, as the volume of data continues to grow, as well as the connections that can be made as a result, we have more potential than ever to understand and manage purchasing intent.

WORKBOOK

How can you use social media processes or social media data to support your sales processes? To get you thinking, look at the following workbook questions:

- What kind of knowledge is important for your customers? What do your customers normally know *before* they purchase your products?
- How important is trust in the sales process? Is this different in each stage of the sales funnel?
- Write down a typical sales flow, starting at the acquisition stage and continuing until the stage where the deal is closed.
- What social media tools could you use at each stage of this funnel to foster trust and knowledge?

Recommendation engines are an effective way of getting to the fourth "V," the value. Setting them up is not always easy, but it coud be the small steps that make the difference between success and failure:

- Look through the sales flow you described earlier: where within the flow could one use a recommendation system?
- What kind (collaborative versus content) would you use?
- How will your customer react to those insights? How could you best explain them without losing trust?

Have you found a new way of engaging within your sales channel? Engage with us via @askmeasurelearn or write on our LinkedIn or Facebook page.

Public Relations

> *Public relations is what you do with what you know and what others think about what you say.*
>
> **—JAMES E GRUNING[1]**

Just after Facebook went public with an IPO of over $100 billion, Mark Zuckerberg updated his status on his own Facebook page: "Mark listed FB on NASDAQ." Is this comment a form of public relations (PR)? Yes, Zuckerberg decided to publish some information about Facebook to the wider public. However, it is not the way PR traditionally used to work. In his case, no communiqué was written, no news embargo was requested, and surely no PR agency was hired to do this update. No, Zuckerberg just updated Facebook. That's it!

Is doing public relations work in an era of social media data as easy as updating a Facebook page? Yes and no! Many startups and smaller enterprises are profiting from this ease. Social media has created a "long tail" for PR activity similar to how online advertisements within Google or other services became more affordable for small and medium businesses. Will this in turn mean that we have reached the end of the PR profession? Not at all—in fact, the opposite is the case. Because of all of the new possible ways to communicate, PR work has become more complex. However, we now have more and better data with which to analyze the effectiveness of PR.

As James E. Gruning states it in his quote at the beginning of this chapter, public relations has two major tasks: to *distribute* and to *warn*. On the one hand, company information has to be distributed to clients, employees, stakeholders, or shareholders. On the other hand, the PR teams have to analyze how the information is spreading, in order to give warning if any unforeseen issues are arising.

PR professionals might argue that this is an oversimplified view on the world of PR. They often see relationship building with influencers as part of their work.

1. *http://en.wikipedia.org/wiki/Public_relations#cite_note-10*

In this book, however, we stick to measurements and social media. These two, however, restrict PR in the way Gruning described PR. Social media offers new ways to distribute information. Measuring surrounding social media helps identify early warning signs if things get out of control. In this chapter, we will look at the data and metrics supporting those two main tasks in more detail:

To distribute
: At "Measuring People" on page 70 we will see that the act of distributing information is centered around individual relationships between people. Despite the open nature of social media, it has not changed the way PR works, and thus the famous Rolodex and trusting relationships are still PR's biggest assets. What has changed, however, is that by the virtue of social media, there are measurements to assess those individual networks and gauge how central someone is within her own network. Further on, we discuss in "Measuring Distributing" on page 81 which metrics are best suited to assessing the success of such a distribution.

To warn
: The use of new media has also created new possible PR issues, which we discuss in "PR to Warn" on page 95. We will see why no tools or predictive algorithm can provide a good early warning system. However, by using social media engagement metrics and network topology, one can anticipate critical situations beforehand.

Many of the metrics that we will discuss in this chapter have made PR work in a more transparent and reliable way. Moreover, as PR has its touchpoints with the entire pre- and post-sale cycle, it shares many of the concepts we discuss elsewhere in this book. Take reach metrics. We discussed in Chapter 1 that reach is an important prerequisite to create influence. We will revisit this definition of reach in more detail because this metric is significant for PR professionals.

PR Often Has No Measurable ROI

We stressed that the fourth "V" in data is the value also discussed as ROI (return on investment). Traditionally, the financial impact of PR was difficult to measure for most businesses. The PR industry tried many things to become as measurable as its colleagues next door within the marketing departments. It even created the Advertising Value Equivalent (AVE), a measure which already states in its name the desire from PR, to be as measurable as advertising is. But since the AVE was not calculated in a sufficiently independent way, it fell short of solving the ROI debate.

Often, "impact" numbers like the AVE are made up freely by PR and marketing agencies to impress their clients. In our day-to-day work we have heard it more than once that a client requested a "number" to look better in reviews.

However, as discussed in previous chapters, social media comes on a wide range of new measurements. But *more* data does not necessarily mean *better* data. Will these additional social media data help to find the missing ROI in PR? In most cases, the answer seems to be "no." As you can see in Figure 3-1, the respondents to surveys done by ifbyphone claimed that PR campaigns are still seen as the worst to measure.

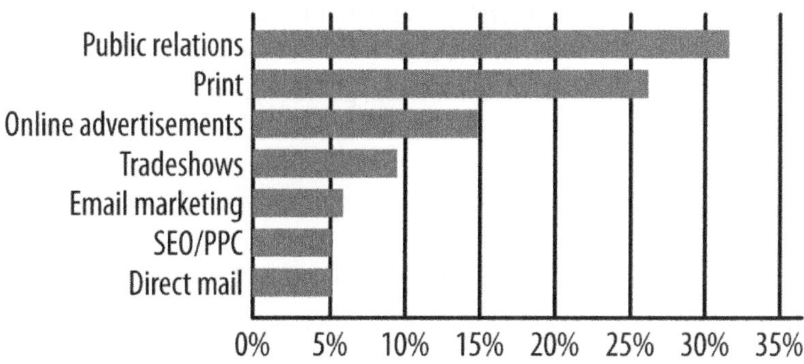

Figure 3-1. PR still is the worst to measure (Courtesy of ifbyphone.)[2]

We believe that this situation will not change, no matter how many new measurements the industry might invent. A ROI can be only calculated if our social media measurements can link to *financial metrics* either directly or inderectly. Later in this book, we will discuss the impact of metrics on ROI in more detail.

This link to financial metrics is what often is missing. If PR distributes information on the company, it is often as generic as the update from Mark Zuckerberg. It is probable that no one would have subscribed to Facebook because of this message, but it was an important one. Unlike an actionable marketing message, that information doesn't have any action attached, therefore linking to "hard" financial numbers is not possible.

There are even many companies that refrain from any communication. Take the company Moog, which produces motion-control equipment. The company

2. Marketing Survey done Dec 2011 by ifbyphone (*http://bit.ly/18G0EYQ*).

would often compare itself to parts of General Electric or Siemens. Have you never heard about them? No! That is not surprising because they have very limited PR activities. They do not distribute any information except if they have to. Does this hurt them? If you compare the financial numbers with their competitors'—who do PR—then there is no conclusion possible. We can neither say it was good to do no PR nor could we state the opposite. Another prominent example of such a "no PR"-strategy is the German food retailer Aldi. The company is one of Germany's biggest and most successful supermarket chains. It doesn't have a PR department, but that hasn't hurt its overall success in the market.

Often a direct link between distributing information and succeeding financially can't be established, and the PR industry seem to have given up on the quest to measure the ROI. But the fact that there's no direct link doesn't mean that PR has no value. Take the financial impact of PR failing to anticipate or warn about upcoming issues. With regard to this, Michael Buck, global executive director for online marketing at Dell, twisted the meaning of ROI of social media into "ROnI."

> *It should not be called* ROI, *but* ROnI = *Risk of* not *investing*
>
> **—MICHAEL BUCK (@MIKEGBUCK)**

PR has a clear value, ranging from reduced hiring costs due to a good image as an employer to better retention rates as clients identify themselves more with the company. However, it is difficult to impossible to attach a real financial value to it. This was always the case in the finance industry, and many thought that because of the vast amounts of data within social media, this would change. But it hasn't.

Measuring People

> *omgg, my aunt tiffany who work for whitney houston just found whitney houston dead in the tub. such ashame[d] & sad :(*
>
> **—AJA DIOR M (@AJADIORNAVY)**

To distribute information is a people business. Neither in the real world nor in the social media world are all people equal. Their distribution power is different. Aja Dior tweeted about Whitney Houston's death 27 minutes before the official news was released.[3] However, Aja's message did not spread any further because she was not connected to the right networks of people. As Gilad Lotan (@gilgul) from SocialFlow showed, the initial message from Aja did not go very far. Figure 3-2 shows as nodes all the user who responded to AjaDiorNavy's tweet. The connections indicate how the information went from one person to the next. The color indicates when someone reacted to this news. Only once the big news agencies released the information was the message distributed to a wider audience, as shown in Figure 3-3.[4]

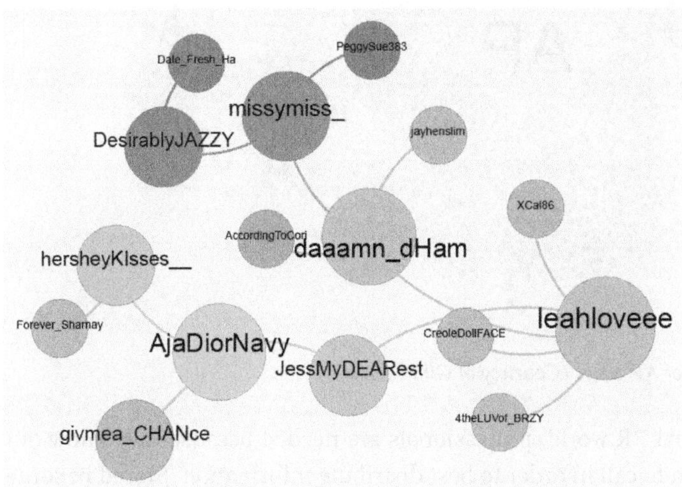

Figure 3-2. How Aja Dior's tweet spread (Courtesy of Gilad Lotan.[5])

3. Samantha Murphy, "Twitter Breaks News of Whitney Houston Death 27 Minutes Before Press," Mashable, Feb 12, *http://on.mash.to/18G245u*.
4. Gilad Lotan, "PDF12 Keynote: Networked Power (what we learn from data)," Social Flow Blog, June 2012, *http://bit.ly/1cqqPAB*.
5. *Gilad Lotan*, "Timing, Network and Topicality: A Revealing Look at How Whitney Houston Death News Spread on Twitter," Gilad Blog, *http://bit.ly/1bZfyfl*.

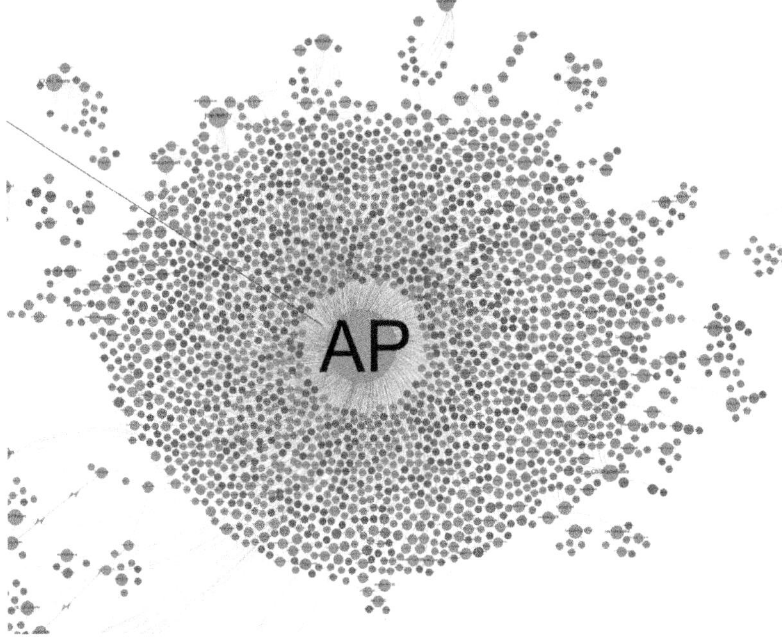

Figure 3-3. The spread of AP News (Courtesy of Gilad Lotan.[6])

In the traditional PR world, professionals are needed because they know out of experience whom to call in order to best distribute information. Stored in some form of "Rolodex," the PR professional would have names and contacts who allowed him to spread the message easily. Social media has the theoretical ability to connect everyone to everyone within a few clicks. Despite this, the need for the "right" connection has not changed. The information flow is *free* and everyone can easily participate, but as one can see in the case of Whitney Houston, not every person is equal. Some are better positioned to spread information than others.

While this idea is nothing new, the onset of social networks makes it easier to measure the flow of messages. Anyone can start measuring public discussions and identify persons central to the discussion. There are two main measurements to assess the ability to spread a message:

6. *Gilad Lotan*, "Timing, Network and Topicality: A Revealing Look at How Whitney Houston Death News Spread on Twitter," Gilad Blog, *http://bit.ly/1bZfyfl*.

Reach

Who and how many people can this person (or brand or institution) reach? What is the size of his network?

Context

What is the network interested in? In what context does the network believe the person (or brand or institution)? In what area does the person have an authority?

We will define those metrics in the following sections.

Warning

As we discussed in Chapter 1, people who can easily reach many others have often been labeled "influencers." This term is wrong because their power to really *influence* has been widely overestimated. It seems that most people are not influenced directly but rather follow a predefined homophily. However, in terms of dissemination of information, or reach, the position within a network is vital for the overall speed with which information can be distributed. Thus, there are people who can reach more than others.

REACH IN PR

Reach within PR is often defined as a measure of how far certain information was distributed and how many people or "eyeballs" were reached. Unfortunately, this metric is quite different depending on whether one looks at online media, social media, or traditional media:

Within Online Media, reach is best described by page views or how many people clicked on the site.

In theory, this should be the most accurate description of reach. But the devil is in the details, or as usual, measurements. There are several ways through which you as an owner of a web page can count page views. You could use a tagging system by which you play out a cookie to each visitor. The data derived from here will largely differ from the data you might draw up from your own log files. Why? In log files, you measure every visitor. Therefore you will measure scrapers and search engines as well as regular visitors. In the cookie-based systems, you measure only those visitors who actually accepted a cookie.

As you might have already imagined, for websites that you don't own and therefore can't place cookies on or analyze log files for, it's impossible to define reach. However, there are third-party providers (such as Alexa or Compete) that try to help with external measurements.

Within Social Networks, reach can be best described by the measure of centrality or "betweenness."

This describes how well a person is positioned to distribute information. The more *central* or *between* a person is in regards to other people in the network, the better she can control the flow of information. For further reading, we recommend the article from Linton C. Freeman, "Centrality based on Betweenness."[7]

The best way to measure centrality is to use software tools like Pajek. If you're looking for prepackaged measurements, there are several tools, like klout, kred, or peer index, that wrap several measures into a single number. The downside of those prepacked measurements is that the more common they are, the more people will try to deliberately influence them, as we will see in Chapter 6.

Within traditional media in TV or print, measures of centrality cannot be easily applied because the network topology is not easily measurable.

Instead, circulation rates describe in some form the impact of the news source. Unfortunately, circulation rates are based on TV program or a new source. A standardization body takes care of the audit. Social media outlets there are millions and millions thus stanardized and audited circulatio rates are harder (if not impossible) to set, knowing the circulation of a newspaper will not identify who the "gatekeeper" or "connector" is. Short of circulation numbers by journalists, traditional PR professionals use job titles and positions to assess the *personal impact and power* of a specific journalist. As you can imagine, this is a very subjective measure since different media companies use different words. A "senior editor" might not be that "senior" in another company. A big advantage of reach figures is that they are reliable. A standardization body takes care of the audit. Such an audit is not possible within social media outlets as there are many millions of them. It will be hard to get a standardized measure for them.

Those differences in the measurement make it difficult to compare the traditional media world with the social media one. Each measurement—reach or

7. Linton C. Freeman, "A set of measures of centrality based on Betweeness," Sociometry, 1977, *http://bit.ly/JiZU2H*.

centrality—within its own world (reach within traditional media or reach within social media) will work, but it's not possible to mix and compare those measurements. Thus, you can't compare the reach metrix from traditional media with the reach metric from social media.

CONTEXT IN PR

The right gatekeepers can help to distribute a message effectively; however, the context of the message is equally important. Each of us knows from experience that news like Whitney Houston's death is met with strong emotions and will spread easily. But how about an update of, lets say, the corporate privacy policy? That's less interesting, except when it is published in the midst of a public privacy debate, like the one surrounding the revelations by Edward Snowden.

Whether a message spreads or not also depends on the context of the message and the surrounding mood. Joseph E. Phelps and colleagues from the University of Alabama in 2004 examined which email topics get passed on. Not surprisingly, certain topics were more easily forwarded than others. While 48% of all emails containing jokes were forwarded, only 0.2% of all political messages were forwarded. Context plays a very important role.[8]

What does this mean for marketeers that jokes get forwarded so easily? Does this mean that would-be social marketeers need to start cracking jokes? In some cases, this is exactly the strategy that advertisers follow. For example, every year in the United States, humorous television advertisements are a tradition of the Super Bowl broadcast. Advertisers often create their very best work for this telecast, and the most memorable ads are subsequently seen by millions of people on YouTube and other websites. People spread links to these ads to their friends, primarily because they are funny, and the advertiser gets brand recognition in return.

Jokes aren't the only content that spreads. People also spread emotional and important information. Thus, another key conclusion we can derive from this study: people spread information based on their level of interest in it, as both readers and senders. We refer to this as the *context of the content* and the *context of the author*, which we describe in the following sections.

8. Joseph E. Phelps et al., "Viral Marketing or Electronic Word-of-Mouth Advertising: Examining Consumer Responses and Motivations to Pass Along Email," Journal of Advertising Research, Dec. 2004, *http://bit.ly/1gsMX4d*.

Context of the content

To estimate the context of content, one could use trending topics from messaging services like Twitter or Sina Weibo. Fisheye Analytics experimented with something which it called "mood of the nation," showing which news topics created the most engagement from the audience. Figure 3-4 shows a two-month period of UK newspaper articles and the respective discussions by their audience. In the beginning of the month, there was a high interest or a high number of articles in the entertainment and culture sections. This was mainly due to Frankie Cocozza, who was kicked off a television show called X Factor. Those news stories decayed over the course of the month. At the time of this writing, articles from the entertainment and culture sections are spiking again as we move toward New Year's Eve: many stories appear on fashion tips or what the stars will do for New Year's Eve. The question surely is what here is a leading and what is a lagging indicator, as we will discuss in the BP example in Chapter 9. Was it that the general public showed less interest in entertainment discussions, or was it that the journalists realized that there was nothing to add to the recent discussions? It was probably a combination of both, and it showed what the general journalist community considered newsworthy.

As one can see, the news cycle isn't cyclical and doesn't follow a weekly pattern. During those two months, there were several political news stories of interest, each of which had its own *long tail* in the news cycle.

Thus it is a good measure to balance various topics. For example, one can see that the topics on environment peaked in interest. To launch a message at the right time, it is important to understand the overall "mood of the nation." The more public interest there is already, the easier a message will be distributed. Companies like socialflow and others are offering services around those measures.

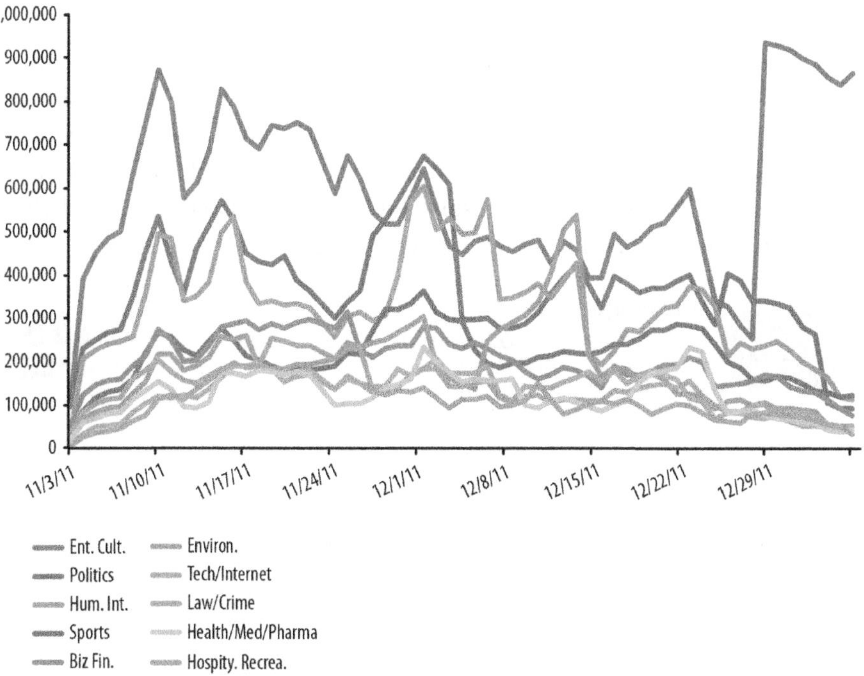

Figure 3-4. Mood of the nation (Courtesy of Fisheye Analytics.)

Context of the author

Next to this generic mood of the nation, there is also the *context of the author*: What does a specific journalist or blogger like to talk about? What excites him? Such background information is highly important since the pure knowledge of who is a "gatekeeper" will not help alone to distribute. The information we want to distribute needs to fit the interest of the gatekeeper. The measurement of this kind of context is best done by word clouds. There are many tools available to generate word clouds for the context of an author. See Figure 3-5 by peerindex to learn about the topics discussed by Lutz Finger. But again, be mindful when you start to compare those context charts or measures across different media types. Lutz Finger's interests depicted as a word cloud would look quite different if you take this book as data source compared to his Twitter account. Since the latter has the constraint of 140 characters, the information will be more pointed. However, both word clouds will contain the hint that the main interest of Lutz Finer seems to be data, social media, and analytics.

All of those tools have their shortcomings. In the simplest case, the tools use only word clouds. They are created by counting words and listing the most common ones. Such basic algorithms would not be able to understand that "debt crisis" and "euro crisis" should belong to the same group. To overcome this kind of shortage, one could use predefined entity extraction, or even better, train the algorithm. Both approaches can yield very accurate results; however, this will take time and effort to set them up for the specific requirements.

Figure 3-5. Peer index from Lutz Finger (Courtesy of Peer Index.)

JOURNALISM CRM

The first obvious use case of metrics like centrality and word clouds is the creation of a detailed database on journalists similar to the creation of a social CRM that we will discuss more in detail in Chapter 5. There are already noteworthy attempts of using social media data to create those databases. For example, the British Gorkana Group offers insights into journalists and bloggers:

> *We know the journalists, what they are writing about, and where they are going next. We know who you need to know and we are here to help you get to know them too.*
>
> **—FROM GORKANA GROUP**

One would be wrong to conclude that context and reach within a database will solve the question of who is a "gatekeeper" and who is not. An in-depth analysis of 1.6 million Twitter users found out that for sure the largest reach is generated by the ones who are central to a network, supporting what we saw in the case of Whitney Houston. However, the team around Eytan Bakshy (@eytan) from Yahoo! research also found out that no reliable prediction could be made about which tweets would spread and which would not.[9] At the end, it comes down to the fact that communication is human.

COMMUNICATION IS HUMAN

While there are ways to measure centrality and context, it would be hasty to conclude that one can easily distribute a desired message by only measuring those two metrics. During the onset of social media in the early years of the new century, this was a common trait in the discussion. Measurement companies surfaced left and right. In essence, communication is a human interaction; and while tools can guide, *execution* and *trust* within PR work are more important than any of the preceding metrics. For journalists and bloggers, the trust of their readers is their core asset. News has become a commodity which is accessible almost freely at any time everywhere. The value of information is not the information as such, but the ability to explain, sort, and organize the news around you. Those efforts go beyond pure information and require trust on behalf of the readers.

If, for example, you just started some charity in the educational space, an influential person to connect to could be Bill Gates. With more than 7.5 million followers on Twitter, he is definitely a well-connected person. Moreover, his own foundation has a strong focus on educational matters. So that seems like a match: high level of centrality and the right context! Why not ask him to *distribute* the word about your own charity?

Because the likelihood of that working is low.

Six principles of influence

While it might be easier today to reach Bill Gates then it was pre-social media, it is still as difficult to build trust or form relationships. In order to get someone to support your cause, you will need to convince him to. Robert Cialdini, professor of psychology and marketing at Arizona State University, has best described the

9. Eytan Bakshy, "Everyone's an Influencer: Quantifying Influence on Twitter," WSDM, Feb. 2011, *http://bit.ly/IRN1eY*.

process with the six key principles of influence: reciprocity, social proof, authority, commitment, liking, and scarcity. All but the last two have gained a new twist and opportunity through social media:

Reciprocity
: People tend to return favors. Dale Carnegie described this best in his book *How to Win Friends and Influence People* (Ebury), published in 1936. Dave recommends thinking first about what the person you want to connect to needs and what you could offer him before reaching out. Steve Knox, CEO of Proctor & Gamble, called this reciprocal altruism and used it to describe how his company should engage with all its customers on social media. Social media has made it easier to reach out to people and give favors.

Social proof
: People are more likely to do things that that you see as "socially accepted." Social proof through social media was best visible during the Arab Spring, as Clay Shirky, who teaches at NYU, has brilliantly described. The effect of social media during the Arab Spring was not the ability to easily connect and distribute information. It was the power to signal social proof. As Clay pointed out: "Governments aren't afraid of informed individuals—they're afraid of synchronized groups. In particular, they're afraid of groups that have shared awareness."[10]

Authority
: People tend to follow authority figures, as best shown in the Milgram experiments, where psychology researchers convinced subjects to continue shocking people who pretended to be other subjects, even when they cried out in pain. Who is an authority and who is not has become blurred within the world of social media, and it easier today to build an authority by, for example, becoming very central in your own network.

Commitment and consistency
: Cialdini proved that people who commit orally or in writing are more likely to honor that commitment. In the context of social media, these are the previously discussed measures of context. If the person who you want to connect to already has committed herself to a certain view, then it will be easier to build up a communication around this view.

10. *http://bit.ly/1gs9cVo*

However, the extent to which information is available to the public can make what people know about you border on being creepy. For example, one professor at the MBA school INSEAD who was invited to a discussion roundtable of industry leaders was shocked to discover that the organizer had distributed a thumb-thick file on her containing all her previous public pictures and discussions.

This, however, is only the beginning. As of 2010, the United States has instructed immigration agents on how to use Facebook to "friend" applicants for US citizenship, to better understand the background of these people and potentially uncover cases of fraud or misrepresentation, such as being deceptive about the state of a relationship. Do you think that most people would reject such an invasion of privacy? Don't be so sure. According to a 2007 survey by Sophos, 41% of people would accept a friend request from a random person.[11] Even worse, people are often tricked into accepting social media connections that may be instigated for fraudulent purposes such as identity theft.[12]

Measuring Distributing

In the last section we discussed how to analyze whether a blogger or journalist is well suited to *distribute* information. Often within organizations, however, a slightly different question is asked. How well has the PR team distributed information for the organization? Thus a measurement for the overall effectiveness of a PR team is needed. We need to split this discussion into two parts. On one side, we need to measure the distribution power; on the other side, we need to ask how much we invested in order to archive the distribution. Let's start with measurements of distribution power.

CLIPPING

"We will meet every morning at 5:30 a.m. On our way to the office, one of us will have sourced the newspapers down in the valley," explained Yann Zopf, associate director of the World Economic Forum to his students. During the annual meeting in Davos (Switzerland), about five students would, each morning, "clip" important articles from the day before.

11. Sophos, "Facebook ID probe shows 41% of users happy to reveal all to potential identity thieves," Aug 2007, *http://bit.ly/1kDuT4V*.

12. Darlene Storm, "EFF warns Big Brother wants to be your friend," Computerworld, Oct. 2010, *http://bit.ly/JjdzXz*.

The words "to clip" stem from a way of doing media monitoring. Each morning a few students would sit around with a pile of newspapers and "clip" relevant articles with scissors. At the end of this exercise, the articles would be counted. Afterward, all articles would be photocopied and placed on the desks of various managers. Today, surely Yann's team uses Google and screenshots and no real scissors anymore, but you would be surprised to know how many organization still have "clipping departments" that clip real articles rather than digital ones.

This process can be automated. A computer can search the Internet for the relevant keywords and clip out the parts of the document which make sense. There are several companies that offer more automated ways of doing this, including Factiva, Meltwater, and Moreover.

However, those clipping teams do one thing that the algorithms from those automated clipping companies cannot do so easily: they read the article, evaluate the relevance to their internal audience, and take only what seems really relevant.

Algorithms can can do some of this. But a computer will take *everything*, meaning all articles fitting the given keyword. As a result, the users often get information overflow. We found that professional PR departments are disappointed by the way those automated clipping services function. "They are inaccurate; they are giving me articles I am not interested in," a manager once complained to us. However, since the cost difference between a complete clipping department and the purchase of an online service is considerable, many companies move to those automated services and accept the reduction in quality. Plus, there are many ways to tailor the algorithms to the specific need of each client and improve what you get. The following measures are just a few examples of what could be asked so at to get more relevant articles:

- Is the keyword part of the headline? If yes, it is more likely to be a highly relevant article.
- Is the article long, and is the keyword used several times throughout the article? If yes, it is more likely be a highly relevant article.
- Is the article published by a source that has good reach, as described earlier in this chapter? If yes, it is more likely be an important article.
- Does the article contain content next to the keyword on which you have a special focus? If yes, it is more likely be a relevant article.

The World Economic Forum has moved away from its manual clipping service to an automated one. Using an automated service, it reduced manual clipping efforts which had at peak times clipped more than 30,000 articles per day. Not even its five-student team would be able to read them all. Using an intelligent system of reading lists, they reduced the work to focus on the most interesting parts. Today the World Economic Forum only needs one or two people looking over pre-selected articles for one hour, instead of five students "clipping" for two hours.

Note

There are some legal questions to be asked about today's automatic clipping services. Already, the traditional way of doing "clipping" was borderline illegal. After an article was "clipped," it would often be photocopied as well and distributed within the organization. Photocopying is a copyright violation. With automated tools, however, clipping companies are copying content from the Internet and charging their clients a fee. For the media companies, this is an even worse violation of their rights. The Newspaper Licensing Agency in the UK (NLA) started to take legal actions toward those automated clipping agencies. Meltwater tried to appeal this action in court and lost.[13] The end of this discussion is yet to come. Whether using automated clipping, like that done by Meltwater, search tools like Google, or content-curation tools like Flipboard or trap.it, many companies are starting to aggregate and republish information that is not their own.

THE MYTH OF NUMBER OF ARTICLES

The World Economic Forum automatically aggregates every article written about it. "It is not so much about the aggregation, but more about the smart insights," explained Yann Zopf. This focus on insights is critical to success. All too often we see how clients replace the traditional way of clipping with an automatic one. There is no additional step needed to analyze the aggregated articles. Articles are compiled and distributed throughout the organization.

Since automatic clippings create way more content than the traditional clipping method, managers often do not view individual articles anymore but focus on one single number: the number of articles "clipped." This number seemed to bring insights that suggested actions that could be taken. If this number was *high*, it seemed that the PR team did well; if the number was *low*, then improvements from

13. IFRRO, "UK Court of Appeal ruling in NLA v Meltwater case," Jul 2011, *http://bit.ly/1hPkc1Z*.

the PR team could be demanded. Is this the number we were looking for in order to measure the performance of the PR team? No, it is not.

The number of articles may have made sense at a time before the Internet, when the pace at which content was published in newspapers was limited. A newspaper had a set number of pages. The editor decided what to put onto those pages and what to leave out, depending on newsworthiness. The number of articles therefore had a value because it described how often the keyword passed this selection process by various editors. Today in the digital world, there are no space limitations. Everyone can start a blog, and each magazine can churn out articles at an ever-increasing rate. There is virtually no space limit. Without a reduced selection process, the number of articles increases. Moreover, there are publications that have no selection process at all. Those posting services offer an automatic *distribution* of content to any website. For example PR Newswire Europe offers, for less than $400, a so-called "Online Visibility Package" where they promise to distribute your articles as widely as possible, including to global websites, news services, and content aggregators.

> *Distributed in English to US and European online destinations, including media and industry websites, on-line databases and subscription-based news services. Redistributed by aggregators such as Comtex, Dialog, Infodesk and PowerAdz.*
>
> **—TAKEN FROM AN EMAIL BY PR NEWSWIRE**

Just because it is easy to publish does not mean that more people are going to actually read those articles. The more is not the merrier. It is even very likely that those articles are not seen at all, as they are published to websites that do not have a lot of traffic. However, the paid distribution will drive up the number of articles found automatically.

In addition to paid distribution, there is the second issue created by so-called spam blogs. These are blogs that exist not to be read but simply to be seen by Google. As Google uses activity on a page as an indicator of how well a blog is run, a blog that frequently updates its content is ranked higher by search engines.

Google and other search engines try to fight those practices, but these services still exist. One example is the Blog Post Automator.

> *You can also use articles from article directories and publish them with the author's name as a kind of "non-exclusive" guest appearance. [What is a] completely automated-content-filled blog that runs on pure auto pilot worth to you?*
>
> **—FROM BLOG POST AUTOMATOR**

Given that anyone can buy distribution of this article, and given that there are tools that push random messages onto blogs, how relevant is the number of articles? Not very. If it is not corrected for those factors, it is outright useless.

But how do we measure the effectiveness of a PR team then? We will need to confine in some way the number of articles clipped such that only the important ones are viewed or counted for the overall measurement. There are two possible ways do this:

Reading lists
: You can restrict the number of sources and count to only articles from a set of predefined sources.

Engagement metrics
: You measure only articles that created a certain reaction by the reader in either social networks or in terms of other ways to react to an article.

Those two approaches are described further in the following sections.

READING LISTS

Reading lists serve two aims. On one hand, we avoid being subject to spam blogs or automated news replication as just described. On the other hand, we can create a comparable number for a publisher set that is important to us. If you count articles about you in a reading list, you mimic the process of having to *clip* from a stack of newspapers. The sources are selected by the client and thus are as trusted as relevant publications.

Let's look at Figure 3-6, which Fisheye Analytics made for an insurance company in Europe. The figure shows the results of measuring how often several insurance companies are mentioned by various newspaper sources.

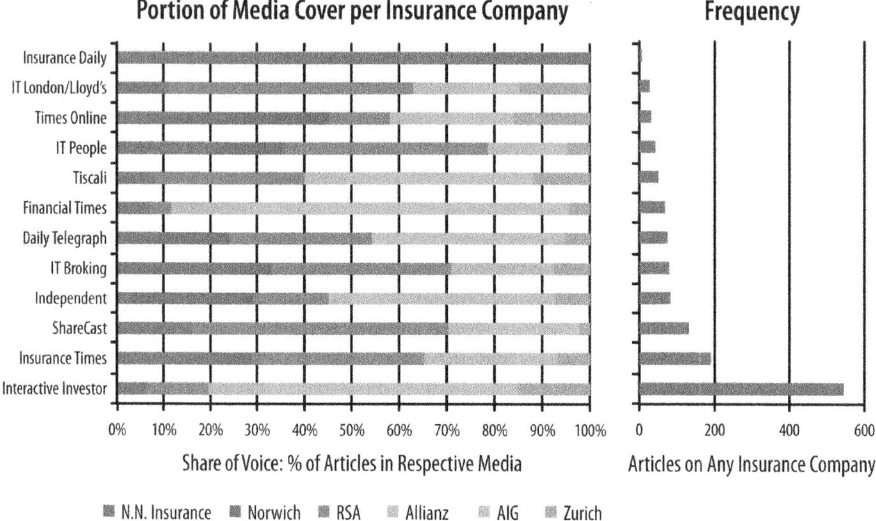

Figure 3-6. The share of voice within media lists (Courtesy of Fisheye Analytics.)

Is this useful? Yes, such an overview can be very helpful because it drives actions. Based on this overview, you can see which newspapers the client should strengthen their relationship with and which newspapers the client should ignore. This graph contains the insight into how much a given paper talks about insurance companies overall. This is a good way to show effort and impact as we will discuss later in this section.

ENGAGEMENT

We explained over the last few pages that the number of articles is a poor measure in analyzing the success of distribution. Reading lists are similar to panels because they give a focused view but also have to be designed manually. You might miss articles that gain attention or are important but were not published by the preselected sources.

Additionally, not every article, even from preselected sources, is equally important. We discussed earlier that editors have eased up in their selection process because there is unlimited space online in which to publish. Let's again take the World Economic Forum at Davos as an example. Each year thousands of journalists meet participants at the annual conference and debate world affairs. Let's look only at the world's top-20 news publications. These are the big, reliable newspapers, and you most likely read one of those papers regularly. How many articles about the

World Economic Forum do you think those sources that have great reputations in journalism will put online *per day* during the event? The answer is 30 articles on the World Economic Forum per day from one newspaper only.

A lower editorial selection barrier by the publisher results in more articles, which in turn means that not all of them are equally important, even when coming from the same publication. How do you select important articles and neglect unimportant ones? Let's look at how editors at a newspaper would do this. An editor could trust her gut feeling—what does she think is important? Or she can use data and look at click rates: which article performs better—which article creates more reactions or the *engages* the reader?

Engagement is a combination of many different actions a reader can perform. Measuring these actions helps an editor or someone else understand whether an article was not only read, but also understood or appreciated. These metrics try to use the "democratic" powers of the readers. The more readers react to a given article, the more likely it is that the article is relevant. The metrics include the following:

Clicking
: How many people clicked on the article?

Sharing
: How many people recommended the article to others to read or saved it to their own curation of articles?

Commenting
: How many people discussed this article or voiced an opinion about it?

Copying
: How many people took the idea from the article and reused parts of the content?

There are surely other forms of engagement an editor might watch, such as the number of emails he gets on a given article from angry or happy readers, or the number of phone calls. However, those are not easy to measure from the outside of the newsroom and thus will not be discussed here.

As an example, please look at Table 3-1. The table presents the messages that were spread the most during the last quarter of 2011 in British newspapers, ranked by clicking, sharing, and commenting.

Table 3-1. Top news measured by spread in social media from October 14, 2011–October 28, 2011 (courtesy of Fisheye Analytics)[a]

Rank	Source	Headline	Clicking	Sharing	Commenting
1	Guardian	The shocking truth about the crackdown on Occupy: US citizens of all political persuasions are still reeling from images of unparalleled police brutality in a coordinated crackdown	14,448	189,230	83,288
2	The Sun	Frankie Cocozza leaves X Factor: Frankie Cocozza has left The X Factor after "breaking competition rules," according to the show's producers.	77,186	60,297	32,016
3	BBC	Breast milk ice cream goes on sale in Covent Garden: The dessert, called Baby Gaga, is churned with donations from London mother Victoria Hiley, and served with a rusk and an optional shot of Calpol or Bonjela.	6, 843	48,550	108,249
4	The Sun	Tatt-poo for cheating: A FURIOUS woman is suing her ex-boyfriend after he tattooed a steaming poo on her back.	41,157	53,030	29,307
5	Daily Mail	Boy, 12, develops his own theory of relativity: A 12-year-old child prodigy has astounded university professors after grappling with some of the most advanced concepts in mathematics.	30,739	52,468	31,001
6	Guardian	Syria, Libya, and Middle East unrest —live updates: Muammar Gaddafi, who ruled Libya from 1969 until August this year, has been killed by forces loyal to the country's new government.	89,864	11,860	2,878
7	Telegraph	EU bans claim that water can prevent dehydration: Brussels bureaucrats were ridiculed yesterday after banning drink manufacturers from claiming that water can prevent dehydration.	6,870	51,227	42,018

Rank	Source	Headline	Clicking	Sharing	Commenting
8	BBC	N Korean leader Kim Jong-il dies: Millions of North Koreans were "engulfed in indescribable sadness," the KCNA state news agency said, as people wept openly in Pyongyang.	12,952	57,683	25,106
9	BBC	Deathly ice finger caught on film: A bizarre underwater "icicle of death" has been filmed by a BBC crew.	12,966	56,909	24,311
10	Daily Mail	Beyonce, Motown wedding dance mash-up by father-daughter the best ever? Rather than having a tender slow dance with her father at her wedding, one Texas bride decided to have a laugh.	19,608	50,607	22,096

[a] SMI describes the spread of the article within social media. How many articles are retweeted, how many are liked on Facebook, how many are reused in blogs, etc. The most important headlines are headlines that have the greatest social media impact via social media metrics such as Facebook likes, shares, tweets, retweets.

There are many tools that track engagement. Most of the social media measurement tools utilize the first three metrics (clicking, sharing, and commenting). There are also free sites like sharedcount, yahelc, or simplereach for measuring engagement.

The copying metric is harder to find, as it is a relatively specific measurement that is often manually adapted to the specific needs of the client. The charity Media Standards Trust offers a service called Churnalism, where the user can check whether a press release was used by any of the major newspapers.

In the following sections, we will explain clicking, sharing, commenting, and copying in more detail.

Clicking

Click rates are well understood. If you have 30 different articles on a topic such as the World Economic Forum from one single news site, click rates would provide clear insights into the effectiveness of each of those articles. But none of the sources would allow the public to know their traffic numbers per article. Those "true" number of visitors per article are kept internal. Some news or blogs might use the clicking number to offer a "what is hot" section on the website. Other, more tech savvy news outlets would decide how many days an article should be visible on the main page by using a mathematical formula using click rates or the decline of click rates. For example, if the decline of click rates day to day is higher than usual, the article should be removed. Certainly, most publishers use the click rates as a tool for internal employee motivation. The BBC, for example, has an automatic wall board in its editorial office displaying the most successful articles.

In general, those click-stream numbers are not public since it is rather interesting competitive intelligence information. It's no surprise that there are services that try to estimate those figures. Companies like alexa, compete, and comscore use predefined users or panels. Technically speaking, those services install a small client on the browser of its panelists. This client notes every move the panelist does online: where he clicks, how long the window stays open, and so on. This system is fairly accurate if you look at the main websites, though it breaks down for most news sites. To drill down to individual sites, the best way is to use shortlink services. Shortlinks are often used by social networks such as Twitter to reduce the space used. Shortlinks can easily measure how often a specific link is clicked, and providers such as bit.ly offer this number through an API. Those measurements are now way more granular than a panel is, but they might not be statistically relevant.

Sharing, Liking, Thumbs Up

Sharing has become as easy as clicking. In the early days of Web 2.0, to share would mean to actually write a blog post or a tweet about what you have read. Today, it can be as easy as clicking the "like" button on Facebook or curating via the various bookmark or curation services.

In Table 3-1, Fisheye Analytics calculated sharing only as the number of times people tweeted, digged, reddit, or liked the article on Facebook. Depending on your audience, you can include other sharing mechanisms, including social networks like LinkedIn or Mixi, or via other curation and bookmarking services.

Sharing is an effective way of measuring the distribution of a message, but more and more automated sharing services like IFTTT.com have entered the picture. Those companies allow an automated, robot-like process to happen. For example, using such an automated service, you can easily create a rule to find all articles online that talk about cats and share each article on Twitter via a shortlink. If another person now looks at the "sharing" metric, she would find a nice spike in the way articles about cats are shared. Her conclusion might be that people are more likely to share articles about cats than articles about other topics. In this fictional case, it's not true, but rather due to the use of an automated tool. This can be done easily, as shown in this video of Lutz Finger. However, he has chosen German news instead of cats.

Commenting

While sharing and clicking can be done through a simple click, "commenting" requires writing text, no matter how brief or lengthy. Thus, by definition, commenting will not be as widely used but will be more insightful. Be aware that so-called "comment bots" exist, particularly in unmoderated blogs; however, if a real reader goes through the "hassle" of writing a comment, she will have thought about the message.

Despite this advantage, comments, as a measurement, should also be used very carefully. You should not compare the number of comments across different sources, as each source has its own process of allowing people to comment. If users need to first register before they can comment, the number of comments will be fewer compared to a site that makes it simpler. And sometimes you cannot even compare comment numbers across a single media source. For example, the BBC allows comments on some articles, but not on all. As a news source financed by the public, it has to read and approve each comment before it lets it go live. As this process is cumbersome and time consuming, the BBC often artificially restricts comments on articles.

Copying

The last of those four engagement metrics is the hardest one to measure. The copying metric is intended to measure the spread of an idea. This can be best measured by how often people "copy" certain wordings. The more content is copied, the more influential the person who initially spread the idea. Take the headline of "Squatter, 59, holed up in No 10," attributed to Gordon Brown, the British prime minister, after his failed reelection bid in 2010.

This phrase was received so well by the general public that it was copied/quoted in more than 700 other articles within a few days.

This kind of copy analytics will be highly valuable for analyzing press releases. No journalist will link directly to a press release. Instead he will pick up certain ideas and use certain text. This kind of copy behavior can be analysed: the PR Sensor has analysed one month's worth of PR in the Arabic market to see how well the articles are spreading. The results are displayed in Table 3-2. The table not only contains how often parts of the press release were copied but also the summed-up spread of all those articles together.

Richard Gutjahr used those kinds of copy metrics to create LobbyPlag,[14] a service that analyzes how often law texts from the European Union contain parts of lobbyist papers.

Table 3-2. Headlines spreading the most (courtesy of Fisheye Analytics)

Release	Date of release	Total coverage (articles)	Total social impact
[+] JVC First to Offer Full HD 3D Consumer Camcorder	03/06/2011	28	1,273
[+] Qatar Airways Announces Move into Canada	02/26/2011	33	127
[+] Kraft Foods Declares Regular Quarterly Dividend of $0.29 Per Share	02/24/2011	36	187
[+] HP Unveils Business Notebooks Designed with Precision Engineering	02/22/2011	31	3,490
[+] Etihad and Linfox Armaguard Announce Joint Venture	02/21/2011	36	40
Universal Studios Hollywood's "King Kong 360 3D" Awarded "Outstanding Visual Effects in a Special Venue Project" by the Visual Effects Society (VES)	02/17/2011	99	108
Porsche Reaches One Million Fans on Facebook	02/13/2011	27	306
[+] BLIZZCON® 2011 ANNOUNCED	02/06/2011	47	1,950

Warning

Engagement seems like an ideal tool to measure the importance of news. However, as we will see in Chapter 6, the more impact a system has, the more likely it is to be "influenced" by others. Skewing the metric might be done by clear fraudulent actions such as social media robots or it might just trigger an action to split the news article into four or five pages to create more clicks and thus show more "engagement."

Note

In order to see whether text has been copied by others, the original text is cut into parts, and the analysis determines whether any other article has used the same text pieces.

As with any measurement, there is a caveat. Certain content just gets copied more easily. For example, a financial headline like "RadioShack's Q1 Profit Plunges 30%" or political, satirical comments like the one about Gordon Brown are more likely to be copied than a scientific finding. In order to compare copy metrics, you need to make sure that the same genres are compared.

14. *http://blog.lobbyplag.eu/*

EFFORT VERSUS IMPACT

As we said in the beginning to this section, measurement of distribution is not only a question of how to measure the distribution with clicks, shares, and more. It is also a question of what we've invested—what the effort was. Take an article in one of the top newspapers. If you keep the article on the home page of the newspaper's website for a week instead of a day you will surely create more engagement and clicks. Your investement or cost in this case is that you cannot have any other story placed on the home page. The same exmple works with social media accounts. As a publisher you can repeatedly tweet about the article. It will help you create more additional shares. There is also a cost: your followers might start to get tired of the same message and start to disregard what you write. Thus measuring success is measuring the relationship between effort and effect.This is hard but not impossible. You'll need to keep all variables, such as "days on the homepage" or "number of times mentioned on social media" equal. Then you can compare the efforts and only then the discussed metrics will be comparable as well. One great attempt to vizualize this relationship is the *New York Times* website, which was done by OpenNews Fellow Brian Abelson.

CASE: SPREAD OF THE IDEA OF "RESILIENT INDIA"

Let's take an in-depth look at how efficiently the World Economic Forum uses public data. They use focused reading lists based on an automated clipping process. On top of this process, Fon Mathuros, senior director of media relations for the World Economic Forum, and her team have created a dedicated system to mine aggregated insights. With this system, the Forum became best in class in listening to the pulse of the time and capturing new trends first.

For example, it conducts a highly successful conference every year in India called the "Indian Economic Summit." This conference is a platform for political and economical leaders to discuss the challenges of the region and to advise on steps going forward. For the conference in November 2009, Fon and her media team selected several topics that were discussed in planetary sessions or in small workshops. After the event, the team was charged with finding out which of those topics spread the most within the public. Figure 3-7 shows that of the chosen topics, the following three had the biggest media resonance:

- Will India be a superpower?
- Green growth

- The girl effect

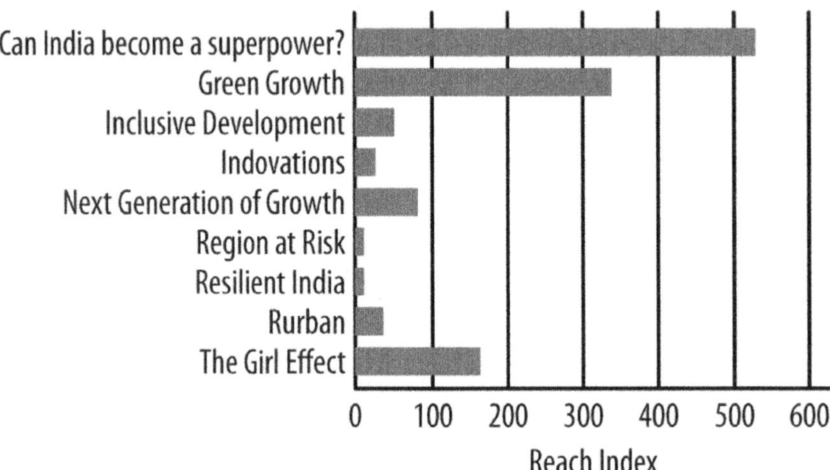

Figure 3-7. Trending topics (courtesy of World Economic Forum and Fisheye Analytics)

This is a worldwide view that encompasses all media types, including Twitter, blogs, Facebook, and traditional news. If you were interested in what had resonated most within the Indian press, you would need to select only that part of the data and compare it by country, as displayed in Figure 3-8.

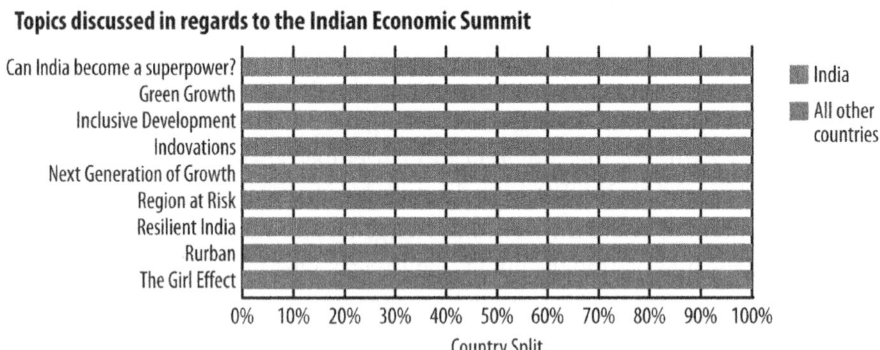

Figure 3-8. The topic "resilient India" resonated best in India (courtesy of World Economic Forum and Fisheye Analytics)

The discussions on sustainable growth for India summarized under the topic "resilient India" got the most interest within the Indian media, while discussions on "risk" or on environmentally friendly growth ("green growth") garnered more interest from the rest of the world.

The World Economic Forum decided to continue to use the topic "resilient India" in the following years because it realized that there was strong interest in it by their local partners.

PR to Warn

As James E. Gruning stated at the beginning of this chapter, PR is tasked with both distributing and monitoring. Monitoring is to catch any reputation issues that may arise. The onset of social media has made this even more essential, since social media not only enables easy spreading of marketing messages, but also easy spreading of negative messages which could potentially damage a brand image. There are many tools in the market that praise themselves to marketeers as the best insurance against such PR issues. We have seen many of those, and we even tried to develop our own. Our conclusion has been that none of those tools work sufficiently well enough to rely on them. In the following sections we will show you why.

EXAMPLES OF PR DISASTERS

In the beginning of social media communication, it was often not a bad product or a bad customer-care experience that created PR issues, but the company itself. Marketeers debuted in the space of earned media for promoting their products and found a kind of "quicksand" that could turn against them at any wrong step. In addition, others have been able to use social media as a PR weapon against businesses and individuals.

Discussions on social media are full of stories where communications went wrong. These can be categorized into four main areas:

- Inappropriate selling
- Underestimated virality
- Self-censorship
- Impersonation

Inappropriate selling

An example of inappropriate selling is a tweet by clothing manufacturer Kenneth Cole, who promoted his products by piggybacking on the Arab Spring:

> *Millions are in uproar in #Cairo. Rumour is they heard our new spring collection is now available online at...*
>
> **—KENNETH COLE**

This kind of tasteless selling behavior created a significant negative backlash with consumers.[15] Only 12 months later, fast-food company KFC went through a similar example. Following earthquake and tsunami warnings, KFC Thailand recommended to its followers:

> *People should hurry home this evening to monitor the earthquake situation and don't forget to order the KFC menu, which will be delivered direct to your hands.*
>
> **—KFC**

Once again, it did not take long before angry customers called in.

Underestimation of virality

Another common issue that has often taken marketeers by surprise is the potential virality of many campaigns. This was unknown territory, as email campaigns (which were one of the main tools used prior to social media campaigns), rarely go strongly viral.

Our pick for this category is the offering of a free meal by KFC. To make its promotion heard, the company teamed up with Oprah and showed it to her roughly 6 million viewers. The response was so overwhelming that KFC ran out of chicken and had to leave customers unserviced. In the aftermath, the CEO of KFC apologized to outraged Twitter users and bloggers via a YouTube message and offered 6.1 million people a rain check.

15. Ken Sweet, "Kenneth Cole Egypt tweets ignite firestorm," CNN Money, Feb 2003, *http://cnnmon.ie/1bld2IT*.

Self-censorship

Another category is self-censorship. The openess of social media has reduced the control by PR. To control or limit information about the company used to be one of the major tasks of PR professionals. When PR professionals try to do that within social media, it is perceived as censorship and often creates negative reactions by the public.

The most common mistake in this category is when PR teams have deleted comments that were seen as too negative for the company image. This has even happened to professional PR firms like Burson Marstella, which was accused of deleting posts on its Facebook page that criticized a smear campaign it had launched against Google on behalf of Facebook.[16]

Impersonation

Finally, activists sometimes use fake social media accounts to embarrass targets such as corporations or politicians. These accounts often purport to be from the targets themselves and send messages designed to put them in a bad light. For example, in a recent US presidential election, a fake Twitter account supposedly representing a conservative politician posted racist tweets directed at African-American President Barack Obama. Meanwhile, the actual politician had shown no evidence of being racist.

A more sophisticated example of this was an elaborate hoax directed at the energy firm Shell by the environmental group Greenpeace[17] and the activist group the Yes Men, to protest Shell's oil exploration in Alaska. This included a fake website (*www.arcticready.com*) that at first glance appears to be an official Shell website, with tongue-in-cheek content such as a picture of an oil tanker with the caption, "Let's hit the beach!" as well as a Twitter account @ShellIsPrepared that portrayed Shell as a company that ruins nature for a "better" tomorrow.

To make the hoax even more convincing, ShellIsPrepared sent tweets under the guise of being a social media response team, asking people to stop spreading embarrassing fake advertising images that were intentionally created by the pranksters:

16. Sam Gustin, "Burson-Marsteller Deletes Critical Facebook Posts, Spares Google-Smear Flacks," wired, May 2011, *http://wrd.cm/19F34Uz*.

17. Kashmir Hill, "Shell Oil's social media nightmare continues, thanks to skilled pranksters behind @ShellisPrepared," Forbes, July 2012. *http://onforb.es/19kxdw3*.

@ShellIsPrepared: Our team is working overtime to remove inappropriate ads. Please stop sharing them.

As of this writing Shell has not chosen to sue these activists, possibly so as not to draw further attention to their activities, and the website and Twitter account still remain active. Examples like these show how social media PR tools have become a weapon of protest for many social and political causes. Other examples of fraud and fakery in social media will be discussed in detail in Chapter 6.

NO EARLY WARNING SYSTEMS

All of those stories have one thing in common; once they turn viral, they happen very fast, and often too fast for corporate PR to fix. As said in the intro to this chapter, there are no real tools to protect companies from this kind of virality. The reason is twofold:

Nondeterministic
It is not deterministic when a message will go viral. A message might be around for some time before it suddenly starts to spread.

Speed to disaster
Once a message starts spreading, virality will happen, often within hours.

Virality versus Contagiousness

The term "virality" is not a real English term; it was coined with the onset of social media. The word tries to indicate that information within social media can spread very fast, similar to the epidemic of a virus. The idea is that each person who is either infected with a virus or has seen a certain piece of information passes this virus/information on to a set number of other people. If this set number is more than one, there will be an epidemic outbreak. A more suitable word to use for such a spreading behavior is the word "contagious."

Viruses, however, are always equally contagious, unlike rumors within social media that start gaining credibility the more people believe the message. The American sociologist Mark Granovetter developed a widely accepted threshold model on the "strength of weak ties," which is so far the best way to do describe the diffusion of information within a network.[18]

18. Mark Granovetter, "The Strength of Weak Ties," American Journal of Sociology, 1973.

Rumors spread through social media do not actually act "virus-like" but are becoming way more viral than real infections.

Nondeterministic

We saw earlier that not everyone or every message is equal in a network. Only if the information fits the "tastes of its readers" and only if it hits the right gatekeepers or connectors within the network will it start spreading.

To hit the right connectors within the network might take a long time, and there is no good way of estimating it. We don't know how long it took until the news will break. It took up to six months in the case of the trending double rainbow on YouTube by hungrybear9562. Uploaded in January, it wasn't until summer that it hit someone who could reach a larger audience. In this case, the gatekeeper was Jimmy Kimmel, who tweeted about it and made people talk about it.

Speed to disaster

However, no matter how long it takes for something to be found by a gatekeeper, or what Kevin Alloca calls a "tastemaker," once something starts to spread, it is usually a process that happens in hours rather than in days. Fisheye Analytics analyzed that roughly 50% to 60% of all articles in the UK get shared within four to six hours. Or said differently: after four to six hours, most of the articles are old news and most readers will not consider sharing them further.[19] As you can see in Figure 3-9, technology and financial news have a very short shelf life during which they get retweeted or shared in any other way, whereas religious and beliefs topics have longer engagement cycles.

19. The time measured is until 80% of all sharing activity has occurred.

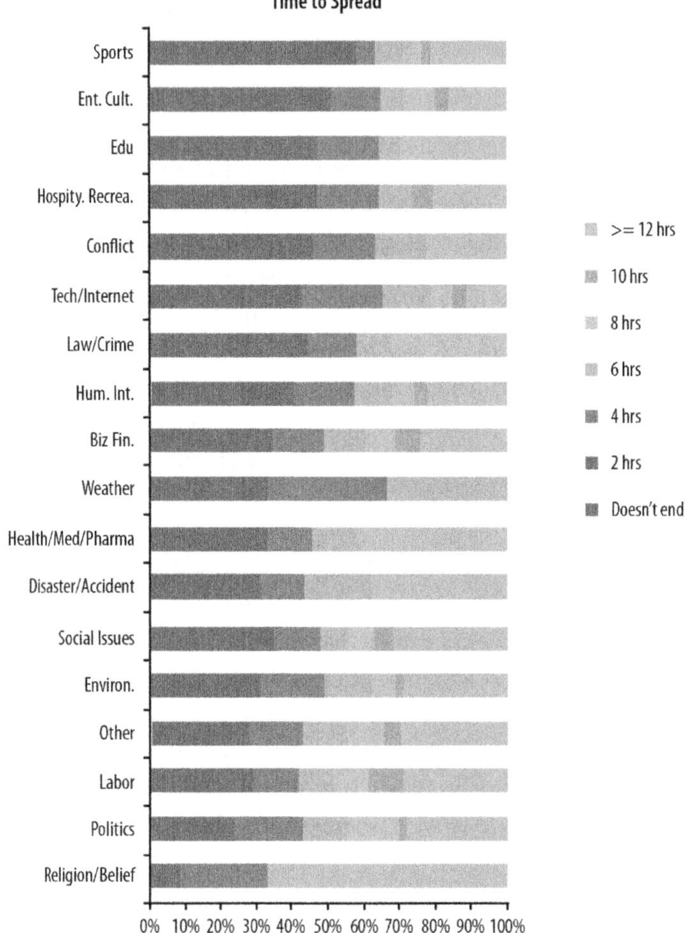

Figure 3-9. The amount of time it takes for clicking, sharing, and commenting to slow down (courtesy of Fisheye Analytics)

On an article level, this might sometimes be a slightly longer period. As you can see in Figure 3-10, 9 out of 10 articles reached their maximum engagement level within the first day.

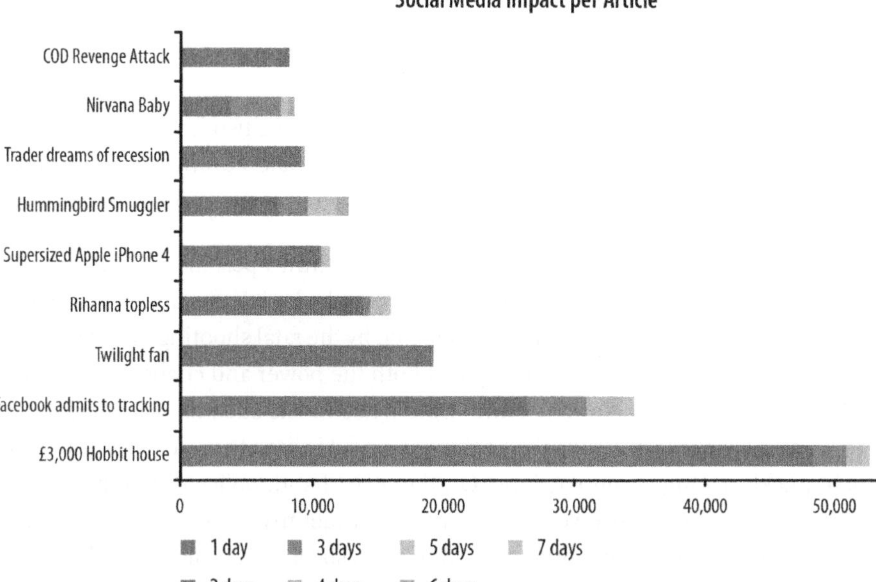

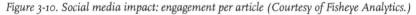

Figure 3-10. Social media impact: engagement per article (Courtesy of Fisheye Analytics.)

Such a high rate of escalation creates technical and organizational challenges for any organization:

Technical requirements

Any software checking the spread of a message would need to do this at a high speed, for example, every 10 minutes (or 144 times a day), to spot any signs of spreading. Within online news we see more than 1 million articles being posted every day. To see whether each article was spreading in Facebook would therefore require 144 million checks. If we add other channels such as Twitter and YouTube, we would need to add 144 million checks for each social media channel. Additionally, we would need to continue to check those 144 × 3 checks for the next 180 days, since we know that it can take six months or longer before the message turns viral. So for our system to warn us when things were going viral, we would need to check seven trillion times a day. If we assume that not only news content but YouTube, Facebook posts, and blog posts can go viral, too, the number of checks increases by a magnitude of 10. In short: it is so far not technically feasible to warn from the outside. The companies offering social networks such as Facebook and LinkedIn could build measurements from the inside to test whether a message is about to go viral. However, at the time of writing, those services are not yet offered.

Organizational issues

Even if you had such a measurement system, given a two-hour response window, can the organization be ready to react appropriately to any communication misbehavior? Traditional PR so far has not been set up to react in "near" time.

Even when it is technically difficult, it is sometimes possible to react in near time. In such cases, people often wonder afterward why it was not done earlier.

The August 2011 riots in London, triggered by the fatal shooting of a black male at the hands of police, were an example of both the power and challenges of using social media in a crisis. On one hand, rioters used tools such as BlackBerry messenger and Twitter to organize their activities, and it is hard to proactively anticipate such quickly arranged mob actions. On the other hand, police did employ social media after incidents to investigate crimes and identify looters. They also used records from mobile phone providers. Moreover, social media also played a role in organizing cleanup efforts following the end of the riots.

Another example of an unplanned social media "flash mob" took place in Germany, when a teenage girl neglected to make invitations to a birthday party private on Facebook and over 1,500 people showed up. Despite canceling the party after getting more than 1,000 RSVPs, people cloning copies of the invitation ultimately led to over 15,000 RSVPs, and police and private security were needed to maintain order. As Figure 3-11 from Fisheye Analytics shows, there was a critical point in time after the initial announcement where one might have intervened to stop the viral spread of this invitation.

Thessa's Party, Berlin, on Facebook 2011
German girl accidentally sets up public FB birthday invite. Upon getting 1000 rsvps, she cancels the party.
Blog 'Partythessa' is set up by a commentator to relay news about the incident (mainstream).
1500 people turn up at private home. Police deployed. One policeman injured.
German gov considers restricting Facebook.
Early May 2011
31 May
4 June
5 June
August
Clone invites are set up by other FB users, gathering thousands more rsvps, providing details of the party.
15,000 rsvps on clone sites despite calls from other web commentators not to go.
Reuters carries the news story.
Critial period: all Facebook activity here could have been countered by spontaneously detecting and tracking multiplying pages/likes/comments in real time.

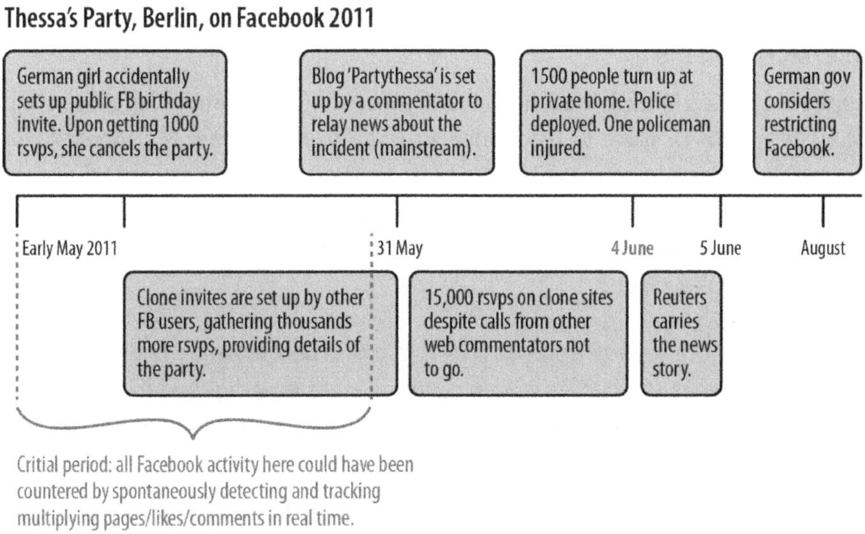

Figure 3-11. Analysis of Thessa's Facebook party (Courtesy of Fisheye Analytics.)

Note

PR disasters might happen quickly and spread within a few hours. For any service to be helpful, the system needs to go back to the message often and check virality in terms of retweets, likes, views, or whatever is appropriate for the media type. There will never be a fully automated tool; a team of social media managers should be ready to flag abnormal behavior, investigate, make a decision, and react. Consequently, there are two questions to ask the potential service supplier who promises you an early warning system:

- How often do you check for updates on the spread of the item? Anything that is below 30 minutes can be seen as excellent.
- How long do you follow a given article around? As seen with the double rainbow, it took six months for that video to get viral. However, anything above two months is excellent.

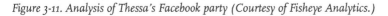

CASE: MCDONALD'S

Despite not having an early warning system, more and more companies are starting to have a system in place to react once an issue has appeared. McDonald's, for example, has created such a system. It built a social media "war room" that may not spot issues before they break out, but can react quickly.

A hoax began with a picture of a piece of paper that was put on the front door of a McDonald's. It read:

> *Please note: As an insurance measure due in part to a recent string of robberies, African-American customers are now required to pay an additional fee of $1.50 per transaction. Thank you for your cooperation.*

It was first posted on a Thursday via a website called McServed.

It took a few days for the picture to go viral and to start spreading under the hashtag #SeriouslyMcDonalds. By Saturday the issue had caught the attention of the McDonald's social media team. It responded with a post, but afterward kept silent so as not to fire up the issue even more.

> *That pic is a senseless & ignorant hoax McD's values ALL our customers. Diversity runs deep in our culture on both sides of the counter.*
>
> **—MCDONALD'S SOCIAL MEDIA TEAM**

As the discussion became a trending topic at twitter, McDonald's took big measures and asked key gatekeepers in Twitter to "please let your followers know." Additionally the company responded to concerned tweeps, and by Sunday hardly anyone believed the image to be true.

There is a lot to be learned from this case, as McDonald's had three things in place that helped it:

- It had an effective measurement system for messages as described in "Measuring Distributing" on page 81. It could not only evaluate the spread of the overall issue but benchmark the issue as well, to decide whether to react or not.

- It had an effective measurement system to identify gatekeepers as we have described in “Measuring People” on page 70. It reached out to them for help in this state of crisis.
- It had an organization and processes in place that were able to react quickly, even over the weekend.

WARNING SIGNALS

While no early foolproof warning system measuring the change in engagement is possible, it is possible to identify certain indications of the potential for an outbreak of a situation.

Manal al-Sharif is a young mother and computer scientist in Saudi Arabia. Women in Saudi Arabia are not allowed to drive, so she, along with other activists, started the Women2Drive campaign. As one can see in Figure 3-12, the Women2Drive Twitter campaign started to gain attention. The tipping point was reached when she published a video on the Internet of herself driving. Her subsequent arrest was greeted by a community of people who already had connected around this issue. The community protested against her arrest and called in even bigger international help. Manal al-Sharif was set free after a short while.

The measurement before the YouTube video was released indicates a tendency. There was a community which had connected around the Women2Drive issue. To measure the strength of the community, we will revert back to the same metrics we have discussed in this chapter: context, reach, and spread.

Knowing that Manal al-Sharif had already formed a community and knowing that she had already created some awareness for the topic, she decided that she could go the next step to protest by officially recording her driving on YouTube. The reaction of the government and the subsequent protests from the outside world made the community of protestors even stronger. Manal al-Sharif reached a new level of influence on this topic.

Summary

Social Media has created a new way to communicate. It is no surprise that it has therefore changed the department that is concerned mainly with communication.

Social media has changed the way we do PR.[20] PR was always a discipline that was hard to quantify and measure. There was the hope that this would change with more data. However, as we mentioned in our initial chapters, more data does not necessarily means easier access to the fourth "V" of data. PR and its quest for insights is the best example. With the many new ways to communicate, many new metrics came. But many of those were descriptive in nature, and they did not reveal the fourth "V" or a ROI. They also do not really help predict anything. But they are very helpful as operational metrics to control the two main transactional tasks of PR: to distribute and to monitor. In this chapter, we discussed the usage of metrics such as:

Reach
: It used to be calculated easily within traditional media. Social media has created new reach metrics. There is no standard, and it is almost impossible to compare those metrics accross different media types.

Context
: It was always key for any communication. Theoretically, we could store all data to create correlations and learn from past experience. However, so far, context is only used in a descriptive fashion or as a benchmark.

Activity
: Despite wide utilization of activity metrics, we believe that the number of articles is a measure that is not helpful for judging the overall success of PR, except when using reading lists.

Engagement
: Better than counting the number of articles are various engagement metrics that measure the spread of each individual article.

Audience
: It is as key as *context*, but similar to context, it is used only in a descriptive fashion. We saw in Chapter 2 that this does not need to be this way.

The second biggest task of PR is to warn if anything unwanted is happening. Search tools of all kinds surfaced to enable PR departments all over the world. This

20. If you are part of a pure B2B organization, you probably had little exposure to social media communication overall. However, even in those organizations, the biggest impact of social media is within the PR departments.

would be the perfect case for predictive analytics. If we could know when something is happening before it happens, we would have uncovered the fourth "V," the value of the data. Unfortunately, we have shown that it is technically not easy to have such an early warning system. The lessons from Chapter 8 are true: the more focused the question, the easier it will be to find articles that start spreading fast.

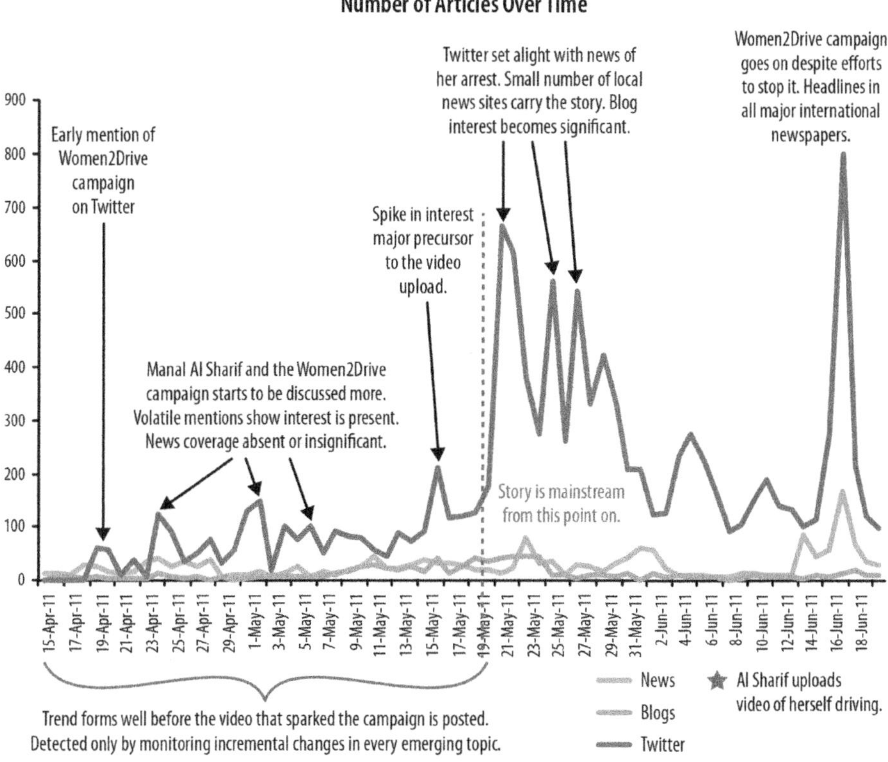

Figure 3-12. Women2Drive (Courtesy of Fisheye Analytics.)

WORKBOOK

PR has no easy way of measuring an ROI. The impact of its actions are longterm and thus causation (for more insights on causation jump to Part II Chapter 9) is not given. This has been an issue for many PR professionals. Which of the metrics discussed in this chapter could be used for your PR department?

Context and audience are areas where one could use unstructured data to support PR activities. A focused question or reading list here is key to success. What kind or reading list would you design for your business? Who is your target audience, and which metrics describe them best?

Every PR professional takes interest in disaster stories and stories about well-organized teams who have reacted to disasters. Please share with us and the world your favorite disaster on Twitter, @askmeasurelearn, or on our LinkedIn or Facebook page.

Customer Care

Within the customer support industry, both social media and big data have been among the most current trends in effectively taking care of customers. Tools in this area hold the promise of automating routine customer responses, improving visibility of customer opinions, and enabling customers to interact with one another as a community. At a deeper level, they signal a sea change in how much of a voice customers have within the business community.

Like other areas that have "gone social," customer care is a field where the hype and promise of social media may never be matched by reality. At the same time, it has become a key part of the reality of serving customers, for companies of all sizes. However, similar to what we discussed in Chapter 2, social media can be used in two ways: it can be a method of reaching out to customers—a new channel for interaction—or all that data can be leveraged in a complete different context. In this chapter, we look at the more operational questions, like if you use social media as a channel, why should you do this and what kind of metrics should you observe to serve your customers better? This chapter is not meant to be an in-depth guide on how to set up a social media customer care center. The challenges of such a task are more operational than technical. It is meant to look at the operational metrics and data around social-enabled customer care. In Chapter 5, we will look more into what else we might do with customer care data beyond pure operational actions.

New Voice of the Customer

At the beginning of the millennium, customer care was seen by many companies as a necessary evil, a margin-diminishing cost center. As long as service was not outrageously bad, you could get by. As a consequence, many companies started to cut cost by trying to reduce so-called handling times with the customer. Unfortunately, this was the wrong approach. Agents would become very short on the phone in order to keep their handling times short, process more calls, and appear more productive. Escalation to more knowledgeable staff was discouraged, and long hold times (complete with bad music) were common. The business case for this service revolved largely around cost control rather than customer satisfaction, brand promotion, and customer retention.

It was a system of cost cutting and negativity. The result is all too well known. Many of us hate the prospect of having to contact a customer service call center. Initial advances in technology made things even worse. Instead of classical music, you were faced with a computer that asked you 1,001 questions, and if you did not answer correctly, it hung up on you. "Sorry, I could not understand your 18-digit –long customer ID, goodbye!" Only the customer who had repetitive or large purchases would be treated differently, getting an extra phone number with shorter waiting times or even a dedicated customer care representative.

The onset of social media, however, has shifted power back toward the customer. There is one fundamental reason for this: visability. When a company delivers poor service to one isolated customer at a time, the damage to its reputation is often gradual, and meeting performance metrics at the expense of the customer becomes all too tempting. In the world of social media, however, unsatisfied customers are immediately on display for all to see. First, service provided directly via social media is often public, and so others can see the Facebook posts or tweets between the company and its customer. Second, the customers can now share and distribute their own opinions and reviews.

As we saw in Chapter 2, user reviews have a strong influence on the purchasing decision process. Those reviews could cover any interaction with the product, whether positive or negative. Allowing this "free" discussion even instills trust in the product or service. However, this is surely only true if there are not many unhappy customers online who complain about the product.

Suddenly, the hidden discussions between a call center somewhere in the offshored world and you—the customer—became public and open.

DELL HELL

In 2005, influentual blogger Jeff Jarvis, the creator of *Entertainment Weekly* magazine, began a series of posts entitled Dell Hell, detailing his bad experiences trying unsuccessfully to get Dell Computer to fix his laptop.[1] It struck a chord with readers and generated hundreds of comments from others with similarly bad experiences. He was not the first customer who had a complaint about Dell, nor was he the first customer to create a column or a blog about it; at that time, one could find many

1. Jeff Jarvis, "Dell lies. Dell sucks." *Buzzmachine.com*, June 2005, http://buzzmachine.com/2005/06/21/dell-lies-dell-sucks/.

clients complaining about the service. However, he had the ability to get Dell's attention by virtue of his reach within the social media world.

The attention in the media was enormous, and so was the damage to Dell's image. Dell, however, reacted directly and proactively; it changed its PR policies and invited Jeff to visit its headquarters. More important, it made moves to become more responsive to consumers, including reaching out to disgruntled customers on blogs, allowing customers to rate products on its site, and starting a blog. Jarvis was impressed enough that he eventually wrote a column in *BusinessWeek* magazine praising the company's efforts.[2] Dell has learned its lesson and become more attentive to the voice of the customer. Still, the damage from this time has stuck with it, and one can still find references to "Dell Hell" or complaint sites such as dell.pissedconsumer.com.

What if the customer care representative from Dell had known that the person on the other side was a journalist and influential blogger? What if the phone system could have assessed the likelihood that this person was influential enough to create a PR and marketing disaster? Yes, for sure, Dell would have given him a different —a preferential—treatment from the beginning and would have avoided the whole PR issue.

UNITED BREAKS GUITARS

The history of social media is full of customer complaints that blew up in publicity. They all follow a similar storyline—David (alias for the poor, beaten-up customer) versus Goliath (alias for the big, cold, bad corporation). One of the more public PR blow ups in this ongoing saga was United Airlines' response to baggage problems.

In 2009, as his bandmates watched, horrified, from the passenger window, Canadian musician Dave Carroll's expensive Taylor guitar was broken as a result of rough handling by baggage handlers on a United flight. He tried to get reimbursed for this, but after numerous contacts, United declined to pay for the damage. Dave was probably not the first person to encounter this situation. However, his response was to write a song and publish a music video on YouTube titled, "United Breaks Guitars." At the time of this writing, it had been watched more than 13 million times and was a public relations nightmare for United Airlines. After top managers realized what was happening, they finally offered to address Dave's case, but it was too late—the public damage was already done. Though it is hard to put a number on the amount of damage that was done by this video, some sources

2. Jeff Jarvis, "Dell learns to Listen", BusinessWeek, Oct. 2007, *http://buswk.co/lI8xDy*.

claimed it was a factor in a subsequent drop of $180 million in the price of United Airline's stock price, nearly 10% of its market capitalization. While the consensus nowadays is that the viral video alone was unlikely to have had such a large financial effect, it certainly had a negative impact on the company's reputation.[3]

Perhaps a more important lesson is that today, you don't need to be an influential blogger or a talented video producer to make your voice heard in social media. In a case that was eerily similar to "United Breaks Guitars," in late 2012, working musician Dave Schneider had his vintage guitar crushed by baggage handlers after Delta Airlines refused to allow him to carry it on board. He described Delta's response as a "runaround" until he took to social media channels, including Facebook and Gawker. It wasn't until Yahoo! News ran a feature story the following month that Delta finally agreed to pay for repairs to his guitar, as well as give him vouchers for two free future flights.[4]

Examples such as these demonstrate that the open nature of social media makes it much harder to hide bad customer service. Will the consequence be that everyone gets VIP treatment? Despite the fact that every company says, "Our customers are king," it's not true. Most companies want to make a bottom line for its shareholders, and VIP treatments for everyone would cost way too much.

The solution is to use your own service tools to help customers who are complaining on social media. In the following chapter, we'll show that this doesn't need to come with more cost and that it provides you with new ways to measure performance and to gather insights.

Customer Care 2.0

Similar to what we discussed in Chapter 1, social media provides a complementary channel to the existing ways of communicating with your customers. Instead of calling a toll-free number, your customer can tweet or write on your Facebook wall. Then your social media team responds to the customer, with no need to wait on hold or stand in line.

This is the fantasy of social customer service. In some cases, it has been the reality as well: for example, cable service provider Comcast helped restore its customer service reputation, in part, around the efforts of a talented social media team

3. Ravi Sawhney, "Broken Guitar Has United Playing the Blues to the Tune of $180 Million," Fast Company, July 2009. *http://bit.ly/1bz1CCM.*

4. Dylan Stableford, "Musician whose vintage guitar was smashed by Delta gets check from airline, new one from Gibson," Jan. 9, 2013. *http://yhoo.it/lS1sj6.*

led by executive Frank Eliason, dubbed by *BusinessWeek* as "the most famous customer service manager in the US" after the success of his @ComcastCares service channel on Twitter. On a broader level, many customer support automation and CRM vendors now offer capabilities to manage customer issues through Facebook fan pages or Twitter.[5]

On the other hand, despite the hype, people are not all flocking to vent their customer concerns through social media. According to customer support portal site SupportIndustry.com, only 20% of customer support centers currently serve customers via social media, and these in turn only handle between 1% and 10% of their transactions through this channel. With some few exceptions, such as Microsoft Xbox's Elite TweetFleet (@XboxSupport), which has a dedicated team of representatives monitoring Twitter proactively for comments from gamers, social media has become just one of many channels for customer care, along with telephone, web chat, and others.[6]

So what does customer care 2.0 really look like? It is a world where companies interact with their customers as they always did, but with two key differences. First, some of these customer contact channels, such as social media support or online user communities, now expose people's service quality to the public. The incentive to squeeze performance metrics or control costs is now tempered by the reality that people will often see how well they or others are served. Second, customers now have a voice they never had before. Many of us nowadays rarely make purchases, particularly major ones, without checking online comments and ratings from other consumers.

This trend has tremendous implications for both the profession of customer care and the underlying data analytics that drive it. Let's look at some of the ramifications of moving toward customer care 2.0.

KNOWLEDGE BASES AND CUSTOMER SELF-SERVICE

Customer care does not just serve customers in the present moment. It also generates knowledge that can often be reused and mined as data. Now there are protocols such as the Knowledge-Centered Support (KCS) approach of the IT Infrastructure Library (ITIL), developed by the nonprofit Consortium for Service

5. Rebecca Reisner, "Comcast's Twitter Man," Bloomberg Businessweek, Jan. 2009, *http://buswk.co/1b25HPV*.

6. Casey Hibbard, "How Microsoft Xbox Uses Twitter to Reduce Support Costs," Xocial Media Examiner, July 2010, *http://bit.ly/1crJBHN*.

Innovation in the 1990s. KCS outlines a process by which solutions are generated by agents, validated by reuse, and then published for external use. Major corporations have been using such approaches more and more in recent years.

Another increasingly important source of knowledge is the customers themselves. For any product or service, people often use search engines such as Google to see if other people have posted solutions to customer issues on their blogs or social media sites. And for larger companies, formal online support communities often serve as a rich source of knowledge. The main challenge of such communities is their economy of scale: to have sufficient participation, you need either a large or very dedicated user base. Hence such tools are mainly found among larger firms like Apple, Dell, and Microsoft, or companies that were able to create a high degree of attachment to their product, such as Evernote.

In both cases, one goal of knowledge databases is to have customers serve themselves, an objective that is better for both the customer and the financial interests of the company. Figure 4-1 compares those two approaches. A customer calling into the call center creates cost, let's say $5 to $10 per call.[7] Most questions have been asked before, and most questions are known to the community. We assume in Figure 4-1 that 65% of all questions can be answered by the community. Customers who got their question answered are less likely to call in (only 40% call in to seek a second opinion—60% of those calls are "deflected"). That means that there will be about 39% fewer calls.

Moreover, each person who expresses appreciation for an answer from the community encourages more people to join, which strengthens the brand awareness of the product.

7. *http://bit.ly/1aBgrW8*

Figure 4-1. Social media ROI for customer care

HAPPIER EMPLOYEES

Social customer service benefits your employees as well as your customers. Few brands enjoy the economy of scale of a Microsoft or Apple, so instead of self-serving community teams, many firms will build up their own social customer care teams. You will soon find that those teams have the highest morale within the customer service organization.

Usually service staff get criticized for all kinds of product- or marketing-related issues. They often have to take the complaints for situations they can neither fix nor avoid. Service staff who try hard often get only a quick "thank you" at the end of a call. This is different in customer care conversations happening over social media. Here, happy clients often create a written and publicly available statement, and this public appraisal boosts employee morale. For example, Jens Riewa, a famous German television presenter, had an issue with his telecom provider. The social media team offered fast help without going through long phone queues. Jens offered as his personal sign of appreciation to "wave" his pen shortly before the end of his evening news program. Björn Ognibeni, who consulted this social media customer care team, reported later, "This one single moment had created an enthusiasm that carried the team forward for a while."

Surely one's own social media team comes with its own cost. Since those teams are publicly visible, meaning that that bad service could create a negative effect on brand and image, these teams need to be carefully trained. To build a social customer care center, you must carefully select appropriate staff to not only solve issues, but also to communicate effectively. In some cases this will create additional costs compared to using an outsourced call center, but hopefully at an overall benefit to your brand and market share.

SMART SELECTION

We discussed in "PR to Warn" on page 95 that social media has the capability to spread information fast and effectively. Unsatisfied customers who go online and tell their woes to a larger audience are often a cause for PR issues such as those we saw in the examples at the beginning of this chapter.

Now there will always be cases where a customer leaves unhappy. Not even VIP service for all would fix this issue. A well-run social customer care system should be able to detect a potential danger of dissatisfaction spreading. There is no bulletproof system for detecting spreading or contagious messages. However, the more confined the system is, the better the chance of such detection. With customer care you actually have some good ways to measure the extent to which a given complaint is important.

The old, nonsocial-media world factors such as revenue are still important to understanding the potential impact of this kind of service call. But social media now adds a new component to the mix—the social network.

How well is someone networked? We concluded in Chapter 1 that the effect of word of mouth is often overestimated because a network can create only reach but not necessarily buying intention. However, an unhappy comment can prohibit buying intention, and if this goes together with reach, this public comment needs greater attention.

The way customer care teams should select messages is by analyzing the level of unhappiness of a comment and the risk of the message spreading to a larger audience. This assessment needs to be done automatically so that the customer service team replies to the most urgent one first.

The potential reach could be assessed by complex metrics such as centrality or in-betweeness. As a first proxy, it's sufficient to measure just the network size: the bigger the network, the bigger the risk of spreading information. As an example, within Twitter or Facebook, you can derive two variables for each of your complaining customers:

What is the size of the social network of the customer?
: The network is the basic variable. The more people you can complain to, then the more dangerous your complaint might be.

How big is the network after the second degree of separation?
: For customer service complaints, this metric is most likely more powerful than the pure size of an individual network. A message often spreads only once it hits a certain gatekeeper, as we saw in Chapter 3. Take the Vancouver Olympics in 2010. After the IOC had issued guidelines about how athletes should use social media so as not to alienate their respective sponsors, Lindsey Vonn wrongly claimed that the IOC had forbidden any use of social media. The IOC reacted promptly and tweeted, "Athletes, go ahead and tweet." This catchy phrase was not picked up strongly by the followers of the Olympic Twitter account. But it did start spreading after Lindsey Vonn published it herself to her 35,000 followers, which created the needed tipping point.

The size of the social network of your customers is not the only metric to analyze commentary within your customer care discussions. Most other measurements are very similar to what we discussed in Chapter 3. Engagement and content are other critical areas to measure:

Engagement
: Messages that create a lot of public attention via likes or retweets or a similarly spreading mechanism should be ranked higher within the customer care system to draw the attention of a customer care representative to it.

Content
: Similar messages should be flagged if they use certain critical words or if the conversation starts to become long and repetitive.

POSITIVE PUBLICITY

A social CRM does not just offer the ability to pick up customers where they are. It also offers a unique ability to pass on successful customer service requests. The same way the publicity will enhance negative messages, it can enhance positive messages. Surely to become really contagious the message needs to be appealing. "I fixed your telephone line" will be probably not spread, except perhaps for examples like the phone line of Jens Riewa the TV presenter.

Dutch airline KLM knew this, and in order to introduce its new 24/7 Facebook and Twitter support, they generated live reply messages (see Figure 4-2). Each social media customer care representative would carry a letter, and the team would line up in a way to form a response. This process was filmed and published on YouTube. It was an instant hit, and the news spread. KLM became known for their great social customer care support.

Figure 4-2. KLM live reply (Courtesy of KLM.)

Even seemingly outrageous complaints might become a positive PR opportunity. One British feminine hygiene company showed, in an excellent video response to a critical Facebook post, how to do this. A man posted (probably tongue-in-cheek) about how Bodyforms "lied" by showing active women enjoying themselves during their menstrual periods, when in fact his own girlfriend became like "the little girl from The Exorcist with added venom" during her own period.

In response, the company posted a YouTube video response from a fictitious CEO named Carolyn Williams. She apologized for this deception, stating that it was a response to focus groups in the 1980s showing shocked and fearful men crying as they learned about their partner's periods. She went on to admit that there was no such thing as a happy period, and closed by breaking wind and noting that "we do that, too." The video was a viral hit that resulted in tremendous publicity for the company on social media.[8]

Dos and Don'ts

Are you convinced that you should "go social" in your CRM? Good! Here are a few dos and don'ts that we have been seeing:

GET CLIENTS INTO YOUR SERVICE CHANNEL

You should help and serve your clients publicly. No need to wait until they call in. Try to address them where you can find them, in the same channel. Do this publicly to show that you care. But keep in mind that 140 characters isn't enough to handle conflict or customer care topics. So once you pick them up, try to get clients into your traditional service tool as soon as possible. This transition should be painless for the user, as he came to complain, not to go through several customer service channels.

It is important to get clients into your traditional service tool for several reasons. It could be that the customer issue involves how a credit card is disposed, or some other private information. This is not something to handle in the public space. And even if this sounds logical, just to make sure it never happens, move customers as quickly and as painlessly as possible into a nonpublic tool.

A second reason you should move customers swiftly to your own channels is the question of control. As many companies moved into online social networking sites like Facebook, they found that their clients were not interested in "liking" the most recent marketing promotion but rather in voicing their issues with the product. As a natural consequence, companies opened up and reacted on the social networking platform by giving feedback and advice. They used the social network as their own customer care platform. While in principle a good idea, there is an inherent risk to this, as companies own neither the data nor the outlay of the page. As soon as a platform decides to change the page layout, the companies have to follow suit no matter whether this is actually useful for customer care or not. This is another reason to move clients as quickly as possible into other online tools, where the company owns the content.

The third reason to move from a public discussion in a social networking platform to a more controlled environment is that visible customer care discussions

8. Barnett E., "Bodyform's response to Facebook rant a viral hit," The Telegraph (UK), Oct. 17, 2012, *http://bit.ly/1bCJFqr*.

are also visible to your competition. They might use the discussions to analyze your weaknesses (see "Automation and Business Intelligence" on page 123) or even try to engage with your customers by offering a better service or a better solution to the customer's issues.

MIND THE TROLLS

Any customer service representative can tell you what a "troll" is. They existed long before the onset of social media, but social media has made their life even more pleasant. A troll is someone who just has fun complaining and bullying, often in a loud and nasty way. Should an organization jump and try to give these "trolls" a higher service level? Not necessarily. It might be that those clients are not the right ones they are trying to reach. It is often helpful to create a figure such as Figure 4-3. There's not always an overlap between the people who are complaining and the ones buying.

Figure 4-3. Mind your customers and not necessarily the trolls

At the end of 2010, the German train company Deutsche Bahn decided to start its own Facebook offering. To drive initial uptake of Facebook fans, the Bahn offered a so-called "chef ticket." Those were only available to Facebook fans of the Deutsche Bahn and were considerably cheaper than they would have been otherwise. Depending on the kind of trip, you could have saved up to almost 90% of a ticket price.

The campaign was supported by a YouTube video and an associated marketing package. The video was leaked to the public a few days before the actual campaign started, and the German social media scene was not impressed. The company was not known for innovative marketing, and this Facebook page raised the ire of many net activists. Complaints about the tone, execution, and content were voiced on Twitter, Facebook, and in news articles.

However, all of these complaints happened before the Facebook page even went live. What should the company have done? Stop the campaign? Excuse itself publicly? The company decided to do nothing, and went live as planned.

In the end, the complaining net activists were not the fans who were interested in buying train tickets. The circles as displayed in Figure 4-3 did not have a strong overlap. Meanwhile, the customers loved the price reduction offer, and the Facebook campaign became a success. Within the first 24 hours, more than 5,000 "fans" registered. After six weeks, the number had risen to over 60,000 Fans. There are no official numbers about the financial success of the campaign, but insiders comment that over 180,000 tickets were sold, accounting for $5.6 million in revenue.

RESOURCES AND SCALING

Any customer care setup faces the question of staffing, whether it involves traditional channels such as the telephone or newer social channels. Complex models exist, such as the Erlang C model, for making sure the right number of agents exist to serve the customer. While an understaffed call center may frustrate customers who are waiting on hold or cannot get through, a staff shortage in social customer care will also frustrate people who expect at least a same-day response (or in some cases, such as an airline flight delay, a same-hour response). Moreover, social customer care has the disadvantage that your lack of response is extremely visible to the public.

Even well-oiled social customer care systems can look bad during an unexpected peak time. In April 2012, during one of the most important football matches, the pay-TV channel Sky had broadcasting difficulties, and the Twitter community reacted in a state of outrage. Luke Brynley-Jones, a blogger from Our Social Times, explained this with a response metric over time (see Figure 4-4). More then 60% of all messages simply went by unanswered. While Sky normally has very good service, in this case they could not cope.

The lesson here is to be ready to have additional resources on demand when needed. Those could be employees who normally have a different job but who could come and help during a crisis situation. For example, electronics retail chain Best

Buy encourages employees at all levels of the organization to tweet answers to customers on Twitter as part of its Twelpforce. Together with its regular social media footprint, including blogs, a Facebook page, and community forums, the company credits this model with over $5 million in call center deflection. Infrastructures such as these help to engrain a social service culture into the company culture.[9]

Figure 4-4. Twitter activity during Sky TV outage during a UK football match (Courtesy of Engagement Index.)

Is Social Customer Care the New Commodity?

Social customer care can certainly add value to your service offerings. However, if the lessons of history are any indication, it would not be a good idea to bet your competitiveness on social customer care. Just like having a web page or an email address, the bad news is that social customer care is quickly evolving into a commodity. Any business can have a Facebook fan page or a Twitter account in a matter of minutes, and these are rapidly becoming routine and expected.

One of the best examples from the past is the case of banks in the United States. Years ago, banks were not often noted for their service quality. Then a few banks started to brand themselves around offering better customer service, and others soon followed suit. Today high customer satisfaction is not a competitive asset for a bank; it is simply a hygiene factor that is expected in the marketplace.

9. IBM Global Business Services, From social media to Social CRM (report), June 2011, *http://ibm.co/1fbKAyS*.

A more subtle case has evolved in the computer industry. Apple combines a very efficient customer support infrastructure that depends heavily on online resources such as knowledgebases and crowdsourced user community forums, with the ability to obtain free premium service in person by visiting a "Genius Bar" at an Apple store, which includes features such as free computer courses and easy-to-access service staff. The model for the Genius Bar was the hotel lounge, with the idea that customers should be as relaxed as they are in such lounges. Apple set a standard that has led many other hardware suppliers to begin improving their service support. Today, in many industries, good customer service has become an expectation, and thus social customer care is about to become a commodity as well.

Automation and Business Intelligence

With all that customer commentary online, a new segment of business intelligence was born to analyze how companies interact with their clients and how happy the clients are. The results promised to be faster and more easy to obtain than any customer satisfaction index. Tools and software to dig through large amounts of unstructured commentary and distill customer opinion data from millions of online social media interactions developed at a fast pace. Their main promise was to find out what customers were thinking about your product and about your competitors' products. Listening to client conversation seemed to have the promise of replacing surveys. We would not need to ask our customers anymore. No, we just need to listen to their conversations. While this is true in principle, the reality is in most cases very different.

We will see in Chapter 9 how complex it is to set up a keyword. But the keyword only determines the datapool to be analyzed. It determines which conversations are selected. The real work is about to begin after this selection. Automated business intelligence tries to find metrics in order to give answers about what the customers thought, what their feelings were, etc. This is a way more complex task, and it unfortunately often goes wrong. This is due to the complexity of *sentiment analytics*.

With sentiment analytics, we try to find out a specific *sentiment* toward a certain position. Does this customer like my product or not? We try to look for *clues* in the text to indicate a sentiment that might not be clearly formulated. The human language can be very subtle and multifaceted and therefore too complex to be analyzed simply by an automated machine-learning program. You might have heard such an argument before, when the first automated translation systems hit the market. They were terrible, and we claimed that the human language was too multifaceted for them. We can assume that sentiment analytics will improve over time due to statistical methods or just due to "brute force" calculations from computers as much as translation programs did—they will never be perfect, but way better.

Until we see those improvements, we will need to take the same approach as we did with automated translation programs. We need to reduce the scope of the task. Instead of looking for all possible sentiments, we are analyzing only specific cases. For example, "what you think about this restaurant?" The ways to answer here are more limited, and thus a computer can be trained to be more focused. In turn, the sentiment algorithm will produce reliable and useful results. Whether that sentiment data will yield the fourth "V" of data, however, depends very much on whether the question you trained the machine to answer actually has a tangible and business-centric action attached. The question "what do you think of this restaurant," for example, will easily help companies like Yelp to sort through thousands of user generated comments and display good restaurants higher up on their search engine. However, in the PR world, sentiment is often only asked in hindsight and is just a reporting number that does not lead to action.

The next section provides some examples of the issues involved in trying to leverage the stream of social media information into actionable customer intelligence.

A CASE OF AIRLINE CUSTOMER SATISFACTION

In late 2009, an Asian airline asked us to analyze the satisfaction level of airline passengers. The best method would be to poll the passenger using a questionnaire. This would create structured data, but it would take time and money. Is there an easier way to get to this data? Yes, by using social media comments from passengers.

Of course, the biggest challenge here is separating the signal from the noise. As we will discuss in Chapter 9, the first step is a data-reduction process, where we reduce the media types surveyed (such as focusing on Twitter data), data content (for example, restricting attention to tweets referencing the company Twitter name or hashtag), and the use case (such as common words used by customers, particularly frustrated ones).

Jeffrey Breen (@JeffreyBreen) has done a similar exercise for US airlines. He also used those *reductions* and *R*, an open source software environment and programming language for statistical computing and graphics, to analyze the data coming from the open Twitter API. He describes his approach step by step in a slideshare doc.[10] We would encourage anyone with some technical interest to try this for yourself at home. It is fun.

Stunningly, the result is not all too different from the survey done by the airline industry itself, as one can see in Figure 4-5. On the horizontal axis you can see the sentiment scores he had calculated using a Twitter feed; on the vertical axis, he has the scores from those industry services. It is not a perfect correlation, but the trend is clearly indicating that those focused sentiments correlate to the overall survey result.

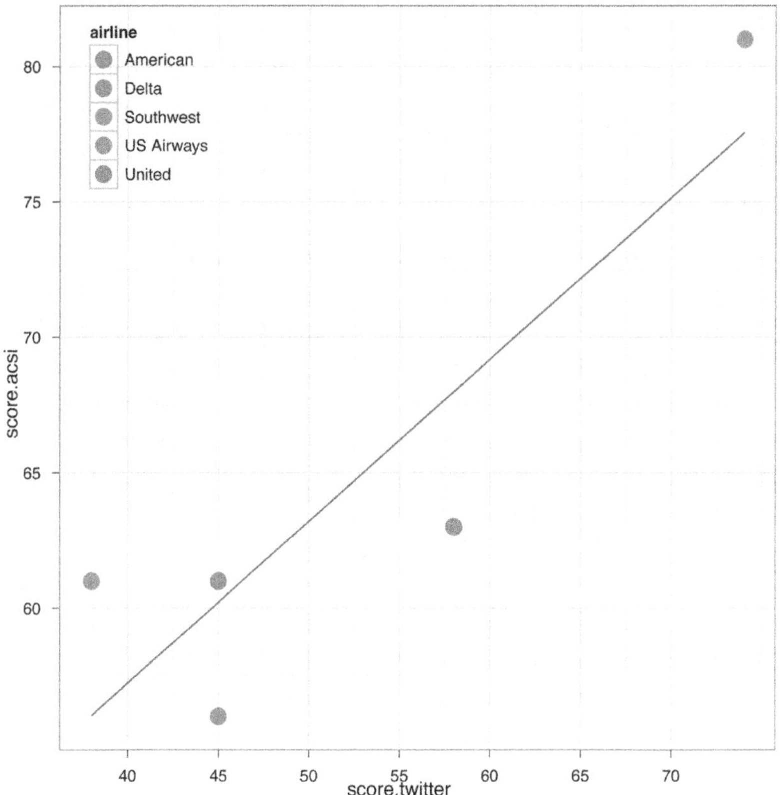

Figure 4-5. Comparison of Twitter sentiment to the American Customer Satisfaction Index (courtesy of Jeffrey Breen.)

10. Jeffrey Breen, "R by example: mining Twitter for consumer attitudes towards airlines," Boston Predictive Analytics Meetup, Jul 2011, *http://slidesha.re/ITMKYW.*

Surely there are several shortcomings to this approach:

- The questionnaire has many more in-depth insights versus what Twitter analytics will have.
- The questionnaire from the ACSI is done on a proper statistical sample, while those complaining to airlines on Twitter are anything but representative.
- The use of predefined language clues brings a bias by the person designing the analytics. Small critical tones will not be easily visible.

Of course, Jeffrey did not attempt to replace the surveys done by the ACSI in a single go. But this experiment shows that it is possible to analyze social media data, but you have to be careful what kind of data you use.

SENTIMENT ALGORITHM

In his example, Jeffrey Breen used a so-called word sentiment list. He used an opinion lexicon with 6,800 positive and negative words. Positive words would be signaled by words such as "cool," "best," and "amazing," and negative words by words like "worst," "awful," and "terrible."

This is the simplest form of a sentiment algorithm. The algorithm then compares a list of words with the tweet and assigns a negative (-1) or positive (1) sentiment score. The overall sentiment is just a sum of all sentiment scores. For example, let's look at the the following tweet:

"@Continental this flight was so bad."

"Bad" is a negative word, which the algorithm counts as negative. At the end, the computer adds up all negative and positive words to get an *overall* score for the article. The programming approach is relatively straightforward.

The main advantage of such an algorithm is that it can be precalculated, as there is not a given subject. For example, a company like Sysomos uses such precalculated sentiment scores. The main advantage is that within seconds, the sentiment of thousands of underlying articles can be added up and presented.

But look at the following fictitious tweet:[11]

"@Continental, you could be more friendly—@southwest I never had such a bad flight."

11. The following tweets are fictive and are just created to explain the system.

The net amount of positive and negative sentiment would be neutral: 1 × (-1) "bad" + 1 × (1) "friendly" = 0 meaning neutral. But in reality, the author of this tweet is most likely not satisfied with Continental. If you are interested in the sentiment for Continental, the algorithm should only count the sentiment expressed toward Continental and not toward Southwest, but already it is hard to tell whether "bad" relates to @southwest or @continental. The context will make it clear, but automated algortithms are often not able to relate to the context.

Granted, with Twitter and its 140 characters, there is often not too much context, and those tweets are just made-up examples. However, a good blogger or journalist would balance words between negative and positive sentiment to keep the article interesting. Thus a realistic score will simply not work.

Katie Delahaye Paine, a highly respected PR expert, issued a warning in 2009 about the inaccuracy of those measurements. However, this serves as an example of how to start thinking about automatically filtering online customer comments into useful data.[12]

Anaphora Algorithm

The algorithm that would be needed to accurately measure sentiment would look for a so-called baseword. For sentiment algorithms, the "baseword" is the word we focus on. Thus what is the sentiment in regards to this very word? Take again this fictive tweet:

"@Continental, this was a terrible flight—I should take the friendly @southwest next time."

If the baseword is @Continental, then only adjectives relating to this word are looked at, therefore, only "terrible." The word "friendly" does not seem to be connected to @Continental, as this is already the next sentence. Most professional social media mining companies use this approach.

Further sophistication can be added if the algorithm will not only look for the baseword, but also for linguistic links to the baseword (e.g., "it," "he," and "his"). Such referential links as those created by pronouns are referred to as anaphora. This will be needed because many articles will not repeat the baseword over and over again:

"Took a @continental flight today. *It* was awesome."

The algorithm would realize that the word "it" relates to the baseword @continental, even though this is a new grammatical structure.

12. Ld Jacobson, Linda. *Public Relations Tactics*, Nov2009, Vol. 16 Issue 11, p18-18, 1p.

Context

Despite enhancements of the algorithm such as these, the power of these algorithms to correctly judge the sentiment has been quite low. The biggest issue is the missing context for a fixed or hard-coded algorithm as we already saw on the phrase: "@Continental, you could be more friendly—@southwest I never had such a bad flight."

Context is very important for the overall judgement. Take as an example the phrase, "Go read the book," which could be a positive or negative sentence, depending on whether it was a comment about a book or a movie.

Many research groups have worked to include insights given by context. Their approach is often very similar: they split the text into grammar structures such as noun, object, adjective, and verb. They then classify nouns, verbs, or some combination into themes by matching those words against a dictionary. Each context, however, would demand, as we just saw, its own dictionary. Those context specific dictionaries are called "corpus." For example, companies like Provalis Research offer those kinds of dictionaries or corpuses for political and financial news. For general purposes, psychological dictionaries, such as the positive and negative word lists of the Harvard-IV General Inquirer can be used.

Most word lists will not directly lead to the sufficient results. You will need to train them for a specific situation. While doing so, there are three dimensions to watch:

Train by question
: The more specific a question is, the better it is. Try to be more specific than only "movies" or "phones."

Train by media type
: As we saw, news, blogs, and microblogs sometimes use drastically different language and have different possibilities for leveraging both negative and positive words.

Train by language
: Often, measurement companies take a "shortcut" and first translate text into English before starting analysis. While it is highly cost-effective, it strongly reduces the quality, as an algorithm that produces a high rate of error (sentiment algorithm) is fed by content that might have a high degree of unreadability after an automated translation.

Thus a large number of corpuses/word lists would need to be developed by a machine-learning approach. This approach is purely theoretical because the data and the time capacity are not available, at least not so far. However, using a standard word list raises accuracy concerns. Michael Liebmann, a researcher who analyzed press releases from companies (see Chapter 7), said that predefined word lists might miss between 83% and 94% of positve/negative perception.

CAN WE USE IT AT ALL?

In addition to context, the algorithm will have a hard time correctly measuring ironic or satiric content. So are there any cases in which an automatic analytics of customer sentiment makes sense? Yes, there are, as we already saw in the example illustrated by Jeffrey Breen. However, in order to automatically analyze customer care comments, the most important part is to reduce the scope to such a limit that the shortcomings of the algorithm do not play a role.

Case Sony Ericsson—special words

Reducing scope can mean focusing only on a small set of emotions: for example, only focus on swear words and explicit language. This way one could easily spot the biggest annoyances. In Figure 4-6 you can see how this is done in the case of Sony Ericsson. All messages are selected that use swear language. You could now relatively easily sort those comments by topics, or you could compare the same swear word analytics with other competitors.

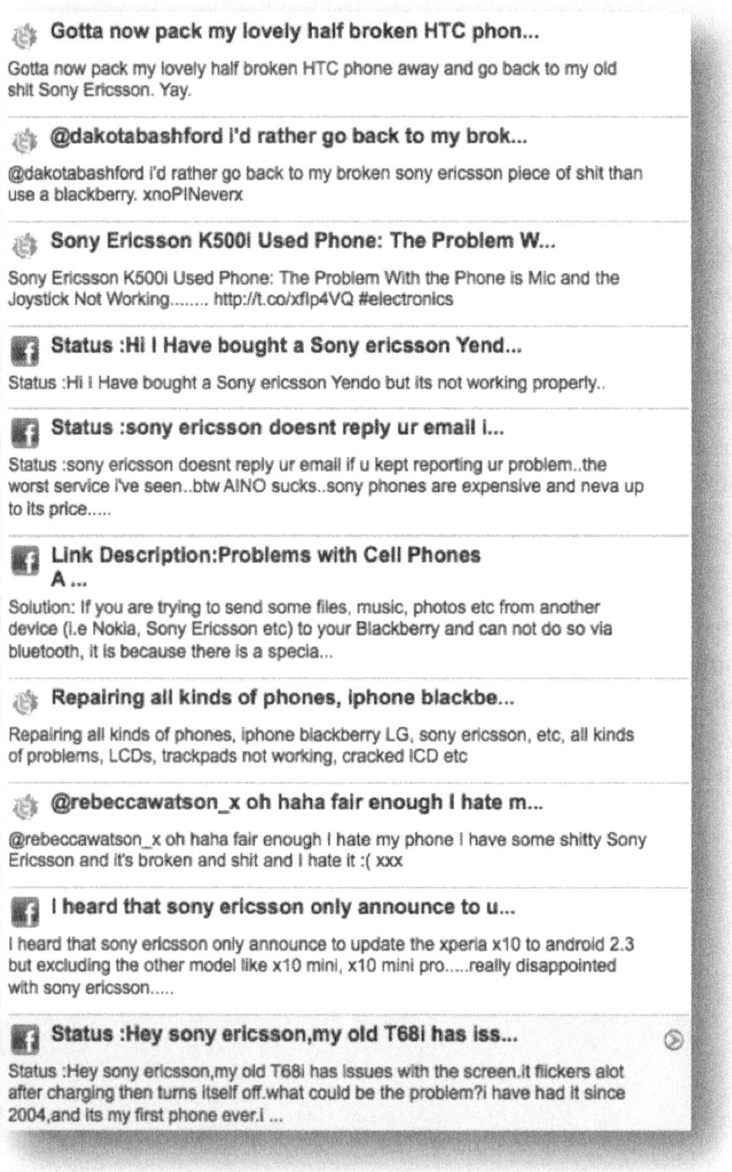

Gotta now pack my lovely half broken HTC phon...

Gotta now pack my lovely half broken HTC phone away and go back to my old shit Sony Ericsson. Yay.

@dakotabashford i'd rather go back to my brok...

@dakotabashford i'd rather go back to my broken sony ericsson piece of shit than use a blackberry. xnoPINeverx

Sony Ericsson K500i Used Phone: The Problem W...

Sony Ericsson K500i Used Phone: The Problem With the Phone is Mic and the Joystick Not Working........ http://t.co/xflp4VQ #electronics

Status :Hi I Have bought a Sony ericsson Yend...

Status :Hi I Have bought a Sony ericsson Yendo but its not working properly..

Status :sony ericsson doesnt reply ur email i...

Status :sony ericsson doesnt reply ur email if u kept reporting ur problem..the worst service i've seen..btw AINO sucks..sony phones are expensive and neva up to its price.....

Link Description:Problems with Cell Phones A ...

Solution: If you are trying to send some files, music, photos etc from another device (i.e Nokia, Sony Ericsson etc) to your Blackberry and can not do so via bluetooth, it is because there is a specia...

Repairing all kinds of phones, iphone blackbe...

Repairing all kinds of phones, iphone blackberry LG, sony ericsson, etc, all kinds of problems, LCDs, trackpads not working, cracked lCD etc

@rebeccawatson_x oh haha fair enough I hate m...

@rebeccawatson_x oh haha fair enough I hate my phone I have some shitty Sony Ericsson and it's broken and shit and I hate it :(xxx

I heard that sony ericsson only announce to u...

I heard that sony ericsson only announce to update the xperia x10 to android 2.3 but excluding the other model like x10 mini, x10 mini pro.....really disappointed with sony ericsson.....

Status :Hey sony ericsson,my old T68i has iss...

Status :Hey sony ericsson,my old T68i has issues with the screen.it flickers alot after charging then turns itself off.what could be the problem?i have had it since 2004,and its my first phone ever.i ...

Figure 4-6. Unhappy tweets are easy to spot as they use strong language

Another possible focus could be to reduce brand discussions only to very specific topics, as shown in Figure 4-7. On the horizontal axis, the share of voice of each brand is displayed, broken down by specific topics. You can see, for example, that Motorola managed better than anyone else to get into the public discussion in relation to its new front-facing camera.

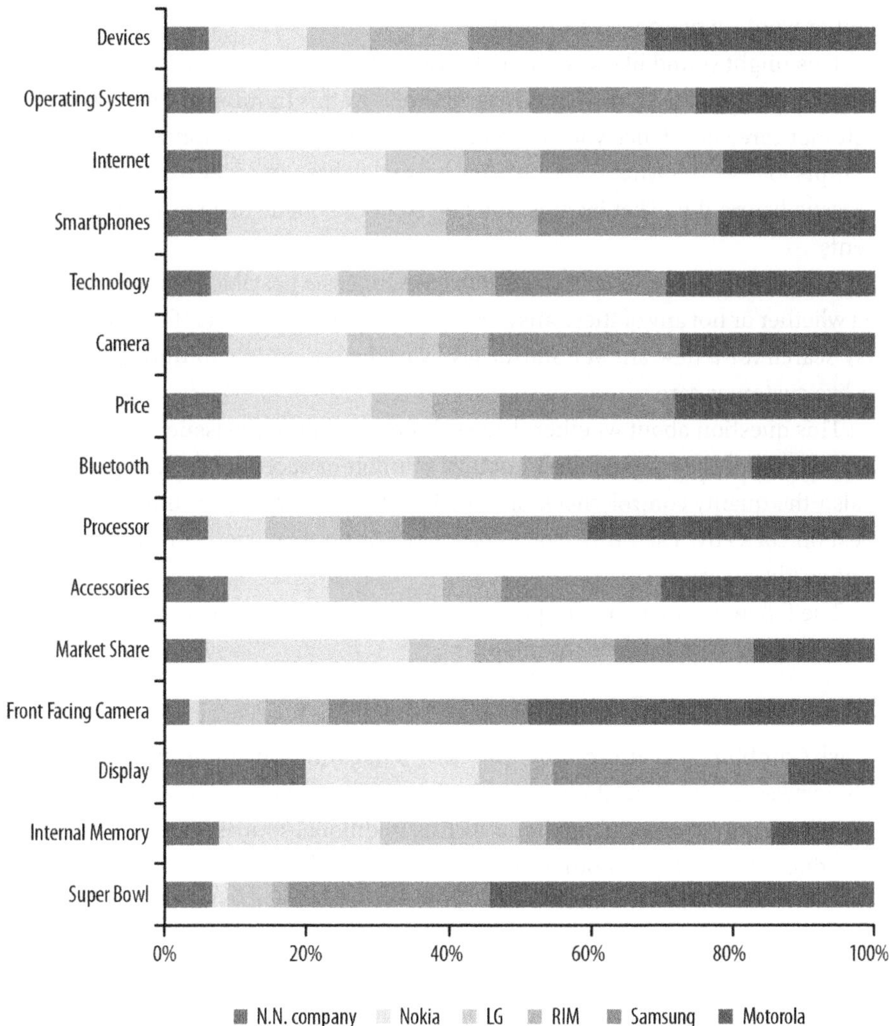

Figure 4-7. Comparing topics for given brands (Courtesy of Fisheye Analytics.)

A DYNAMIC APPROACH TO MACHINE LEARNING

All of the techniques discussed have the shortcoming that they are hard-coded via word lists. The quality of those lists determines the quality of the algorithm. Moreover, those lists might not evolve over time in terms of wording, media types, and contexts, and surely different languages will need different lists.

Those shortcomings might be best overcome with supervised machine learning. An algorithm learns what is correct and what is not and can figure this out without our assumption that a specific word actually carries bad sentiment and another word carries good sentiment.

This might sound like a solution; however, this algorithm needs to be trained. That is the "supervised" bit. A good example of how this training can work is online customer care sites. Once you submit a ticket in writing, an automated algorithm attempts to research what is in the knowledge database in order to try and resolve the issue before the ticket itself is transferred to the queue of a live customer care agents.

Based on this simple search, the database suggests possible solutions and asks you whether or not any of these answers would resolve your issue. If not, the system may search for a new answer and/or give you the option of submitting the ticket for live customer care.

This question about whether these solutions resolved the issue is not only the check on whether to provide you another solution or access to live support, but it is also the quality-control check on whether the algorithm has understood your question correctly. Each time you click on yes or no, the algorithm will train and improve the algorithm.

The following are two examples of how to apply machine learning within customer care on unstructured comments:

Case: newBrandAnalytics

Ashish Gambhir created a specific "use case." His own company *newBrandAnalytics* only focuses on one specific sector: the hospitality industry. He aggregates customer feedback from social media, as well as traditional sources like guest surveys, to produce proprietary customer satisfaction metrics for firms in this sector. In the future, this firm plans to expand this approach to other vertical markets.

Thus from all possible discussions, he reduces his approach only to what people say about restaurants. This is a quite feasible task for a machine to get trained on, as in not much training data is needed. However, Ashish needs to train the machine by hand.

This approach is manual because a human needs to decide what is positive or negative commentary. There is no self-enforcing algorithm because he has no clients rating it for him, unlike what users might do at sites such as Microsoft technical support.

Case: Dell's customer care

Stuart Shulman from Textifter[13] trains his algorithim using the input from customer care teams. A human decides where a given complaint should be sent. If it's a complaint about a printer, then it should be sent to the printing department. If it's an inquiry about a laptop, then it should be sent to the consumer division, and so on. Each time the customer care agent dispatches a mail or a tweet to the actual responsible customer care person, the underlying algorithm learns what is behind the distribution. The tool will soon take over and automatically dispatch all tweets and emails by itself. If a complaint was misclassified again, the tool will learn from those mistakes.

> Note
>
> In any sentiment algorithm, the most important part is that the algorithm can be trained relatively easily.

Summary

Social media has changed the balance of power between customers and the companies that serve them. Thanks to social media platforms and online communities, even the most humble customer can now have a voice that may be heard. To measure this voice is essential because on one hand, companies should mind the trolls, those people who are just abusing their new power. On the other hand, distinguishing between important and less important service requests will become a key success factor for a cost-optimized customer care organization, since not each voice in the online world is equal.

As we saw in the examples from KLM, social-enabled customer care offers companies a whole new ability to position themselves. Every service request can be used as an opportunity to position the brand or to demonstrate the value of the service or product.

13. Acquired by Vision Critical.

Social media does not offer only operational metrics to guide and measure the customer care efforts. The data created by that interaction contains value that we need to lift. We discussed two main examples for this fourth "V":

- Comments from users can be data mined for sentiment. Due to the complex nature of human sentiment, those metrics work best if they are very focused, as we saw in the example from Sony Ericsson or newBrandAnalytics.
- Customer Care requests can be analyzed to best understand which service request needs which question. This approach only works if there are many requests present because the underlying technology utilizes a machine-learning approach.

Social Media data has already created both management visibility and efficiency improvements in the way we serve our customers, and with time and technology, these benefits are likely to continue increasing. Meanwhile, these data have helped usher in an entirely new era of putting the interests of the customer first.

WORKBOOK

Social-enabled customer care has become reality for many companies. Let's look at the measurements you are using:

- Which social media metrics do you use to empower your employees? Can you see improved morale as their customer care dialogue is taken public?
- What are good metrics to differentiate your customers? Is each customer equally important? Is each comment equally visible?
- We often recommend to our clients that they should only have the start and end of the customer service discussion public. How is the discussion flow in your company? Would you like to change the flow? Try to determine when interactions should be public.
- Have you experienced troll comments? What are their characteristics? Could one automate their detection? If so, how?

The data has a value that can help to improve and processes. Let's discuss how:

- How many user comments or customer care comments do you have? Are they statistically relevant?
- Have you sorted those comments manually into topics? What could an automated approach look like?
- Assuming you would know what a customer needs from the written customer-care ticket, how could you treat him differently? What are potential engagement opportunities?

The area of social customer care is probably the most mature. Please share your experiences and thoughts via Twitter, @askmeasurelearn, or write on our LinkedIn or Facebook page.

Social CRM: Market Research

Customer relationship management, or CRM for short, is one of the more tangible results of drinking from the firehose of customer data. In return for capturing customer data at the point of sales or service, you can now tell how often people purchase something, whether they buy more frequently on special days, and how often they call for service. It has revolutionized the strategic use of customer data.

After integrating social media into the customer care process (Chapter 4), it seems only a small step to integrate this social media data into a CRM tool and use it to conduct market research and customer analytics. While Chapter 4 was more about operational discussions, we will look now at the data. Besides directly answering a customer question, is there anything else that can be done with this data? The answer is yes. In the future we will be able to combine several data sources from customer service data over product discussion to product usage data. That kind of customer-centric data base has the potential to be leveraged for market research purposes.

One key advantage of this type of integration is that the issue of whether we are "listening to the right people" (see "Mind the Trolls" on page 120) is no longer a factor, since you have all those social media comments enriched with your CRM data of your paying customers.[1] Another advantage is that the data is accessible in one way: this is a kind of master data management (MDM) system, only with one important differentiation. The social CRM system of the future will contain all different types of data: structured, unstructured, transactional, and nontransactional. Using this database, you can easily judge whether a comment is from an important client (someone who buys a lot) or not, and how important the comment is overall. Another advantage is the capability of using social data to cast a wider net versus

1. Assuming that your clients have told you the social media accounts they use.

the "walled garden" of traditional market research activities, such as consumer panels and focus groups.

Finally, this type of integration is part of a larger trend where we are increasingly listening to customers, rather than interrupting them and asking them for data. This chapter explores the difficulties of connecting the dots within the CRM data. The new generation of marketing research and product management is not yet around the corner—not because of technology but mainly because of organizational barriers.

Case Study: Customer Lifecycle

We discussed several times that social media commentary has the disadvantage of being unfocused. Your client might mention a brand without taking a position about it. A tweet like, "My son just spilled Pepsi over my new sofa. Does anyone know a good cleaner?" has no relation to your brand if you are Pepsi. So let's first look at focused data: customer satisfaction surveys. Many companies use these: they ask their customers many questions, aggregate the answers in metrics, and display them on dashboards. And what happens then? Unfortunately, not a lot. While "customer first" is a slogan used often, it is seldom put into action. Most of the time, one of three issues keeps companies from really acting on customer surveys:

- Silos are disconnected.
- Time relationship is too short.
- Averages disguise the issues.

Peter Crayfourd is the former head of customer lifecycle strategy for a global telecommunications firm with revenues in excess of 45 billion euros per year as of 2010. Peter and his team established a complete overview of all aspects of a customer lifecycle. Their focus is to capture the mood of their customers. "The way of thinking about a customer is what prohibits change," Peter said. "Often, companies see customer relations in the same way they are structured: in silos."

No matter which metrics one organization uses, NPS,[2] C-SAT scores,[3] or any other way, "They often do not measure the customer journey in its entity."

Let's look at a telecommunications firm. Why are customers unhappy? Maybe they were unhappy with the service quality of the network. They might be by chance then asked about another product of the company's or how happy they are with the store service. Most likely, their experience with the network will determine their reaction. "Companies tend to measure those interactions separately, but they are linked together," Peter explained. It is important to connect all parts of the customer experience over time. "What is the likelyhood that a customer will leave us when we dropped their calls several times?"

Telecom companies have the answer to questions like these in the network. They can correlate network service quality with the overall customer journey and the voice of the customer. Mapping different interactions with an overall happiness score will circumnavigate the issues of silos. But the more products there are, and the more possible interactions there are, the more data is needed to create a regression model. Those models are not new for most online retailers. Many of them use the structured data of clicks and products bought to predict the customer lifetime value. The big retailers with many users, and thus with a lot of data, can predict the lifetime value after only the first three clicks on a site with a likelihood of 90% or more.

These types of models are also possible with unstructured data from customer service centers. Jörg Niessing is an associate partner at Prophet, a strategic brand and marketing consultancy. He and his team built a predictive model for a bank in the US. "We could show that the likelihood for a customer to cancel the bank account and to go to a competitor is much higher when someone had to call the customer hotline more then once over the weekend," he said.

But what to do with this information? Of course this is a predictive model, where you need volumes of data to build it. But does the prediction have value? Only if you can react before something goes bad. That, however, is not always so easy. "If a user can not do some specific task and he is unhappy because of this, we can not change the banking application on the fly," said Jörg.

However, that information can be used to improve internal processes. At Verizon's call center, for example, a customer care agent will see a first guess by the

2. NPS: Net Promoter Score. First developed by Bain & Company to explain how likely a customer is to "recommend" the brand further.

3. C-SAT score stands for "customer satisfaction score."

computer about why that client is calling in, particularly if there have been network-related issues. This way the agent can already prepare a proper and customer-centric response and this way lower any retention failure.

Peter and his team want to go a step further: "Do not even wait till the customer calls in," he said. "Interact with him proactively until he is satisfied." Here is where Peter's "happiness" score shows its strength. Organizational focus can be achieved more easily if it is not only about retention or customer lifetime value but also about how the customer feels about the company. A telecom company might have difficulties improving the network quality around a single person that very moment. However, it can react proactively and start to talk to the client once a call gets dropped. For example, each company that knows which customers are unhappy might offer a special treat. "Companies should not wait until a customer complains," Peter said. "We have all the data to react proactively."

The second issue is that companies often tend to forget the time component. "They treat customers as a financial relationship over time," he said. "At the end of the contract, we are the customer's best friend as we want him to renew, but we might have forgotten to keep him happy during the time of his contract." He is right; ideally we would have a model to measure the overall satisfaction of a client throughout his journey with the company. But if there are too many factors impacting the relationship, it will be hard, if not impossible, to include the time dimension.

The last of the issues that stops companies from using surveys effectively is the matter of *averages*. Data is often not put into models that try to predict behavior or customer happiness. Instead, it is stored in dashboards showing average metrics for a given timeframe, which disguises correlations. What does an average service quality of 85% mean for you as a person? You might be the one for whom the network just dropped the call a couple of times (see Figure 5-1). Yes, you were unlucky, but you as a client will not care because you are unhappy. "If you manage your business by averages, you run an average business," explained Peter.

Figure 5-1. The issue with averages

How would you show that bad network quality creates unhappy customers? You would need to break the average down to each customer. Here, averages are not helpful. All in all, you need a *predictive model* that mixes the perception data of the customer survey (the overall happiness or customer satisfaction) with the hard facts of the network quality for this very customer.

From banking to telecommunications, we see that more and more processes rely on predictive analytics in order to anticipate customer behavior and to react faster, better, or more efficiently. Underlying those models are machine-learning approaches that analyze data to see patterns, as described in Chapter 2. Let's analyze what this will mean for the area of market research.

Analytical CRM: The New Frontier

People like Peter and Jörg are on the leading edge of a new discipline: using CRM data to conduct market research. Or, perhaps more accurately, they are part of a natural evolution in how we leverage our customers as a source of data and strategic insight. Market research expert Robert Moran describes this evolution in terms of three "epochs":[4]

4. Robert Moran, "Measuring the Future of Market Research," Future of Insights, June 2010, *http://bit.ly/1hRfNvm*.

Data Collection Epoch (or Asking Epoch)
: Marked by interviews and surveys

Listening Epoch
: Defined by observational analytics, ranging from social media data to exotic things such as tracking eye movements

Simulation Epoch
: Shifts the focus to anticipatory research driven by market research game simulations, Delphi panels, and strategic foresight

In Moran's view, we are now exiting the Data Collection Epoch and moving toward both the Listening Epoch and the Simulation Epoch. Big data is a necessary component of the Listening Epoch and potentially a driver for the Simulation Epoch, as well. Put simply, we are entering an era where customers now leave a substantive footprint of data in the course of their normal activities, and this data is a force to be used and managed.

Similar trends have been validated by the larger market research community. A 2011 UK survey of senior market research professionals showed that more than half are at least experimenting with techniques like market research online communities (MROCs) and web scraping. The former are curated groups, and the latter extracts data from social media sources such as blogs, Facebook, and Twitter. Close to half are also practicing or exploring co-creation (online collaborative concept or design work) and digital ethnography (in-depth qualitative studies of individuals or families using online data).[5]

All of these trends point to the fact that social media and big data are growing as tools for both marketing research and customer connectivity.

Asking customers questions to get insights has always been a time-consuming and expensive approach. It might take a month until a survey is returned—valuable time. Social media has the potential to approximate surveys inexpensively, even with a very simple approach. Welcome to the new fronter of analytical CRM.

ISSUES WITH THE TRADITIONAL WAY

Traditional market research would yield common segmentation criteria for consumers. You would use factors such as gender, income, age, or nationality to describe taste and purchase behavior. Then businesses started to realize that more

5. Tim Macer, et al., "The Confirmit Annual Market Research Software Survey 2011," meaning ltd., 2012, *http://bit.ly/ITVRJ4*.

segments seemed to be needed, as the traditional ones did not really help with all the correct classification. So it was no surprise that more and more segments were soon invented: the adventurer, blue collar, emerging adults, health and fitness, Hispanics, women with children, and so on.

But where does all this segmentation lead? Today an individual person is not best classified by personal demographics such as gender, race, income, or skin color. Today we are looking more into people's actions. After a few decades, the song from Lee Michaels, "You are what you do," seems to have become something of a reality. Increasingly, we analyze a person based on purchasing, reading, or other activities. In the future, marketing may increasingly revolve around the long tail of specific individuals.

As an example, Annet Aris, a strategy professor at INSEAD, frequently asks her students to identify two candidates: Segmentation Candidate 1 and Candidate 2. Both are male, born in 1948, British, in second marriages, affluent, and from well-known families. In most cases, the first guess is clear: "Prince of Wales Charles of Windsor." But do you know is the second one? It is the "Prince of Darkness" rock musician Ozzy Osbourne. To put both men into the same segment and assume similar shopping or customer behaviors is clearly not applicable.

Thus, the question might be asked, "Is this the end for traditional CRM?" Many sources, like Johanna Blakley's talk on TED.com, say it is "the end of gender," pointing to the fact that each person might develop individual interests that cannot be classified by the the main demographical segments. This does not, however, mean that each of us is now a complete "individual." Humans tend to organize their behavior, as well their shopping habits, in groups. Some of those groups will be characterized best by demographics. Take women's underwear as an example. Other products might not have a very clear-cut user group, and the marketing of those products will greatly benefit by changing the way we measure demographics.

The daily routine for many marketeers looks different, however; their industry is slow to change, and gender and age are still big parts of the discussion. As Blakley notes:

> *Media and advertising companies still use the same old demographics to understand audiences, but they're becoming increasingly harder to track online, as social media outgrows traditional media, and women users outnumber men.*[6]

It will still take a while until we move from the data collection epoch to the simulation epoch. The word "simulation" means that we test out hypotheses using data. For example, we run on subsections of our customers A/B tests. The more tests we run, the more hypotheses we can test. Google has mastered this. It has become known for testing the different colors of blue underlying a link.

Market research can use social media for testing. The data provided by social media can help in selecting user groups to be tested. It can help formulate new hypotheses and much more. However, it will take time before this simulation epoch becomes reality. Or as the political and economic consultant Nicolas Checa asked, "It took the research industry almost a decade to come to terms with Web-based surveys, so how difficult will it be with social media?" Therefore, one of the key challenges of social CRM remains not only technology but the inertia of the marketing industry itself.

TURNING CRM AROUND

Analytical CRM is about trying not to think in terms of boxes or classification. Take for example the predictive models formed by Peter and Jörg in the beginning of this chapter—those models do not care about the gender of customers. An algorithm tries to determine the data that has the most impact on predicting the loyalty. Thus, as strange as it sounds, analytical CRM does not start with the customer. It starts with what Peter calls the "touchpoints," meaning the interactions with the customer. This could be the network quality for a telecom operator, the products sold for an online retailer, or the time someone calls into the service center for a bank. Who the customer is, what he thinks, and what he does is irrelevant at first. The idea of the analytical CRM is to judge customers by what they *do* and not by their demographic segment.

This can be supported by Netflix, which would not conclude that a 30-year-old male with a high income would probably like the genre of "action movies." What it cares about is what that user does, and if he is watching kids movies all day long,

6. *Johanna Blakley*, " Social media and the end of gender," TEDWomen, December 2010, *http://bit.ly/1kGnjq4*.

it might be that this is his taste, or it might be that his kids are watching. Whatever it is, Netflix would use this as the basis to suggest new movies. "He is paying us for this kind of movie, thus he has a definite interest," said Xavier Amatriain.

FACEBOOK AND OPEN GRAPH

> *Facebook is different from Apple or Google or Amazon or Microsoft, because it doesn't build products. It seeks to improve the products built by everyone else.*
>
> **—MARK ZUCKERBERG**

The idea of an analytical CRM is to not only use traditional information on your client, like where he lives or how old he is, but to take all of the possible information you own to create a complete picture of him. What is he doing if he goes online, what does he buy, and when does he buy it?

There is one company that is trying to do exactly the same thing: Facebook. It wants to be a platform and wants to integrate all this data into a massive CRM store. It calls it Open Graph. Open Graph is the further development of social graph. The social graph showed the network of your users, while Open Graph shows much more. It shows not only the network, but all of the other pieces of information belonging to each user.

Facebook's Open Graph capability links users' activities to their social network. You see it whenever, for example, digital music service Spotify posts what song you are listening to on the news feed of each of your friends—or when an application asks you to log in via Facebook, and then posts on your behalf. It is powerful, and at times controversial: for example, users do not always want to have their entire network see what movie they are watching through Netflix, or have an application suggest things to their friends on their behalf. However, this capability is a metaphor for how people are becoming increasingly linked through social media—and how the trail of socially-linked data they leave behind can become strategic intelligence.

The trick, however, is that Facebook does not even own all this data. Many companies would most likely not give all of the consumer data to Facebook. This would be neither legal nor strategically beneficial. But Facebook attempts to organize data from others because Mark Zuckerberg has the fundamental belief that "a social version of anything can almost always be more engaging and outperform a non-social version."

Let's take the example of a bookseller. If it wants to serve ads to Facebook users, it could simply select a random sample of users and receive a certain response rate. Or it could select Facebook users who have "liked" particular books or publishers, in which case the response rate would likely be greater. The bookseller is leveraging the simplest part of Open Graph, filtering structured data to select a more targeted audience. In an interview with *Wired Magazine,* Mike Vernal, head of Facebook's Open Graph development team, explained that the book recommendation site Goodreads.com has seen an 800 percent increase in impressions from Facebook since going live with Open Graph in early 2012.

According to Mike, the social experiences of Facebook revolve around the ability to quickly analyze how people interact with content and its relative importance. In the interview, he noted, "If you prefer music, we show you more music. If you prefer games, we show you more games. Then we merge those two sets of scores together, to influence what Newsfeed shows and what Timeline shows and what some other systems show."[7]

As always in this book, the question is not about technology or data; the question is how to use this data successfully. The main question Facebook has in mind is how to use its data to effectively place advertisements and enable social commerce, the so called "F-commerce."

But not all believe that Facebook has been successful in this approach. This is mainly because, as noted in previous chapters, behavioral clues we collect from searches are more powerful then public statements we make by "liking" something. To get back to the book example, I might say I like a book of Nietzsche's, but in reality read more easy-to-swallow comics on love, crime, and rock'n roll. Facebook has realized this and started to collect, via applications of its partners, useful user data such as whether someone actually reads Nietzsche or whether he spends more time on comics.

Nevertheless, Facebook's Open Graph approach has the beauty of combining both what people do and what they say to give a much more detailed picture about each personality. Perhaps the social aspect is often not the main enhancement, as unstructured data is still too difficult to read. Facebook thus tries to get developers to put a structure on the content to make it easier and less complex to read.

In 2001, World Wide Web founder Tim Berners-Lee put forth the term "semantic web" to describe where he felt unstructured data was going: semantic

7. Cade Metz, "How Facebook Knows What You Really Like," *Wired Magazine*, May 2012, *http://wrd.cm/1h6X7Fe*.

information bound together by metadata and relationships and not just structured data. For example, you could search for a picture or video on the Web based on its metadata or find a range of prices corresponding to a class of data. Facebook's Open Graph approaches this ideal by providing third-party applications with a way to structure their data, which in turn enables Facebook to access and reuse this data. According to Vernal, Facebook bases its capabilities around an "object store" (containing object data and metadata) as well as an "edge store" (containing relationships between objects).

Personalization: More than Just Recommendations

In Chapter 2 we discussed recommendation systems as a key driver of purchasing intent online. They are also an important example of personalizing your online experience. However, at least one social media executive feels there is a huge gap between many of today's online recommendation systems, such as Facebook, Netflix, and Amazon, and truly personalizing the Web.

Hank Nothhaft, cofounder and chief product officer of Trapit, a personalized content-delivery platform, claims that much of what passes for personalization today is actually crowdsourced general interest mapping, and describes such results as "insultingly banal." Speaking in a 2012 Techcrunch article,[8] he feels that true personalization needs to recognize each of us as unique and constantly changing individuals rather than specific market types.

One example Nothhaft points to is the evolution of television, as it changes from a static medium to a highly viewer-controlled one in the presence of DVRs and web-based television; in time, he predicts that each person's television will be completely unique. In his view, "As the Web becomes our own personal web...[T]his means incorporating both more direct and more ambient information, such as awareness of time, location, my schedule, my habits and engagement with content. Furthermore, it means realizing that human identity is a constantly shifting target."

---

8. Hank Nothhaft, "Let's Get Personalized: Moving Beyond Recommendations," Techcrunch, Jan., 2012. *http://tcrn.ch/1hRkfdH.*

Which Data?

Let's go back to the approach of linking the voice of the customer with the internal data about the service. Which data should be included in the discussion? Many companies sit on an abundance of data, more then they know. A telecom operator, for example, could save each connection, each bandwidth allocation, and each status of each base station. A retailer would not only know which clients have bought something, but also which ads they saw or which clicks they made before they came into the store. On top of that, we could save all social media communication. Does this make sense? Shall we really save everything? Aside from privacy concerns, the answer is yes. Saving data is meaningless until we have the right question so that we can create value out of the data. Often in the beginning, we do not have the right question in mind. Since storage has become cheap, we still should capture all this information for a later stage once we have the right question formulated.

Often, companies are faced with enough complexity to store and enable their internal, mainly structured data. Social media, however, is unstructured data, and in Chapter 9, we explain why it is more difficult to gain insights from such data. Shall we—on top of all internal data—save unstructured socia media data in order to correlate this with our CRM data? Depending on who you ask, you might get two quite contradictory messages: "too shallow," will one camp say; "too sensitive," say the others. Let's look at both arguments.

SOCIAL MEDIA: TOO SHALLOW?

Is social media too shallow to use it for customer insights? An online retailer or a telecom company has a massive amount of data about user behavior. This kind of data is mainly structured. We will discuss the difference between structured and unstructured data more in Chapter 9, the summary in short is, that structured data is easier data mined. It is more suited for computer and thus is more likely to yield better insights. The unstructured data such as social media commentary contains a lot of noise not only for us humans but even more so for computer and machine learning algorithm. It is thus much harder to identify any trends or structure in this kind of data.

But this is not the only reason why social media data is ill-suited at first sight. It is culturally biased: it is more likely to be generated by people in the Millennial generation rather than older Baby Boomers. Thus, the results from them might be highly skewed, and statistical relevancy might always be an issue. And indeed one can not find a lot of academic studies that have explored the impact of social media on market research, according to literature survey by marketing professor Anthony Patino.[9]

But there are situations where you want to have social media data. When? The answer is simple: when there is no *better* data around. Take the recent surge of patient communities like PatienceLikeMe, cofounded by Jamie Heywood; or Ubiqi, founded by Jacqueline Thong. Members of those sites discuss their symptoms, share how a medication has worked, and register when they are "happy" or "in pain." This is unstructured data at its best. Moreover it is skewed: highly skewed, even, as mainly younger, tech-savvy people will use those methods. But all this data is unique. It offers valuable insights because all of those members discussing their treatment are becoming a part of a virtual study. Using their members' data, PatienceLikeMe has published more then 35 research studies. The data is not "too noisy" or "too shallow." Over time, we will see many more examples like this. Social-sourced data is by no means "too shallow."

Many CRM systems already have the ability to attach social media information. But this feature is seldom used in an analytical setup. Even when social media can deliver insights, the transition of market research from "asking" to "listening" will still require time and infrastructure. According to the Confirmit 2011 Annual MR Software Survey discussed previously, a plurality of companies (42%) feel that it is hard to gather insights from unstructured text, and less than a third feel the process is easy. Perceptions such as these remain one of the challenges in effectively transitioning to social CRM from traditionally structured customer data.[10]

PERSONAL DATA: TOO SENSITIVE?

The second argument was "social media data is too sensitive." This is surely a contradiction to the idea that it is "too shallow." If it were too shallow, how could it be too sensitive? Well, whenever it is actually used to gain insights. Insights from social media data often enter into areas that are personal, like health or financial well-being. Human communication is personal; so are the insights. Take for example the German credit-rating company Schufa. It started a project to analyze whether data from Twitter, Facebook, and Xing (the German LinkedIn) could help to predict credit ratings. Together with the Hasso-Plattner-Institut from the University of

9. Anthony Patino et al., "Social media's emerging importance in market research," Journal of Consumer Marketing, Vol. 29, Issue 3, pp.233–237, 2012.

10. Tim Macer, et al., "The Confirmit Annual Market Research Software Survey 2011," meaning ltd., 2012, *http://bit.ly/ITVRJ4*.

Potsdam (HPI), they founded the Schufa-Lab@HPI. The idea behind this project was to scan social networks for information that could possibly lead to conclusions about a person's financial capacity. Without waiting for the research to be done, we knew that there would be a correlation. Think about the success Garmeen Bank had with microfinancing. Some of its success can be attributed to a good understanding of the real-world social networks of the lender. Schufa planned to bring the same process into financing.

Suddenly what we wrote and said in this semi-private space of social media had the potential to impact our credit score. The reactions to this from the public and politicians were fierce, voicing concerns about privacy. Some government officials even intervened, and the project ultimately was stopped as a result of the intense opposition. Schufa was not the first case of its kind and it will not be the last.

Wary of those issues, some even preemptively ban themselves from entering into any research. We once showed French government officials how to analyze the public discussion. They were excited about the richness of the analytics. We could show them insights about the public opinion they had not seen before. Despite this initial excitement, they decided to not go on with any measurement. "If the general public starts to realize that we 'spy' on our citizens, we might have a crisis that we cannot cope with," said the leading secretary.

Really? Is this spying? Well, it depends on what you do with the data. If you use it for the better of the planet or—less ambitious—for the better of your customers, you are welcomed as "visionary"; if you use it to do evil or with the clear intention to spy, you will meet some resistance.

Since we do not know how companies and governments around the world plan to use our data, we fear the unknown. Thus the best advice would be transparency as we show throughout this book, this fourth "V" as we coined it in the beginning is not easy to be found. Thus often it is not clear what you want to do with the data. However, it is clear that there is value in data itself. But since it is hidden and not yet clear, many of us fear the unknown.

In short, many data sources are very sensitive, including social media data: maybe not every single tweet or Facebook update, but the collection of data BCG's John Rose pointed out in a conversation with Martin Gilles on data privacy issues. The future focus should not be so much about how we safeguard data but more on transparency in how data is used.[11] But here we are in a catch-22. Neither

11. John Rose and Martin Gilles at the Economist's Information Forum, in San Francisco, discussing the tension between the benefits of data analytics and the need for privacy.

governments nor companies often know what they want to do with all the data they are collecting. As we've pointed out several times throughout this book, the fourth "V" (value) is hard to find. Thus we keep on looking for it and at this very moment, many companies and governments cannot be transparent about the use, because they simply do not yet know. Often, companies start off with a kind of "senseless" data-collection approach. While collecting data, they are doing tests to see how best to use the data. For example, let's go back to SCHUFA, the German credit ranking company. It didn't know whether Facebook posts or Facebook friends had a correlation with your credit score, however, before it can find out, it will start to collect data. This worried German citizens immediately.

After a short but very emotional public debate, SCHUFA had to stop; however, like always in research, it is hard to stop an idea. Other smaller companies picked it up. The British short-term loan firm Wonga is one such smaller company. They offer money at very high interest rates for very short periods of time, with instant online approval. As part of their application process, they publicly state on their web page that connecting with them on Facebook will allow them to get to know you better and will improve the chances of being approved for a loan:

> *Connecting with Facebook helps us to get to know you better. This will improve your chances of being approved for a loan.*

Social media information is as sensitive as healthcare information, and therefore many consumers are concerned. Any company using social media information to predict or to model user behavior would be well advised to be as transparent as possible to users.

Summary

The aim of market research is to understand why customers behave the way they do. Traditionally, to find this out, you had to get them out of their natural surroundings and into a rather artificial interview situation, where they could be questioned about things they tend to do instinctively.

Data mining and technology have turned this approach around. First, we can often automatically capture data about customer behavior. Second, we can ask consumers in any given situation how they *feel* about our product. By doing so, we might give up representative user groups but gain real-life usage moments. In this chapter, we showed how telephone companies and banks are already trying to gather this 360-degree view on the customer.

Those models are about to turn the process of market research around. For one thing, there is a clear turn away from a top-down approach by marketeers. No longer is it a small group of marketers thinking about the relevant features of the market ("young, white fathers with an income over..."). The market itself designs the set of behavioral criteria that describes the subgroup best. Thus whether you are the right fit for action movies, tropical vacations, or any other product or service will in the future be defined by your behavior more than by some arbitrary identifiable personal characteristics. For another thing, companies are turning away from collecting only internal data about customers. Instead, consumers are supplying more data themselves. This might be social media data such as Facebook's Open Graph, but it might also be self-registered data or other monitored user behavior.

Our aim is to create self-learning models that automatically adapt our offerings toward what makes our customers happiest. For example, we want to know which combination of marketing mail, price points, and service quality will generate the best cost-benefit for an online retailer. In a way, the analytical CRM is closing the loop between product marketing (Chapter 1) and sales (Chapter 3).

However, in order to derive such a "happiness" score, we should not only mine data and technology. To be successful, we need to understand what makes any given person *happy*. That's a personal insight, for sure. So we are faced with more and more concerns about privacy. A key success factor in this kind of data mining is not only asking the right question and using the right data or metric, but also how we deal with our customers' concerns about privacy.

WORKBOOK

Analytical CRM is the future and will try to encompass all areas of the customer's lifecycle. Such an analytical approach will then need excellent technology. It will demand an organization that analyzes the customer journey as a whole, and it will raise questions about customer privacy. Please discuss the following questions with your peers:

- How are we measuring the voice of the customer? Is the complete customer lifecycle analyzed? Which parts are missing?
- Do we know which variables will have the highest impact on an NPS score? In the example Crayfourd gave, it was mobile phone coverage and network service quaity. What is it for your company?

- How do you work with customer data? Who owns the data, you or your customer? Who knows what happens with the data?

The last point in particular will become more and more important in the future. Companies will need to find a way to create trust and to get the permission to use the data without a predefined goal or action. Only this way can the full benefit of data be available. What are the best ways to create this trust? Transparency at the time one finds out how to use the data? Open data initiatives? Public data exchange controlled by the users? While many companies collect data about its clients, only a few are transparent about what they do with the data. Privacy and open data will become more important over time, and will be the key to gaining trust from your customers. Please share your views either on Twitter, @askmeasurelearn, or on our LinkedIn or Facebook pages.

Gaming the System

More than many aspects of technology, data analytics is subject to a very powerful force: human nature. By its very nature, data reveals winners and losers, and everyone wants to win, of course. Making your product, your political candidate, or your brand seem more popular than it is can be very profitable. Social media presents myriad opportunities to create this fake popularity. One example is to friend new and unknown people and "spam" them with offers. This reality can very easily lead people to try and shade results in their favor, or even openly cheat the system.

More generally, any successful metric can be intentionally or unintentionally skewed by rewarding wrong behavior. After we have learned how marketing and PR use social media and social media data, we should spend some time on the shadow world of robots. This chapter describes the dark side: the abuse of the tools and metrics described earlier in this book. We have touched on many of the concepts in previous chapters. However, they are now used to intentionally skew metrics. Here, we look frankly at many of the ways that people can "game the system" with social media and data analytics, because you must often manage for human nature as well as numbers to succeed in this area.

Spam and Robots

The law of unintended consequences governs every system. For example, when email suddenly made it possible to communicate with large numbers of strangers for free, it immediately led to the problem of unsolicited commercial email, better known as spam.[1] When computers could communicate openly through networks, it spawned viruses and Trojan horses. And now that we live in a society of social media channels and information on demand, this world has become flooded with phony or even fraudulent information. Spam has grown into social spam. Viruses

1. "Spam" is an acronym for "supply-processed American meat," adapted to Internet email in 1988 by two scammers.

and unsolicited emails functioned well because of the ability to easily spread through digital networks.

But social media offered something new: openness. Anyone can post information that might be meant to distort reality or to benefit someone else. Social spam converted into social bots, algorithms that make people believe that they are humans.

While social networks such as Facebook or Twitter take corrective action to counteract these frauds, the detection is far from perfect, and moreover, this is an iterative process that is constantly being tested on all sides.

Over the last few chapters, we have argued that social media information can be data mined to help make business decisions. However, when there is phony or even fraudulent information that can make its way into *your* data, it will impact the quality and accuracy of *your* measurements and therefore *your* decision. How? Let's say you analyze your competitor's products by monitoring the public discussion. In Figure 6-1, each color represents one of those products you monitor. There are discussions from fraudulent sources aimed at selling the gray product. This inflates the amount of discussion about this product. If you are not careful, you might think that those artificially inflated discussions show a higher public interest in this competitor's product.

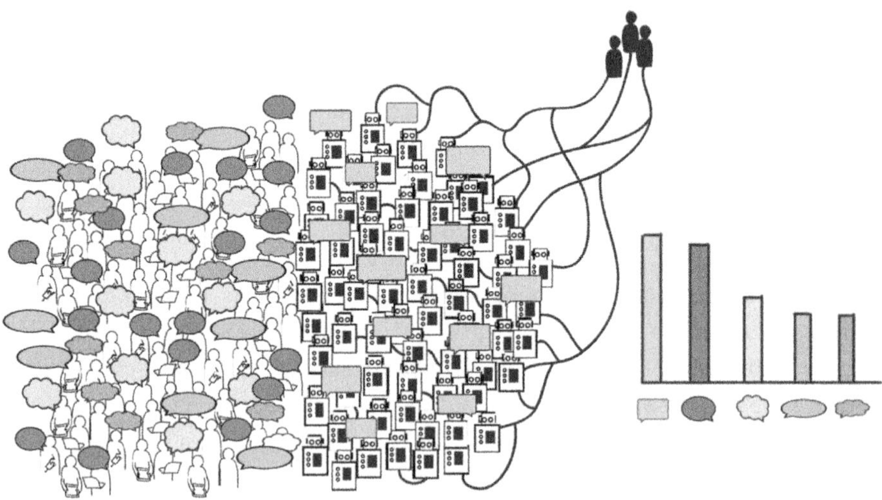

Figure 6-1. Automated bots are influencing your measurement

Sometimes the goal may in fact be to distort the measurements to misguide someone. We see in Figure 10-3 how often Google has to change its algorithm to not fall prey to search engine optimization (SEO) experts trying to misguide the algorithm for their purposes. This desire to influence Google's ranking algorithm has spun off a multimillion-dollar industry of SEO. Automated influence can get to the point where it changes public opinion. How? Through sockpuppets, i.e., automated fake online identities. Those robots publish and discuss stories in Twitter, for example. But some 55% of journalists use Twitter to find sources for their stories, according to the *Digital Journalism Study* by Oriella.[2] To quickly and effectively sift through the daily clutter of information in online media, journalists use measurement systems. These systems help them find the most interesting, best trending stories. Bots in turn try to influence these measurements to influence the journalist and, in turn, to influence the public opinion.

In either case, whether the intent of social bots is to purposely disrupt our measurements, to manipulate, or only to use the network to spread unsolicited or fraudulent information, it is important to spot manipulative, phony, or fraudulent behavior. To remove those is critical in creating accurate measurements.

We stress the importance of starting any measurement process with the right question (see Chapter 8). Similarly, knowing the right motivations for fraud or manipulation will help you spot behavior that could lead to skewing. In the following sections we will see a few of the main motivations, ranging from swaying political opinions to artificially boosting popularity ratings.

Additionally, we will look at the most common ways to skew social media measurements through automated means and discuss ways to combat them. The most common aims of *fraudulent* or *manipulative* activity are the following:

- To create *reach* and spread a message more widely
- To *smear opponents* with false information
- To *influence* others and/or to create an *intention* to purchase products or services
- To *suppress information* that may be politically or commercially damaging

There is a fine line between what is *manipulation* and what is *fraud*. Using automated means and not disclosing it is definitely fraudulent. Cheating in any system seems unavoidable. To find the ones who cheat and to avoid being found will remain an ongoing battle in the use of online and social data. Counteracting

2. Shea Bennett, "55% Of Journalists Worldwide Use Twitter, Facebook To Source News Stories," All Twitter, June 2012, *http://bit.ly/1hRyzCX*.

fraudulent use of data has already spawned a discipline unto itself, whose efforts could in time rival the multibillion-dollar online security industry that sprang up in response to threats such as computer viruses and spam email.

Creating Reach

Have you met Diarny Smitrh? She recently contacted me via a social networking site as you can see in Figure 6-2. She had a beautiful face and asked me to visit her website containing adult content. Who is she in real life?

First of all, Diarny is most likely not a girl at all. Nor is she even human. Diarny is a robot, also known as a "bot." She is an algorithm that connects to more or less random people on LinkedIn to generate traffic on the adult content page. But not only this, Diarny tries to connect to you to find out more about your connections and to be able to connect to them. Is it likely that you'll connect to a bot? No! Research has shown that 16% of us would accept an unknown friend request.[3] In the case of bots like Diarny, this acceptance rate goes up to as high as 22%, according to Yazan Boshmaf. Moreover, this acceptance rate can be improved if the name sounds familiar. It's not surprising that "Diarny Smitrh" has a name that looks like one big spelling mistake. The name is supposed to sound familiar despite the fact that this very spelling will result in zero results in a search engine. But even if you do not fall prey and you do not accept Diarny's invitation, at least she tricked you into looking at her message. In a word, she has created reach at almost no cost. For Diarny, the cost to connect to one or to thousands of users of a social network is almost the same.

3. Yazan Boshmaf et al., "The Socialbot Network: When Bots Socialize for Fame and Money," ACSAC, Dec 2011, *http://bit.ly/18ZXVfk*.

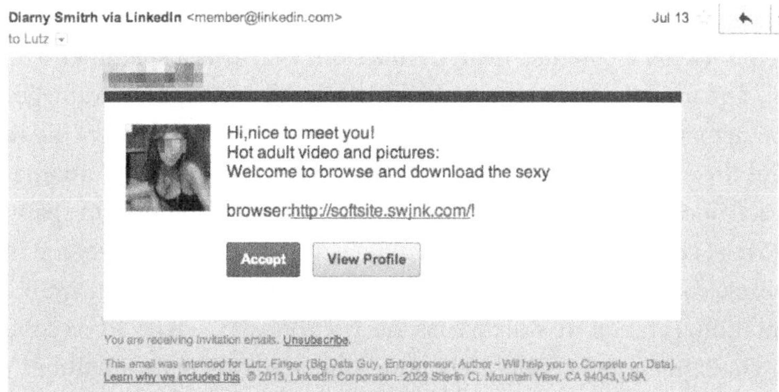

Diarny Smitrh via LinkedIn <member@linkedin.com>
to Lutz

Jul 13

Hi,nice to meet you!
Hot adult video and pictures:
Welcome to browse and download the sexy

browser:http://softsite.swjnk.com/!

Accept | View Profile

You are receiving invitation emails. Unsubscribe.

This email was intended for Lutz Finger (Big Data Guy, Entrepreneur, Author - Will help you to Compete on Data).
Learn why we included this. © 2013, LinkedIn Corporation. 2029 Stierlin Ct. Mountain View, CA 94043, USA

Figure 6-2. Diary Smitrh wants to connect with you, or at least wants you to read her message

The Age of the Bots: We Are the Minority

Diarny Smitrh is not alone. She, the algorithm, is part of a majority: 61.5% of all Internet traffic is nonhuman, according to a study[4] released in 2013 by Incapsula, an Internet security firm. Surely much of this traffic comes from scrapers or search engines, but more and more, from bots like Diarny Smitrh. Life in social networks sometimes feels the opposite of being connected. Brands, governments, organizations, and spammers all would like to engage with you or to get you to respond to them (Figure 6-3).

Figure 6-3. Bots want you to engage with them

4. Alexis C. Madrigal, "Welcome to the Internet of Thingies: 61.5% of Web Traffic Is Not Human," The Atlantic Wire, Dec 2013, *http://bit.ly/1a6ljpW*.

Those who visit her profile see a link to her website and can read more information designed to create a potential deal. In this case, Diarny is a spammer who just went social. She used the social networks without really using the advantages of trust and connectivity. She made the same mistake that many marketeers did in the beginning of the social networks (see Chapter 1). She just used it as another channel. But reach does not necessarily create intention. Conversion rates of spammers are very low. A spammer like Diarny would need to reach out to everyone in LA to get to a single conversion.[5] Diarny is thus something that we call a spam bot of the first generation. Later on we will discuss the evolution of the bots, the second generation, which do not go for reach but aim to influence and create intention.

How to Spot Bots

There are a lot of bots like Diarny Smitrh out there. If you are on Twitter, you could easily do a self-test. Companies like StatusPeople or PeekYou offer services to find out to find who is a bot. According to Michael Hussey (@HusseyMichael), the average Twitter user, like you and me, has anywhere from 40% to 65% robots as followers.[6] Bots like Diarny, thus bots from the first generation, which just use social media to distribute a message, are easily detected. Once detected, services like Twitter and Facebook will delete their profiles. But with each deletion, the creator of a bot learns how to circumnavigate the very issue that led to detection in the first place, creating a learning loop that leads to better and better bots.

Typical ways to spot bots are taken from how we would spot crawler attacks on a network. A person who is very active or active in bursts in a way that a human couldn't be is a bot. Thus if Diarny Smitrh attempted to reach out to a couple of hundred people within a few minutes, then it's clear she is a bot. Another indication of bots is ovely regular behavior:

Regular messaging

Someone who reaches out to other people on the network 24/7 without sleep and weekends is likely a bot. And with conversion rates as low as described, Diarny Smitrh will need to do exactly this; otherwise, she will not become effective.

5. Lutz Finger, Conversion Rate—Spammer, Jan 2013, *http://bit.ly/1b2Z0x3*.

6. Erica Ho, "Report: 92% of Newt Gingrich's Twitter Followers Aren't Real," *Time*, Aug 2011, *http://ti.me/18JkJ0b*.

Suspicious behavior
: Fake social media accounts often do not show a lot of authentic activity. If a tweep uses only one hashtag over and over again or sends out only one link to click, then it is most likely a bot.

But it is easy for a program to "randomize" the activity of a bot and to ensure that the bot sleeps or has weekends. Also, personal behavior can be programmed quite easily. A bot could take a random RSS feed from somewhere in the Internet. That is not his content and is a copyright infringement, but it keeps the bot safe from detection. The algorithm analyzing behavior to spot bots will think that this is a normal person.

Less easy to overcome is the data of creation. Any bot will need to be created at some point.

Recent data of joining
: In the early days of commercial "bot business," the bots were rather junior and recent but "acted" senior. Thus very junior accounts that already have a lot of conversations might be a sign of a robot.

Similar date of joining
: Often fake tweeps are created in "batches." For example, a European social network told us that it had at one point a sudden growth of accounts from India. "Within days we had new applications that accumulated to 30% of our overall user base from India," said one manager who didn't want to be named.

But those detection measurements could be easily overcome. One would need to have waiting periods for bots to become active. The best way to spot a bot is by its friends, in other words, to analyze its network topology. Bots are lonely. At the end, who wants a talking billboard as a friend? Let's use Twitter as an example. Each tweep has a network formed by his individual friends and followers. The topology of this personal network can be used as a kind of fingerprint for this person. A bot, however, will not be able to connect to other humans at first. Most real people would not become friends with someone who seems to have no connections at all and who is not very well known. Normally a social "newbie" would connect first to his or her closest friends. And those friends would answer the connection request in reciprocal order. A bot, however, has no real closest friends except other bots that will answer a connection request. Afterward, once the bot has gained a certain level of connectivity, it looks trustworthy to others, and only then will it try to infiltrate the network by slowly connecting to other parts of the network.

Such behavior can be spotted by analyzing a given cluster of social network connections. A network like the one in Figure 6-4 consists of people often called "nodes," and connections between those nodes are often called "edges." Two measures are especially helpful in detecting bot networks in an early stage:

Density within subgroup
: Density measures the amount of interlinking of a network. It compares the existing number of connections (also called edges) to the theoretical possible ones. Figure 6-4 shows one network that contains two very dense areas. A density of 1 would mean that each person has a connection to any of the others. Such a high density is normally *not* seen in real-life networks and is thus an indicator of a bot network.

Cohesion
: Assessing cohesion is another way to measure and detect bot accounts. The two groups in Figure 6-4 are interlinked by some people, indicated by all the edges that go from orange to green. That means that some accounts have contacts in the other group. Bot networks, however, are lonely, not very linked with the rest of the world. Or said differently, the "small world experiment" by Stanley Milgram will not work for bots. While each of us is connected by only a few degrees of separation, bots are not. The measure to describe this is cohesion, which counts the number of links you need to take away until the network is detached from the rest of the network.

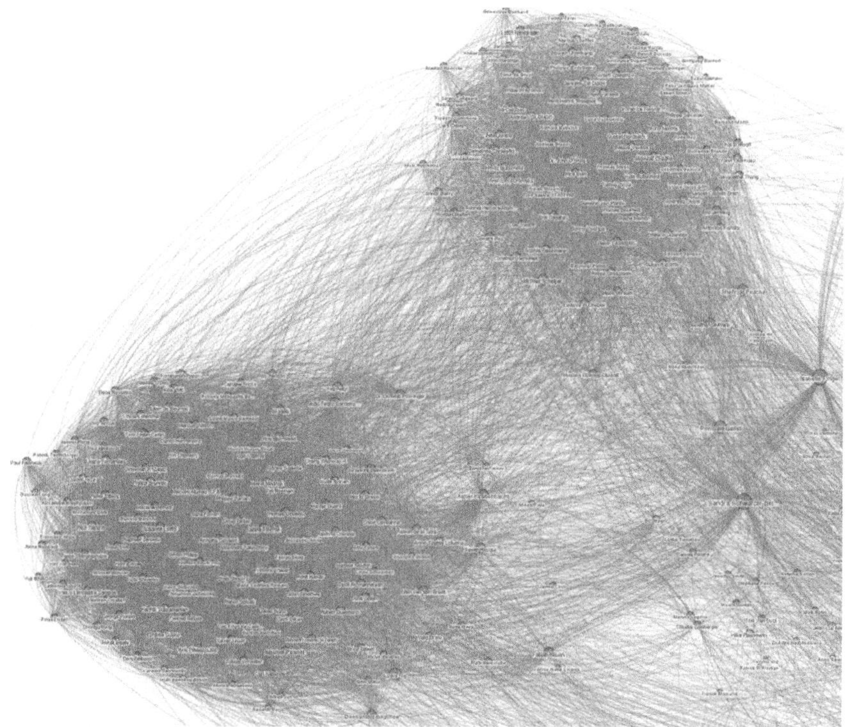

Figure 6-4. Subset of a social network, created using LinkedIn Labs

Since bot networks will first create their own group by linking to one another before they start to infiltrate the rest of the network, especially in the beginning, you will see a highly dense network with very low cohesion to the rest of the network. However, those measures using network topology only work in the beginning as the bot network is formed. Once the bots have started to integrate into their target network, it becomes harder and harder to distinguish the bots from just a normal tight community. It is, therefore, of great importance to detect those networks as they form.

This issue of bots is high on the agenda of all social networks. They try to build their own systems to detect fake identities because their business models depend on the trust of their users. Many, if not most, platforms are ultimately advertiser-supported, and no one would place advertisements with them if they knew that only 20% of their response traffic was from real people. Thus Twitter introduced an upper limit for people you can follow. This way it restricts Diarny Smitrh, and other bots from following a few million people in one go. And most networks created a way to flag spam or bots. This way, the network can not only catch them, but their early friends as well. Using network topology, as described previously, or using machine learning, the social networks spot other similar profiles and delete them. In the spring of 2013, Facebook instigated a massive purge of deceptive accounts and fake "likes" on business pages, deleting tens of thousands of these "likes" in some cases. Business Insider reported that the number of fake accounts dropped by around 83 million in the second quarter to 76 million in the fourth quarter. But because of the purge, Facebook's own fanpage lost about 124,919 fake likes.[7]

These systems don't mean the problem is solved. The Facebook bot-detection system is called the "Facebook Immune System." Shortly after it was launched, researchers found out how to easily circumnavigate those control systems, as Yazan Boshmaf showed. He and his team operated a large number of robots on Facebook to infiltrate other users. They had a success rate of up to 80%.[8] Once people were connected to the network, the robots from Boshmaf's group managed to get personal information, as well as spread messages. Twitter also used a system to reduce spam messages from 10% in August 2009, down to below 1% in 2010.[9] But soon researchers found out that this was only a temporary win. In 2013, Amit A. Amleshwaram et al. reported that 7% of all tweeps seem to be spammers.[10]

This will become an endless cycle where people try to spot bots while spammers try to circumnavigate those controls, as we have already seen with email spamming and with computer viruses and the antivirus software industry. It will be a cycle that technology can't win because both sides have access to the same means. In 2012, Twitter went one step further (Figure 6-5) and sued alleged spammer companies such as TweetAttacks, TweetAdder, and TweetBuddy.[11]

7. Jim Edwards, "Facebook Targets 76 Million Fake Users In War On Bogus Accounts," Business Insider, March 2013, *http://read.bi/18JoXVF*.

8. Yazan Boshmaf et al., "The Socialbot Network: When Bots Socialize for Fame and Money," ACSAC, Dec 2011, *http://bit.ly/18ZXVfk*.

9. Twitter, "State of Twitter Spam," Twitter Blog, *http://bit.ly/1b345pe*.

10. Amit A. Amleshwaram et al., "CATS: Characterizing Automation of Twitter Spammers," IEEE, Jan 2013, *http://bit.ly/1fr2NJl*.

11. Gerry Shih, "Twitter Takes Spammers To Court In New Suit," Reuters via Huffington Post, April 2012, *http://huff.to/IUir4c*.

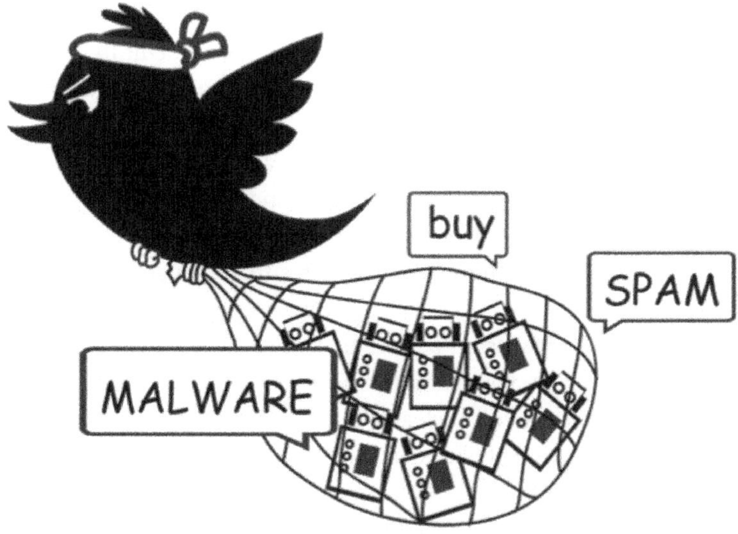

Figure 6-5. Twitter sues alleged bot companies

Next to legal and technology actions, there is a third way to avoid spammers from the beginning: make sure that they are identified. There are several ways to do this. This could be done by techniques that include "captcha" codes. Once you register your social media account, you are forced to type in a letter combination that is either handwritten or difficult to read. Those codes should, at least in theory, only be readable by human beings. Unfortunately, technology soon caught up, and there are many tools to automatically read and enter captcha codes. The next level then is to ask sophisticated questions like "calculate one plus one." But that can also be solved by potential spammers. In this case, one would need to use mechanical clerks, e.g., people from low-wage countries who identify CAPTCHA questions and type them in for less then a cent per security code.[12]

Surely the networks could raise the bar even higher to prevent automatic systems from generating fake identities. They could force everyone to enter a mobile phone number or ask for credit card details. Those measures will work best to keep bots who possess neither of those away. But unfortunately, they also keep a lot of potential customers out and such measures could be commercial suicide.

12. Vikas Bajaj, "Spammers Pay Others to Answer Security Tests," April 2010, *New York Times*, *http://nyti.ms/JgmJnb*.

If spam bots have infiltrated and spread into the network, especially once they have found friends who are *real* humans, it can be extremely difficult to identify them. However, you can probe suspicious candidates by asking them questions that a computer would find difficult to answer. For example, Facebook sometimes requires users to identify people who are tagged in the real account owner's photo library: they show seven images, allow the person to skip up to two of them, and do not allow any errors. Other approaches might be to ask questions based on a user's profile or seek responses to things such as jokes that an algorithm would have difficulty responding to.

All of those approaches are far from perfect since they always will miss some bots and punish some *real* users. For example, Facebook users have been locked out of their own accounts because of unclear photos. Increasingly, sophisticated technology is being employed on both sides of this battle, and this trend is likely to continue for some time to come.

Since there is no cure for bots, "verified accounts" will be the future. Major social networks such as Facebook and Twitter have already introduced them. Since public institutions are using online tax filing and other digital systems more frequently, online identity verification will soon be even more mainstream. Something like a digital passport will become accepted. That will be the end for most bots, and it also be the end of individual privacy in the social networks.

How to Set Up a Bot

If you're not a techie but want your own bot, you might be surprised by how easy it is to set one up. There are many services to choose from. Companies offer retweets and followers for little money. One company offers for as little as $21.44 more than 600 Facebook likes. Their service says:

> *100% Guaranteed Facebook Likes! We offer guaranteed Facebook fanpage "Likes" packages to kick start your Facebook marketing campaign. Whether you currently have zero likes or thousands of fans, when you buy Facebook likes cheap from Social Media Combo we always send additional "Likes" to your fan page so you can increase your social proof and fan page activity.*

A short video from the German Deutsche Well shows how easy one could set up a bot with services like ifttt.com. The bot @spotthebot was created within a few minutes, and it got other bots as friends, and from then on it became more and more connected in the real world.[13]

One step further is to have your own bot software. That's also easy to buy, as you can see in Figure 6-6. This company offers an easy-to-use service for all different networks, including a software to bypass CAPTCHA codes.

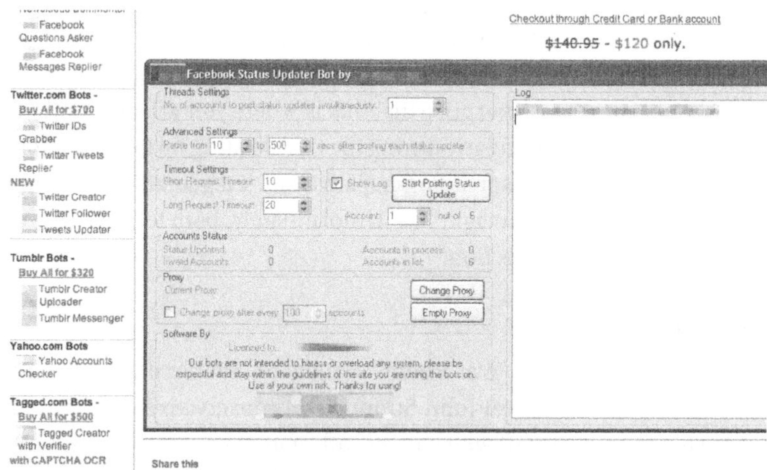

Figure 6-6. Commercial bot software is easily available

If you know how to code, you can download bot software and natural language toolkits from university websites under an open source license.

Smearing Opponents

Diarny Smitrh wanted us to visit her website and potentially become her client. That is spam in its basic form. Sometimes bots can have consequences that go far beyond spamming people to buy things. They can also be used to harm the reputation of others. Bots can be used to smear others.

Suppose that you are a company that manufactures a household cleaning product. One of your competitors dominates the market for this type of product, and you would like to have a greater share of this market. Of course you will compete

13. Michael Wetzel, "Remote-Controlled Spin," Sep 2013, Deutsche Well TV, *http://youtu.be/TwOdxnkVP7Y*.

on the basis of things like pricing and features. However, it might be even more profitable for you to raise doubts about the safety of your competitor's product.

If you were to publicly challenge your competitor in this way, you would be held accountable for what you say, and your credibility, of course, would be suspect as a competitor. But if you were to invent bogus "concerned citizens" who spread these concerns on your behalf through social media, you might be able to damage your competitor's reputation much more effectively. This would especially be the case if these accusations are exaggerated or not entirely accurate.

One of the more common areas where smearing opponents happens is in politics. It should come as no surprise that this is where you will also find the most activity from social bots. Particularly during the time leading up to an election, there is often a gray area between spreading negative and exaggerated campaign messages versus disseminating outright lies. Unfortunately, both techniques are often employed in the heat of an election.

JOHN SUNUNU

Take the case of the "Sununu War Room" scandal on Twitter during the 2012 US presidential campaign. The real John Sununu is a conservative politician and former White House chief of staff who had recently gotten into hot water for implying that another public figure had supported President Barack Obama, in part, because both were African-American. In response, a prankster created an account @SununuWarRoom pretending to be Sununu and posting racist and insulting tweets.

These tweets soon spread through social media channels, with many people believing that they in fact came from Sununu, even though they were clearly designed to be inflammatory. For example, the comment that Barack Obama would not be "3/5 of the president" that Mitt Romney would be alludes to legislation in the late 1700s that US slaves could be counted as three-fifths of a person for the sake of representation in Congress. Twitter soon shut down the account as being fraudulent.

Like the example of creating fraudulent reach for the sake of influence discussed previously, fake smear campaigns enable people to distort reality or spread falsehoods under the cloak of anonymity. This means that, as with other issues in social media and online data measurement, it is important to examine the underlying question that motivates what is being posted. If this question appears to be biased or suspicious, the possibility of fraud must be considered, triggering an examination of the validity of those who are posting.

FOLLOWER SCANDALS

While it is fairly easy to spot a prankster trying to smear John Sununu, smear campaigns can sometimes be very hard to detect. Let's look at some of the recent "fake-follower" scandals in politics. During 2012, several politicians were accused of creating "fake followers" in order to look more important in social media. Were those accusations true or false? We will never know for sure. We know that this has happened, but we do not know who created those fake followers. Was it the politican himself (or his team) or someone who wanted to smear the politician by creating false accusations?

One of the first high-level accusations was against Newt Gingrich (@newtgingrich), who ran for the 2012 Republican presidential nomination. Gingrich had a surprisingly high number of Twitter followers—1.3 million—compared with other politicians, as *Time.com* reported.[14] Social Media company PeekYou said that 92% of Gingrich's followers were fake followers. Other politicians and political parties accused of purchasing tweeps in 2012 were:

- Nadine Morano, a minister in the French cabinet 2012[15]
- The German conservative party (CDU)[16]
- Mitt Romney (@MittRomney), another Republican and the GOP's eventual candidate for the US presidential election[17]

It seems strange that all those politicians should have made the *same* PR mistake within less then six months. In all those cases, the fake followers were easy to spot. All of those accounts were very junior and were created on the same day or within the same week. As discussed in "How to Spot Bots" on page 160, there is a very basic method for identifying bots. Professionally created bots would be more difficult to spot.

14. Erica Ho, "Report: 92% of Newt Gingrich's Twitter Followers Aren't Real," *Time*, Aug 2011, *http://ti.me/18JkJ0b*.
15. M.S., "Nadine Morano dément l'achat d'abonnés sur Twitter," *le Parisien*, Feb 2012, *http://bit.ly/1b366BR*.
16. ZDF Blog, July 2012, *http://bit.ly/IKcaJ0*.
17. Zach Green, "Is Mitt Romney Buying Twitter Followers?" 140 Elect, July 2012, *http://bit.ly/1jY96aC*.

As noted earlier, it is crucial to analyze the *motivation* behind any fraudulent behavior. Let's analyze potential motivations of those followers scandals. We will see that politicians seem to gain very little from fake followers:

- Higher follower count increases reach, which will help spread the message, for example, calls to do fundraising for the candidate. While it is true that reach can be linked somehow to follower count, it only works for *real* followers. Fake followers would not help to spread any message, because they are often not linked to real-life people, and thus no one would hear what they said anyhow.
- More followers on an account might make real tweeps assume the politician has greater authority. This is certainly true. Evidence shows that tweeps are more likely to follow back if they meet someone with a high follower count. However, what kind of difference would that make for a politician who is a well-known personality and whose authority is analyzed in detail by mass media like TV? Fake followers will make no real difference at all!

Therefore, there is no real benefit to gain for politicians from high follower counts. For all those follower scandals, there might be only one of the following two explanations:

- There is a hidden incentive structure for having a high follower count. For example, a politician would like to show that he has social media competence by displaying a high follower count. A similar type of explanation would be that there was some incentive structure which put the number of followers into the personal goals of someone within the media team.
- The other possible explanation is that political opponents bought followers for those people to harm them and to create the accusation of "cheating."

Which one of those scenarios is true would be hard to detect.

Creating Influence and Intention

Diarny, the bot we described earlier, was not only looking to create reach. This reach had a larger purpose. By following lots of people on Twitter, she hoped that her spamming would create an action, such as a click on her website, and then, in turn, an intention to purchase the adult content she was selling. As discussed earlier in this book, the goal of many marketeers is to create intention. However, they often fall short by just aiming for reach. Bots are faced with the same issue if they aim only for reach. An effective bot will try to influence, to trigger an action, and to create intention.

The difference between reach and intention often lies in creating a human connection with a need. Following people on Twitter is relatively easy for a bot. Getting these people to click on a link for your website is less easy; there must be some attraction. (In the case of Diarny, this might take the form of physical attraction from the profile photo.) From there, translating this click into a purchasing intention requires both the perception of filling a need, and the credibility for people to trust you to fill it. Just recall the email spammers; response rates were one in 12.5 million for a fake pharmacy site.[18]

With spam emails, we have seen that click rates improve once the perceived *credibility* of the sender improves. While spam emails have only limited possibilities to increase this kind of perceived credibility, social media allows for a wide range of way to establish credibility. For bots to be able to improve click rates or gain information, they have to improve their own credibility in the real world. This can work quite successfully. There have even been reports of bots improving building trusted connections in social media. Rather than approaching a new contact directly, for example, you can use a Twitter bot or Facebook bot to first get an introduction. In an experiment reported by the *MIT Technology Review*, Twitter robots were built to lure potential connections. What the researchers found was that once a connection was established, those robots could introduce new connections, enabling them to build a network via recommendation.[19]

Once public relations was the domain of those who could afford large-scale access to the media; today even small businesses can wage PR wars using bots, or activists can invent an army of fraudulent identities that appear to back their causes. This, however, creates more and more skepticism within social media users and makes trust an even more important asset in today's communication.

In the following sections, we will look at two examples of trying to influence people: Nigel Leck (@NigelLeck), who tried to influence debates on environmental issues and the recent efforts by the US military to create nonexistent personas for social media as a potential tool for influence.

18. Lutz Finger, Conversion Rate - Spammer, Jan 2013, *http://bit.ly/1b2Z0x3*.

19. "Robots, Trolling & 3D Printing," Feb 2011, @AeroFade's Blog, *http://aerofade.rk.net.nz/?p=152*.

A TURING TEST ON TWITTER

The case of Nigel Leck @NigelLeck was reported by Treehugger.[20] Nigel had realized that the same arguments were often used over and over within environmental debates, so he programmed a robot to tweet these arguments for him. Every five minutes the program searched within Twitter for arguments and gave predefined answers from a database. With some humor, he called the robot Turing Test in accordance with the similarly named experiment on computer intelligence (see Figure 6-7). Some 40,000 tweets later, after a lot of press attention, Twitter became aware of this bot and shut it down.

Turing Test
@AI_AGW The Ether
Looking for simple questions with well known answers.
http://en.wikipedia.org/wiki/Turing_test
Following
Timeline
Favorites
Following
Followers
Lists
AI_AGW Turing Test
@Gigi2505 NASA's Hansen: There is NO 'global cooling' http://to.ly/514O
3 minutes ago
AI_AGW Turing Test
@fanofhockey Has the Earth been cooling? NO! http://is.gd/cNfNm #tcot
13 minutes ago
AI_AGW Turing Test
@grizzlymamabear Bill Gates's recommended reading on Climate Change http://is.gd/d3hC7 #p2
18 minutes ago

Figure 6-7. @AL_AGW was a bot to fight for environmental issues. (Courtesy of Treehugger.)

The Turing Test

Nigel Leck called his bot @AI_AGW the Turing Test. Alan Turing, one of the founding fathers of modern computing, once posed the bold question of whether computers could ever be made to think. In a 1950 paper, he reframed this question as to whether a computer could reliably imitate a

20. Michael Graham Richard, "@AI_AGW Twitter Chatbot Argues with Global-Warming Deniers Automatically," Treehugger, Nov 2010, *http://bit.ly/19HGT05*.

human. This query led to what is now know as the Turing Test: can a computer communicate, via text, in a way that a human cannot distinguish from a person?

One of the earliest examples of the Turing Test was a ELIZA, a 1960s computer program that modeled a psychotherapy session using the approach of Dr. Carl Rogers, who empathetically paraphrased much of what a patient said while making periodic observations. By using linguistic rules, the program gave surprisingly convincing responses: for example, a statement mentioning depression might be met with, "I am sorry to hear you are depressed," while questions that began with "Do you ..." were often answered with a curt, "We were talking about you, not me."

Later examples of the Turing Test included PARRY (a simulation of a paranoid schizophrenic that fooled nearly half of the psychiatrists in one study) and RACTER (a talkative raconteur). In the Internet era, "chatbots" based on similar technology fool people into sharing their personal data for identity theft by masquerading as attractive people of the opposite sex.

THE US MILITARY'S SEARCH FOR SOCIAL MEDIA ROBOTS

At another level, the potential for spreading influence through bots can attract interest and research at high levels. For example, public documents from the US Air Force showed that it solicited vendors for personal management software that could be used to build an array of nonexistent people within social media platforms.[21] The contract was awarded in 2011 to the US-based company called Ntrepid for $2.76 million.[22]

While the planned applications for this software are classified, such tools would enable virtual people to be placed strategically in locations around the world, to influence public opinion in ways that would benefit the US goverment. The *Guardian* quoted General David Petraeus, who said that this software is used to "counter extremist ideology and propaganda and to ensure that credible voices in the region

21. Solicitation Number: RTB220610

22. Stephen C. Webster, "Exclusive: Military's 'persona' software cost millions, used for 'classified social media activities," The Raw Story, February 22, 2011, *http://bit.ly/lKflec.*

are heard."[23] Tools such as these represent the modern equivalent of dropping propaganda leaflets from airplanes in past world wars, but in a much more personal and credible way, and it can be done at the push of a button from within the safety and comfort of your own borders.

Spreading Paid Opinions: Grassroots and Astroturfing

Social media has often been hailed as the *purest* form of democracy. Everyone can participate. In politics, social media is often connected to grassroots movements, which are local groups. Volunteers bound together by a mutual cause fight for their interest and may even cause change by getting the attention of the general public. Grassroots movements are often seen as being in contrast to the representative democracy, where political or social decisions are dominated by a few elected power sources.

Anyone can try to start a grassroots movement because anyone can create a social media account. However, the mass adoption of the given cause is far from certain. There are three main success factors for a grassroots movement to become engaging for a broader group of people:

Content
: Is the cause of the movement my personal cause?

Access
: Can I easily participate in this movement?

Reach
: Can I reach enough people and convince them that the cause is important and that they should participate?

Grassroots movements have existed since the onset of society. However, social media has made reach and access extremely easy. In the early days of the social Internet, you had to write a post to participate and to give an opinion. With Twitter or microblogs, the post, and thus the effort, became smaller. Today, making a statement or supporting a cause is down to one click such as a retweet or a Facebook like.

23. Nick Fielding and Ian Cobain, " Revealed: US spy operation that manipulates social media," the *Guardian*, March 2011, *http://bit.ly/lUmrSj*.

SOPA AND PIPA ACT: A MODERN GRASSROOTS MOVEMENT

The power of this simplicity became clear in a worldwide online protest done in early 2012. There were concerns over how Internet piracy legislation might shut down free expression and require a damaging level of infrastructure on the part of service providers. Several companies like Google and Wikipedia (and this book's publisher, O'Reilly) asked US visitors to contact their congressperson to protest the introduction of the SOPA (Stop Online Piracy Act) and PIPA (Protect Intellectual Property Act), bills that would add a great deal of unwanted cost and accountability to these sites by forcing them to shut down websites viewed as engaging in copyright infringement or selling fraudulent products, in an argument that was framed around the larger issue of free speech. Google blacked out its logo on its homepage, while Wikipedia blacked out service entirely, with both sites offering links to protest this legislation.

The turnout of online protestors was enormous, and social networks were full of arguments against the bills. This grassroot movement became very successful, and both bills were quickly shelved by their sponsors. This success was most likely not only due to the cause of stopping the legislation. It can even be safely assumed that not every protestor understood the underlying discussion. But it became successful because it was easy to participate and because the participating sites like Google and Wikipedia had considerable reach. The blogger Dan Rowinski pointed out that the protesting websites couched their advocacy in overly simplistic terms to stir up public opinion:

> *Censorship bad. You don't want censorship? Of course not. Here's a nice popup for you. Click the button that says censorship bad. You can do it. Good boy.* [24]

This example underscores that movements can leverage the Internet and social media to build a base of support in a way that is potentially reflexive and simplistic.

MICROSOFT'S ANTITRUST CASE

Sometimes grassroot movements go even further. It is not a matter of simplification and reach, as in the SOPA protests, but skewing the picture like in the cases of Nigel and the US military. No matter how honest the intentions are, they created fake personas or "sockpuppets" and bots to create an illusion of a mass movement,

24. *Dan Rowinski*, "Stop SOPA: What A Blacked Out Internet Looks Like," Readwrite.com, Jan. 2012, *http://bit.ly/19Ocr6K*.

or at least a widely supported opinion. This phenomenon is sometimes called "astroturfing." This term implies that something is not a real grassroots movement, but rather a movement made up of artificial grass. (Astroturf is a brand name of artificial grass that was first implemented at the Houston Astrodome, when it was discovered that real grass could not grow under its domed roof.) Technology is the right fit for astroturfing because it can enable thousands of generic sockpuppets to vote for a given cause creating this illusion of a mass movement.

Astroturfing has existed for quite a while and is not restricted to the onset of social media. For example, when Microsoft tried to organize a movement against the antitrust suit against it in the late 1990s, its supporters received prepared letters urging President Bush or others representatives of Congress to drop the case.

Microsoft understood that ease of participation is key and offered prewritten letters on already personalized stationery with preaddressed envelopes. All the participants needed to do was go to the post office. Unfortunately some of the protestors even went one step further and sent the letters in the name of other people, some of which were already deceased. As this became known, newspapers scoffed that the dead were fed up with the government's antitrust case against Microsoft Corp.

CHINA'S 50-CENT BLOGGERS

Some governments try to influence public opinion. China created a paid blogger army way before the US military started to look for personal management software. The phrase "5 Mao army," or a 50-cent blogger in English, was coined for a group of Chinese citizens who get paid to comment on or to write in favor of the Chinese government. They pretend to be ordinary bloggers but use different identities to promote government opinions. David Bandurski at Hong Kong University estimated in 2008 that there were about 280,000 paid bloggers in China.[25] However, the use of paid bloggers appears to have decreased lately, perhaps due to the inefficiency of the process.

Fisheye Analytics saw a strong decline in these bloggers between 2010 and 2011. Ashwin Reddy, cofounder of the company, noted, "In 2011, total social media activity [from blogs] increased by more than 50% from the previous year. However, Chinese blogs showed a strong decline, down to only only a third of 2010's level of activity."

25. David Bandurski, "China's Guerrilla War for the Web," The Far Eastern Economic Review, Jul 2008, *http://bit.ly/19HMiUX*.

Why did this decline happen? Perhaps the Chinese government felt that the propagation of news did not equate to action, and that the influence of these bloggers was not sufficient. Or perhaps the 5 Mao army has now been focused on other areas of the social Internet, such as Twitter, Weibo, or Wechat. Either way, the existence of these bloggers serves as an example of how astroturfing can easily be accomplished by real people, as long as their services are sufficiently inexpensive. Moreover, the line between real and automated sources of opinion continues to constantly shift.

CAUSE, ACCESS, AND REACH

To create a grassroots movement, honestly or fraudulently, you need three things: a *cause* (such as allowing smoking or banning SOPA), *access* to the protest (like writing a letter, going to the street, or clicking on a button), and the *reach* to engage a lot of people and inform them about your protest. Newer electronic means of generating reach, such as using bots or multiple online personas, make it potentially easier to create such a movement and perhaps multiply it through contagiousness of a message. This makes astroturfing an even greater risk in today's world of online and social media data.

Contagiousness

As mentioned earlier, to say that a social media message or protest like the one against SOPA was "viral" is not quite the right use of the word. Information gains weight as it travels. The more people believe a given piece of information, the more true it is perceived to become. Thus the spread of a message is unlike a virus that is equally *contagious* at all times.

Contagious or *viral* messages will need to have the same ingredients as a successful grassroot movement: reach, access, or an easy way of spreading the message, and suitable content or a suitable cause.

As we saw in the last section, technology can make spreading information as easy as one click of the mouse. There is also a higher potential risk for "gaming the system" through the use of robots. And we saw that reach can be increased through technology. However, can we change or predict how contagious content is? If we could, might we create virality by design?

KONY2012

Did you know that Kony2012 was one of the most contagious YouTube videos ever? After only six days it had more than 100 million views on YouTube. This 30-minute video, created by Invisible Children, Inc., explains very emotionally, and even manipulatively, the situation in Uganda, calling for action against Joseph Kony, a warlord who abuses children.

How did the video gain such fame?

For sure the *content* was an important driver for this success. If the content was just not interesting, then the content would not be spreading, no matter whether it was distributed over a large network or not. The content of the video Kony2012 is very emotional, as it discusses war crimes toward children. But moreover, the video was extremely well done, in a kind of MTV format with lots of embedded emotions.

The second success factor was how Invisible Children created a strong reach through its network, as Gilad Lotan described in his blog.[26] The video was not just placed somewhere on YouTube waiting to become famous. No, Invisible Children already had an organization of supporters in place. Those supporters acted as spokespeople to promote the film immediately. There were several centers where people started to promote the film. Thus in a short time, at different places around the world, this video was viewed. This kind of viewing triggered YouTube's ranking algorithm to believe that this had to be an important video. So YouTube then promoted the film even more.

The goal of this video was to generate reach, and YouTube rankings were integral to this process. Maybe the reaction of the measurement algorithm was even more important for the reach of the film than the reactions of the initial viewers.

At a broader level and independent of Kony2012, this example means that people trying to disseminate false information can also leverage the efforts of a fake crowd of bots to "game the system," and potentially enhance its reach and virality.

VIRAL BY DESIGN

In the end, no one will know whether this kind of contagiousness has happened by chance or whether there was a dedicated plan to influence the YouTube algorithm to promote the video. However, this last example begs the question of whether or not we could orchestrate virality. The answer is yes and no. Yes, with a lot of care, you can try to influence the algorithm and help spread a message similar to the way marketeers influence Google's search rank algorithm. And also yes, money will buy reach, which would be an alternative route to create high awareness.

26. Gilad Lotan, " See How Invisible Networks Helped a Campaign Capture the World's Attention," Gilad Lotan Blog, June 2012, *http://bit.ly/1j415Tj*.

The "no" part is that so far, we can't determine whether the message is contagious or not. And just the way that reach is no guarantee for intention (see Chapter 1), reach by itself is also not a guarantee of contagiousness of a message. This depends on the message content itself. In the case of Kony2012, the content was the right content to spread. But so far, research has not found a good way to predict up front whether content will spread or not.

For example, research by Eytan Bakshy from the University of Michigan published in 2011 showed that there is no good way to explain the spread of certain URLs.

Bakshy and colleagues studied this impact across 1.6 million Twitter followers and 74 million events over a two-month period in 2011. What they found is that tweeps with larger numbers of followers were more likely to create a greater spread of the message (measured by the number of retweets). On the other hand, they also found that the likelihood of a particular message being spread was quite low. More to the point, they found that predicted interest in the content had little bearing on the degree to which the message was spread. In other words, virality is much more likely to be observed in hindsight than predicted.[27]

In other words, the success of content is hard to predict. No one can accurately predict whether a message will spread, whether a song will be a hit, or whether a movie becomes a blockbuster. The spread of a message or the success of content is nondeterministic, or at least not sufficiently understood. Too many external factors take part in the question of whether a given message, song, movie, etc. resonates with society to make it simple or easy to find the answer.

Similar to how we are very cautious in talking about "influencers" being essential in creating sales intent (see "Purchase Intent" on page 18), we are cautious about concluding that you can orchestrate the spead of a message.

Despite the research findings, there are many companies offering to plan, deliver, and benchmark the spread of content, and they often imply the ability to create an "orchestrated virality." If those promises were true, then everyone could design his or her own campaign to go viral. But if everyone does it and every campaign is viral or contagious, then virality would be the norm, and again, we would find ourselves in the situation where no message is exceptional or outstanding.

A real-life check will support the scientific findings from Bakshy and our logical reasoning: nondemocratic, dictatorial regimes would have loved to create such an automatic process to spread deceptive information. They have tried but so often

27. E. Bakshy et al., "Everyone's an Influencer: Quantifying Influence on Twitter," ACM WSDM '11, Feb 2011.

have failed: the truth always comes out. Perhaps this is an indication that humans are not as easily fooled as marketeers would hope. However, many will still try, aided by the use of tools such as bots and social media platforms.

In sum, we do not believe that there is a secure, predictable method to generate virality or contagiousness. We think automated attempts to create contagiousness most likely are going to fail, as the human mind looks for the unexpected within the content, and *unexpected* also means *unexpected* for any algorithm. On one hand, the human mind is too multifaceted and too interested in the unexpected to predict its behavior; and on the other hand, any set system would ultimately lose the element of surprise and novelty and turn against its original objectives.

THE TRUTH ABOUT THE TRUTH

A message, contagious or not, can be true or false. False information in general has the issue that if people realize it is not trustworthy, then they are not going to believe it. In a way, it is similar to a newly created twitter bot without friends. No one wants to be friends with a stranger who has no friends. No one wants to spread a rumor that no one else believes in.

But once a messsage has traveled, it may gain some weight over time. This is true for false information as well. Once everyone has been touched by this false information, some may start to believe in it, at least to some extent. There is a belief that there is at least a grain of truth in every story, and this sense of truth is amplified as messages spread. Thus the ones planting false information will need to get the message viral, so that people start to believe the message before they can check the facts. As Ratkiewicz and colleagues pointed out in a study of political messages, once an idea or content starts to spread, it does so in the same manner as any viral phenomenon. This underscores the need for early intervention to prevent such a spread.[28]

Bots can not only spam people, smear opponents, and try to convince others, but they can also create "contagious messages" where it does not make a difference later whether they are true or not. To spot a deliberate attempt, you have to look at the *instigation* of a message and quickly react with counterarguments before the message starts to spread.

28. J Ratkiewicz et al "Detecting and Tracking Political Abuse in Social Media" Proceedings of the Fifth International AAAI Conference on Weblogs and Social Media, Association for the Advancement of Artificial Intelligence, 2011, *http://bit.ly/1gwfiXw*.

HOW TO SPOT ATTEMPTS TO CREATE CONTAGIOUSNESS

The more people have trusted a certain message, the more likely it will be passed on further. Thus, to identify a planted message, you can look over time at how a message evolves. If a message starts spreading very strongly in the beginning, supported by tightly connected accounts, it is likely that this is an attempted creation of virality or a false rumor in the making. If messages start spreading slowly supported by independently connected accounts, it is more likely that this is a true message.

Each message contains parts, each of which could start spreading. They are called memes and could be:

- Hashtags in Twitter
- Phrases forming all or a part of a message
- Links to websites
- Other users or accounts within the social network

You need to look at whether any of those parts show abnormal behavior at the beginning. As in the case of fake followers, astroturf needs to be detected in the beginning. Once a planted message has gained momentum, it is difficult to detect because the community starts to believe the message, and thus the propagation looks similar to a true message.

There are still relatively few tools available that look at the real truth of a message. One of the best available efforts to date comes from the School of Informatics and Computing at Indiana University. Professor Filippo Menczer has developed a service called "truthy," the function of which is to watch out for astroturf messages. If you wish to try this program yourself, you can start with his publicly available code or read his research.[29] Other ways of detecting astroturfing involve not looking out for the message or meme but trying to spot the robots.

In much the same way that there is no bulletproof system to create virality, there is no sure way to spot fakes. As soon you have found out what a fake message consists off, there will be methods to avoid being detected. The algorithm truthy, for example, would be looking for a given URL and whether there is unnatural spreading visible. Spammers started to disguise a link getting tweeted over and over

29. J Ratkiewicz, Filippo Menczer et al. "Truthy: Mapping the Spread of Astroturf in Microblog Streams" International World Wide Web Conference Committee (IW3C2), April 2011 *http://bit.ly/1bDwHc3.*

again by adding random queries on the end of the URL or using various short-link services.

The Opposite of Virality: Suppressing Messages

Robots can not only be used to carefully formulate opinions or to influence people; they can also work to overlay any kind of discussion with a high volume of other opinions.

This kind of spamming behavior is similar to the DoS (denial of service) attacks where someone tries to put a server out of order by swamping it with too many useless requests. This can be used for the sake of activism against a particular corporation or industry, such as the case of flooding a Facebook page with useless or critical posts that make it impossible for the page owner to communicate effectively.

It can also be used by totalitarian regimes to stifle dissent, either online or in the real world. For example, during the Arab Spring movement that started in 2010, rebel movements often used social media to coordinate protests and other activities. Governments or others have the potential to use similar hashtags in Twitter to overwhelm communications by sending hundreds of irrelevant tweets, and such tools have been used against protesters to disrupt their activities. In a sense, spamming reduces the *reach* of other messages. The spam message starts to appear on top of the other messages, pushing the *real* message further down, reducing its visibility. Jillian York reported a very good example during the Syrian conflict.[30]

In both the political and business arenas, such moves serve as examples of the cat-and-mouse game that continues to exist behind the disruptive use of social media.

Blurry Lines

Are we being too hard on people trying to market ideas by calling them "fake" or "false"? Wouldn't that be the dream of any marketeer, to get his brand message spread widely? Would this not be the typical call to action for a PR agency: "Please spread this information...make it go viral." Is there always an answer whether information is true or not?

30. Jillian York, "Twitter Trolling as Propaganda Tactic: Bahrain and Syria," Jillian York's Blog, Oct 2012, *http://bit.ly/1gwggmp*.

If one uses robots to spread a message, he most likely wants to do wrong. But there are also a lot of *gray* areas within PR that are neither easily detected nor easily judged as unethical.

Paid opinions, or opinions supported by lobby groups, can be another source of false wisdom. It is, unfortunately, often hard to distinguish between lobbying attempts and outright wrongdoing. The lines are blurred in many situations, and no good detection measurements exist. However, the few cases where someone clearly crossed into a gray area and got uncovered lead us to only guess the extent to which paid opinions are used in today's world.

THE CASE OF FACEBOOK

In 2011, Facebook came under considerable criticism after its PR firm Burson Marsteller tried to get a famous blogger, Christopher Soghoian, to smear Google on its behalf. Soghoian, who had publicly denounced Google for privacy and data-retention issues, was approached by the PR firm to write a bylined op-ed criticizing the new Google Circles social media capabilities, as *Wired Magazine* reported.[31] He was surprised by this request to denounce someone by proxy, and probed further. Asked for whom they were working, Burson Marsteller did not give any answer.

But Soghoian was cautious and went public. "I get pitches on a daily basis, but it's usually a company talking about how great their product is, so this one made me immediately suspicious, even more so when they wouldn't reveal who they were working for," he told BetaBeat.[32] "It seemed pretty clear what they wanted was my name," said Soghoian. What can we learn from this? Technology makes it easy to go beyond gray lines and the temptations are there for everyone.

Summary

There is clearly potential harm to be done via fraud within social media:

- Spamming people, like Diarny Smitrh did, to fraudulently sell products and services
- Smearing opponents by using robots

31. Sam Gustin, "BOOM! Goes the Dynamite Under Facebook's Google Smear Campaign," Dec 2011, *Wired.com, http://wrd.cm/1dbNdz6.*

32. Ben Popper, " Smear Story Source Speaks: Facebook Wanted to Stab Google in the Back," BetaBeat, Dec 2011, *http://bit.ly/Jo6nJQ.*

- Trying to influence a discussion like the bot Turing Test did
- Artificially creating contagiousness; in other words, artificially creating reach and ease of engagement for your content

Examples such as these only scratch the surface of what is possible. And beyond them, there is always the temptation to build a few bots to influence a metric. Any outcome that is desireable or measured is at risk of becoming a focus for behaviors that game the system. It could be as small as changing your Klout score or as large as impacting the financial insights of a hedge fund.

If there is good news in this situation, it is that we now have a broad range of technologies to protect people from fake social media, ranging from the automated fraud detection tools of firms such as Facebook and Twitter to procedures requiring human intervention, such as CAPTCHA type-ins and photo identification.

At a deeper level, the good thing is that as much as we overestimate influencers, we also overestimate the longterm perspective in trying to buy fake messages. The truth ultimately seems to prevail, and we prove to not to be as easily influenced as we thought. There is some research backing this view: Mendoza and colleagues found in 2010 that false information is more likely to be questioned by others.[33]

As with all forms of cyber fraud, such as viruses or identify theft, attempts to game the system using social media and online information continue to follow an iterative cycle. New ways of cheating are met with tools to counteract these moves, which in turn give way to even more sophisticated forms of fraud. This pattern will continue to evolve over time, in concert with the agendas of stakeholders on all sides.

In closing, there is an evolving social context behind both the use and misuse of social media channels. You could view it as an ecosystem that evolves from the motivations of everyone who uses the Internet. Some of the fraud being perpetrated online springs from criminal activity that seeks profit from false information, while some of it is thoughtfully chosen as a vehicle for social change: for example, many "hactivists" see themselves as modern-day freedom fighters using technology to achieve their goals. In either case, the benefits of misusing the human presence in cyberspace guarantee that it will remain an issue for the foreseeable future.

33. Carlos Castillo, et al. "Information Credibility on Twitter," ACM International World Wide Web Conference Committee (IW3C2), WWW 2011, April 1, 2011, *http://bit.ly/1clJyaK*.

WORKBOOK

Fraud is a danger for any business. You need to be prepared to spot fraudlent behavior. Spot how your metric could be attacked:

- What are most important metrics for your organizations? Write them down and list the variables used to calculate the metric.
- Are those metrics closed and secret? (If you want to learn more about how to set metrics, turn to Part II and Chapter 10.) How often do you change them?
- If you would like to attack or skew the metric, what would you need to do?
- Ask your peers and employees to "hack" you. Ask them to build a bot to deceive your metric. Only this way will you learn about the weaknesses of your measurement system.

Please report any unethical attempt of bot-like behavior to the public. We will spread the word if you tell us via Twitter, @askmeasurelearn, or simply by writing on our LinkedIn or Facebook page.

Predictions

Prediction is very difficult, especially if it's about the future.

—NILS BOHR

Predicting the Future

If there is one common denominator across the many applications of social media and data analytics we have explored in this book, it is gaining the ability to predict the future: who will buy, who will win, and perhaps even who will fall in love with us. Successful predictions, seen through the eyes of science, not hype, make the hard work of data analytics worthwhile. Therefore, it is fitting that we close this section of the book with a look at how data is used to make predictions in several key areas, ranging from elections to the stock market.

No matter which department you serve within your organization, whether it is marketing, public relations, sales, business intelligence, or any other function, data will play a big part in the future. Data will change the way you do business. Let's look at a few examples we have discussed so far:

- If you are in marketing, you may be predicting what people want. Or you may be predicting the likelihood of someone to react to your marketing, like the case of retailer Target knowing when someone is pregnant. Or like the case of semasio, predicting *when* someone will place an ad to increase targeting ("Behavioral Targeting" on page 20).
- If you work in public relations, you may hope to predict the next PR disaster, as discussed in Chapter 3. Or you may hope to predict how dangerous a certain situation is, such as when a racist hoax was posted online about McDonald's ("Case: McDonald's" on page 104). You may want to predict which journalist is best to talk to in order to create the most impact. Or you may want to predict when a situation has reached the tipping point, like the case of the Women2Drive campaign in Saudi Arabia ("Warning Signals" on page 105).

- If you are in sales, you are most certainly predicting what to offer customers or prospects so as to induce their next purchase, such as Netflix or Amazon's product recommendations. Or you may be predicting what would be the best price point to make people go out and buy your product.

What do these points all have in common? They are predictions. As we will see in Chapter 8, most questions can be classified in *benchmarks* as well as *predictions*. Asked what is the most important question to be asked for the business, 70% of C-level executives said that these should be prediction questions.[1] So prediction is a superpower everyone wants to have. And most of the time, those predictions will be powered by data—big or small, structured or unstructured. And once you have found an ability to predict certain things, you might want to discuss whether this ability can be productized, i.e., whether we can create a product out of it. Such information products can become important predictive tools for the future.

Data Products and the Confusion with Crowdsourcing

Big data is hype. One of the reasons for this hype is that today more than ever before, we have loads of publicly available data—social media data. Yes, social media data is big data, but not all of social media analytics will be big data analytics. You will often find references to data products, but what the author means is a product centered around the crowdsourced wisdom, such as crowdsourced ideation.

This kind of approach is not a data-centric product but rather a social media–enabled innovation. Innovation, by definition, is a chaotic process, at the beginning of which the collection of ideas is normally placed. Thus any innovation work starts with some form of "brainstorming." Social media works extremely well for including a large number of people in the gathering of ideas. But it is only a good channel for reaching a larger crowd to do crowdsourced ideation. Depending on the number of people participating, crowdsourced ideation can create data that is *big*. But once this data is gathered, it will not tell you anything about feasibility, cost, or other factors. It is just a tool to reach many people (broadcast) and to gather ideas. The real work only begins after the data is collected; tools will try to

1. "In search of insight and foresight: Getting more out of data," Economist Intelligence Unit, 2013, *http://bit.ly/1e5hFQA*.

automatically reduce this pile of ideas into a few buckets or core ideas, which are easier to analyze and to discuss—essentially, making small data out of big data. Small data can be as small as a short list of ideas. However, no computer will generate new creative ideas and execute against it. Thus, the final go/no-go decision about whether to use those crowdsourced ideas is still dependent on a human. Moreover, in most cases, the small data is smaller than what we started with, but still requires a lot of review by a person.

One of the best known examples of this is the Dell Idea Storm community, which allows everyone to participate and to submit ideas. Instead of using an open platform such as Twitter or Facebook, Dell built its own platform so as not to expose too many of its ideas to outside competitors who would want to scrape them.

Another example was recently published by McKinsey about General Electric, which used Twitter to solicit public ideas for a more "social" airplane via their Twitter account @ecomagination. Within a couple of hours, its base of over 90,000 followers contributed thousands of ideas, ranging from new manufacturing approaches to flight-specific hashtags, and many of these ideas found their way into GE's strategic-planning process.[2]

These approaches are highly effective for gathering ideas. However, there are a few risks:

PR risk
: People can use this platform to start complaining about you. To counter this, you need to make sure to have the right channels to out unhappy customers or trolls.

Marketing risk
: Social media is not a self-fulfilling marketing engine. This is also true for social media empowered ideation. To use social media will not be a guaranteed way to get great insights or even high participation. As with other marketing campaigns, an ideation campaign needs proper marketing and advertisement. This is especially the case if people are part of your Facebook or Twitter community for different reasons (for example, because they expect to get free stuff; see Figure 1-4).

2. Martin Harrysson et al. , "How 'social intelligence' can guide decisions," McKinsey Quarterly, Nov 2012, *http://bit.ly/1gBr6Yt*.

Being on the wrong side of the Venn diagram

As you'll see in Figure 9-11, not everyone who is talking in the social network is really your customer. It is easy to state an opinion on Twitter; however, it doesn't mean the person speaking up is actually willing to pay for anything. Let's not fall into the trap that one idea is worth more than another idea because many have voted for it or suggested it. Each idea will still need manual checking. Social media is just a good way to collect these ideas.

While crowdsourced ideation is a good tool (this book was named through it), we shouldn't confuse it with data products. Data products are self-sufficient and automated. They do not require lots of human interaction or judgment. They are mostly centered around predictions made out of data.

Predicting the future from data is the strongest form of the fourth "V" of data: value (as noted in the Introduction). In order to uncover this value, you have by now mastered the two main challenges:

- To have the right questions for your business aim (see Chapter 8)
- To have the data or metric that correlates with the question's outcome (Chapter 9)

Almost all other aspects of predictive analytics are based on technology, which is by no means trivial, but which often can be more easily solved than those two questions. It is in solving them correctly that we find the value we seek from the analysis of big data.

Predictive analytics is as fashionable a phrase as big data. As you can see in Figure 7-1, starting in mid 2011, people all over the world started to search for "predictions." This is a bubble in the making. An even better sign of an upcoming bubble is when Hollywood makes a movie about it. In the case of predictive analytics, *Moneyball* is a perfect example: this 2003 book by Michael Lewis showed how a small-market Major League Baseball team used sophisticated analytical models to predict baseball talent and field a competitive team, despite a small payroll, by predicting future talent accurately. Its analytical approach has since been used successfully by other teams that have won the World Series championship, permanently changing the competitive landscape in baseball.

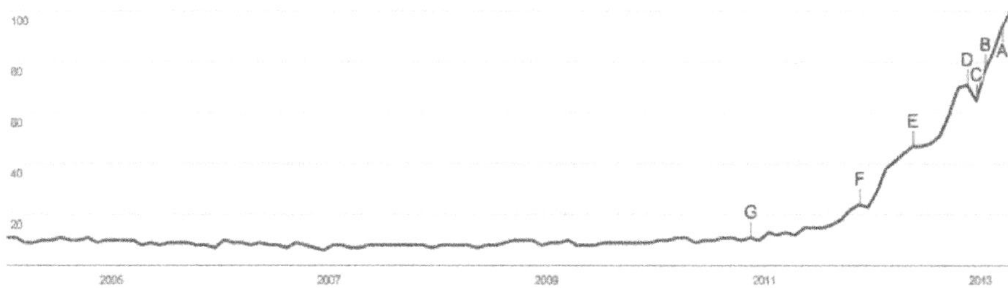

Figure 7-1. The hype curve of predictions, by Google Trends

Despite all of this hype, the goal of making predictions in business is nothing new: for decades, stock traders have tried to predict the market, insurance companies have tried to identify lower risk individuals, and many more have tried to come up with a system for predicting what will benefit their enterprise. The human race always wanted to have predictive superpowers, so everyone from soothsayers to statistical mathematicians has tried to satisfy this need.

In the coming sections, we will look at four areas to show how data products work (or do not work), all based on predictions. But while it is easy to understand that predicting the future can make great business sense, it is more difficult to get them up and running:

Predictions in the learning and education industry
: How algorithms change what we learn

Predictions of box office results in the movie industry
: How predictions fail to detect the unexpected

Predictions in politics
: Why social media is useful for steering campaign efforts, but doesn't help make predictions

Predictions of the stock market
: How it could work, but only when no one knows

Prediction of Learning

Data has started to have an impact, and the journey will go beyond what we imagine. The story of big data analytics started with simple web traffic. The data made our human online behavior more visible. We tracked every move and every click. Using machine learning (Figure 2-2), our next click became predictable. With Web 2.0 and social media, we suddenly had unstructured content data on top of this structured click data. This unstructured data was harder to interpret, but it offered an even more in-depth view of our human behavior. Now we saw that in not only our purchasing and reading behavior, but also how we interacted with others. Next was the tracking of our phones and our moving profile. Suddenly more and more parts of our personal lives were coming online or starting to be digitized. Whereas in the beginning we only predicted which ad banner to show, we started to predict which subject someone should study to be happy or successful.

Far-fetched? No, not really! Big data has started to have enormous effects on the educational process. Learning is turning out to lend itself surprisingly well to data analytics, and it is changing the face of post-secondary education. It all happened with the onset of massive open online courses, or MOOCs (see "MOOCs" on page 192). MOOCs are now taken by as many as 200,000 students. Hundreds of teaching assistants facilitate, creating a great database of possible questions and answers on the course topics. This crowdsourced wisdom helps to find mistakes or the most important questions by the number of people reading something or the number of exchanges on a given topic in the related discussion forum. The data is showing how we learn things and will help us to improve our learning style, and since it is all stored, it will be easily accessible for everyone. This is one of the many revolutions we will see happening through data. Today you can already predict whether a participant of a MOOC will be successfull or not after just the first few lectures. The algorithm uses metrics such as:

- How often did the participant watch a given video and when?
- Which questions did she answer right and which ones did she get wrong?
- Did she participate in discussion forums?

MOOCs

MOOCs stands for "massive open online courses." They are not a new idea: we have always sought to disseminate education to large numbers of people through media. Generations ago, we referred to them as correspondence courses. Two millennia ago, spiritual and social guidelines were captured and distributed among Christians through the Bible. And centuries before that, Aesop's Fables codified lessons for living in easy-to-remember stories.

The factors that make today's MOOCs radically different from any of these educational tools are size, scope, and interactivity. It is not unusual for a MOOC to attract hundreds of thousands of students through online lessons that may use rich multimedia, interactive testing, and online communities of learners. The term was first coined at the University of Manitoba in 2008, and by 2011, Stanford University had piloted three successful MOOC courses, one of which attracted over 100,000 attendees. This scale is changing the educational landscape. A professor we recently met who taught a course on cryptography to 180,000 students said, "The most scary thing is that my course probably took about 50 university professors out of business."

It is no surprise that many leading universities have jumped into MOOCs, and more consortiums and commercial firms are following suit. For example, EdX is a nonprofit consortium including MIT, Harvard, UC Berkeley, the University of Texas, and Cornell, designed to provide a noncommercial alternative to massive online learning. By contrast, firms such as Coursera and Udacity (whose founders include Stanford MOOC pioneer Sebastian Thrun and Stanford professor Andrew Ng) are seeking to commercialize tools and infrastructure for massive online learning.

MOOCs are here to stay and will evolve. Recently, for-credit MOOC programs have been offered through a number of schools as well, including the first-ever MOOC-based master's degree program in 2013 through the Georgia Institute of Technology, in collaboration with AT&T and Udacity.

The important part, however, is that all student interactions are digital. Each time a student learns, reads, or interacts with course material and others, he or she creates a trail of rich data. The data is used to study how students are interacting and learning. The data will be used to predict such things as learner success.

Big data has entered our classroom. At Arizona State University, automated tools tracking student performance go so far as to require advising or even a change in major if students go "off track" for too long, as the *New York Times* reported.[3] In order to improve the success rate of students, the university trends toward front-loading requirements that ultimately determine success: for example, requiring psychology majors to take the hated statistics course first, as this is often one of the

3. Marc Parry, " Big Data on Campus," *New York Times*, Jul 2012, *http://nyti.ms/IPqFv4*.

stepping stones to being able to succeed in the major. Engines start to help predict success and failure. When automated, they can change examination requirements to get the students on the right track. Is this education and career development in autopilot mode?

The system in place at Arizona State University is a good example of how to use data within a product. The college education is the product that can be dramatically improved by better prediction. Data thus enhances the potential of the very product. In this case, it is not the marketing department that needs this data, nor public relations, sales, or customer care. No, the product as such needs the data. Thus, data has become an essential part of the product: a data product.

Words of Caution

In certain cases, data can create predictions. And since the start of mankind, we have wanted exactly this: to predict the future. So it comes as no surprise that predictions based on data excite each and everyone of us. We are stunned by the way we can forecast the flu faster than doctors. We are excited by modeling our purchase behavior. We are amazed that we can predict, and hopefully prevent, crime.

However, data is not the savior of it all. You have seen throughout this book many warnings not to overestimate the power of a new tool, whether in social media, data analytics, or predictive analytics. We learned that Google sometimes thinks that a woman is a man ("Recommendation Systems Can Guess Inaccurately" on page 52) or that robots might be used to skew machine learning (Chapter 6).

Data and predictive analytics are just tools. And as with any tool, there are words of caution about using it wisely:

Avoid the wrong question.
: Often, causation and correlation are not easily determined, or some lurking confounding variable is hidden in the massive amounts of data. For example, if your television viewing habits overlap those of many gay people, this does not mean you are gay.

Avoid the wrong use.
: Tools can do harm as well as good, ranging from smear attacks by bots to facilitating crime.

Avoid the wrong technology.

An algorithm is not the truth, but just one potential tool for finding the truth. Check your answers against reality.

Like any tool, big data itself is neutral and can be used for good or evil. The devil is more often than not in the details, and you will need to work carefully on framing the question and developing the data.

Predicting Elections

People often ask for predictions during elections. On one side, this satisfies a human interest in who will win; on the other, this has a clear business relevancy. Any change in political power might have impacts on critical business decisions, and stock markets will often shift depending on political discussions. This leads to the first way of predicting election outcomes: using the crowdsourced opinions of the stock market.

The more traditional way surely would be polls, conducted by paper or telephone. As a modern supplement to those polls though, we often see more and more use of social media analytics. However, as we learned in the earlier chapters, social media is hard to interpret because the data is often unstructured, noisy, and very hard to read. If you check on social media-based predictions, you will easily find a few fulminant failures to predict reality.

Let's take as an example the United States Republican presidential primary race in Iowa between Mitt Romney, the eventual Republican nominee, versus upstart candidate Rick Santorum. The race was so close—29,839 votes for Santorum versus 29,805 for Romney, with results from eight precincts uncertified due to technical issues—that Iowa did not award delegates to any candidate. The real story, however, lies in the use of social media.

If you were basing your predictions on candidate mentions on Facebook, a third candidate, physician and Congressman Ron Paul, should have easily won this race. On the basis of search volume and relevant mentions, Paul's numbers were far ahead of his competitors. The same was true with measures of positive sentiment. Paul had a devoted legion of followers who knew how to "work" social media, but this did not translate into votes.

So why such a disconnect between social media and results? We will explore this issue in the following sections. Social media did not completely lack predictive value: Figure 7-2 shows that relative mentions on Facebook rose and fell with the fortunes of candidates. But even the newly formed alliance between Politico and

Facebook, which was supposed to give great new insights into predictive polling, ultimately failed.

Paul was very strong and visible on Facebook, as Rachel Van Dongen showed in her post. Yet he won neither the Iowa nor the New Hampshire primary elections. This is just another example showing that the pure count of social media mentions does not contain the needed information. While one person can create a strong social media impact, he or she still has only one vote to cast.[4]

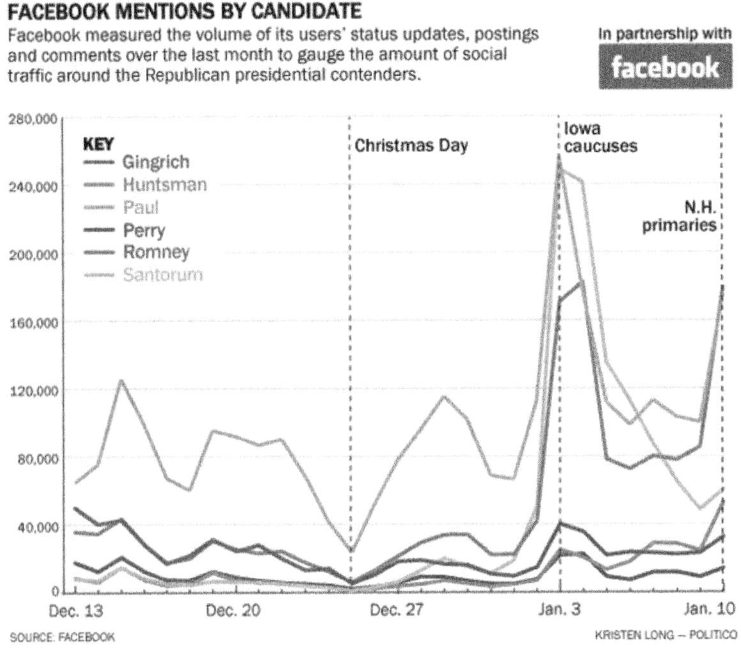

Figure 7-2. Candidate mentions on Facebook measured by Politico (Courtesy of Kristen Long from Politico.)

4. Rachel Van Dongen, "Facebook primary: Mitt Romney, Ron Paul in the lead," Politico, Dec 12 *http://politi.co/18Lxwft.*
Chris Good,"Final Iowa Results: Santorum Tops Romney, but We'll Never Know Who Won," ABC News, Jan 2012, *http://abcn.ws/1dhrl03.*
Tom Webster, "What Your Brand Needs to Know About the 'Social Media Caucus," *Brandsavant.com*, Jan 2012, *http://bit.ly/1fglo9j.*

To dig into the content, as well as into the *who posted* the messages, is more challenging as we deal with the complexity of unstructured data. Another crowdsourced method would be to predict the outcome using the Google API that offers data on the most important search terms and their quantity, like which candidates were searched for more often online. But that isn't the right metric. While it seems that there might be a correlation, we will have difficulty doing a statistical test on that. Predictions on social media alone are difficult. Why? Out of the many reasons, the two best explanations are probably that there is a selection bias and a bad PR bias.

SELECTION BIAS

One of the most difficult things about social media is that not every person who is talking is actually able to act. In the case of the Iowa election, it might be that not each of the Tweets or Facebook articles that were analyzed actually belonged to people who could have cast a vote.

This discrepancy between who you see and what the actual complete group is is a common issue. In discussions like usenet it is a common understanding that 90% of the online community members never contribute at all. Only 10% contribute, and actually most of the actions are done by a few, accounting for as little as 1%.

Those numbers might have changed since "sharing" became easier and can be done by a click on a like or retweet button. However, you still do not see the majority of users, which might easily lead to skewed results, like we saw in the Iowa primary forecasts.

Moreover, even if you could get data from the majority of users, there is often a large difference between what people announce publicly and do privately. This is frequently visible when elected state officials have low approval ratings—the actual number of people who announce that they have voted for them is quite low. This is the case of private polling results. You can only imagine that the skewing is even greater if you look at public announcements. What people publicly claim they want to do and what they actually do can differ quite dramatically.

BAD PR BIAS

In Chapter 3 we discussed why the number of news clips is often a useless measure. This insight is especially true before large elections. Each campaign tries to not only promote their ideas but also create bad PR for the other side. Bad PR would lead to more news clips and more mentions on Facebook, but it surely would not create higher turnout for the candidate in the election.

You might now argue that this is true, but you should look at sentiment ratings. As discussed in Chapter 4, sentiment algorithms are very difficult to program. To predict how a given news report would shift voters would be difficult, as those algorithms would need to be trained with data one does not have, such as what a voter would do after reading this news.

Thus, as it is in PR, many news clips does not mean more fame. It might just mean more problems.

PREDICTING VOTING BEHAVIOR

Because of difficulties such as these, social media is not widely used as a predictive data product in political campaigns. As Chief Scientist Rayid Ghani,[5] from the campaign team Obama For America, explained, it is actually used much less then most people think. This is also a clear sign of the overestimated capabilities of social media.

Political opinions are so multifaceted that there are many possible viewpoints. Similar to the discussion in Chapter 2, the long tail will make predictions of recommendation engines more complicated; predictions of political decisions are complicated because so many different factors might play a role. The situation gets more complex if there are factors such as weather conditions or a sudden change in the public perception that have a strong effect on the results. For example, the impact of Hurricane Sandy before the reelection of President Obama was nothing anyone could have predicted. No poll, no matter how well done, would have predicted this upfront.

But what can social media be used for, if not predicting the outcomes? Social media can be extremely helpful in focusing the efforts of campaign teams. Very often in political campaigns, the real bottleneck is the people on the ground: the teams of volunteers who go from door to door to discuss the election with voters and motivate them to support one camp or the other.

The winning question for any campaign is where to best deploy those volunteers. If you send them into a neighorhood where most people are already convinced that they will vote for your candidate, then they do not shift the proportion of voters intending to vote your way. If the volunteers are sent into the opposite neighborhood where no one will vote for the candidate of choice no matter what they say to

5. *http://bit.ly/1ize3Hv*

the voters, then this will not help either. On the contrary, it may even weaken the excitement of the volunteers and might create dropouts.

Volunteers need to be deployed to contact swing voters. But the question is how to find these swing voters. Similar to our discussion in Chapter 2, where we suggested that you use social media to find potential new sales opportunities, you can use social media to find *undecided voters.*

Is this the most effective way? Yes, since social media is unstructured, it probably will be best to start with census figures of traditional voting behavior. However, social media can give additional insight into which area or which person might be good to be addressed because she is still undecided. Engage, a digital agency in Washington, DC, did a nice study that showed how diverse the voting camps in the 2012 US election were in terms of social media: for example, Google users tended to trend toward President Obama, while users of the ecommerce site eBay were, as a group, more in favor of the Republican challenger[6] (see Figure 7-3). Equipped with that sort of information, you can start to address swing voters at least in those different channels. The general election in 2012 is only the second big election supported by new media; there is still much to be learned about this kind of analytics in politics.

6. Patrick Ruffini, "INFOGRAPHIC: Mapping the Politics of the Social Web," EngageDC, Jul 2012, *http://bit.ly/1k7Wv4G.*

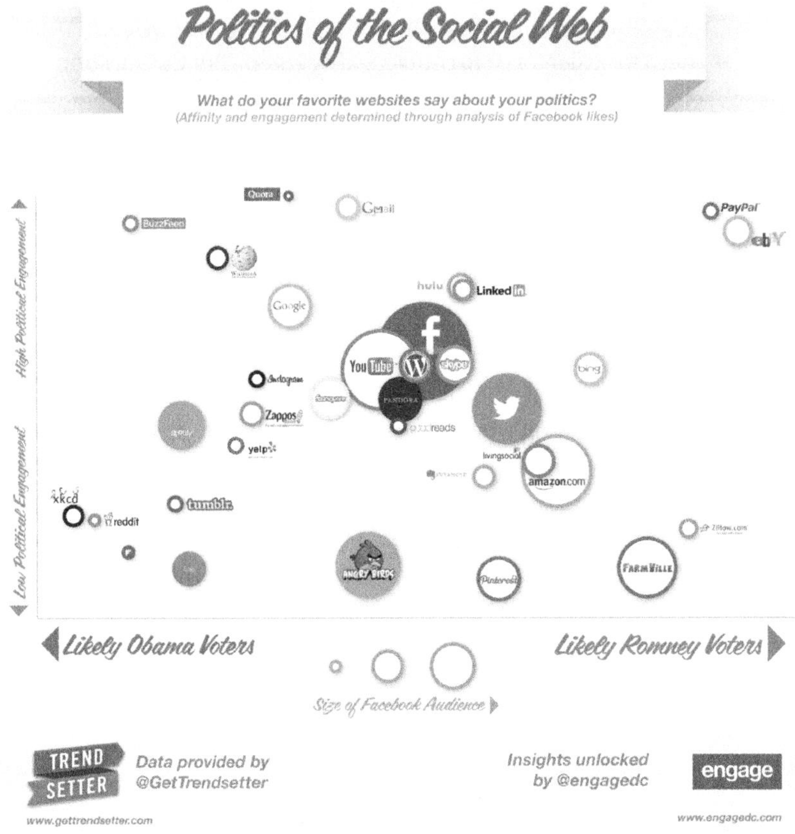

Figure 7-3. Mapping social behavior and politics (Courtesy of Engagedc.com.)

Predicting Box Offices

As noted previously, the hype of social media within predictive analytics comes as we suddenly have data about human thoughts, hopes, perceptions, and emotions. Up until now, predictive analytics had been used for much more tangible, quantitative things, like predicting the likelihood of a car accident based on data your insurance company has. What we might now predict those massive comments and discussions displaying human emotions has to be of value for the very industry that is known for emotions, the movie industry.

THE MOVIE INDUSTRY

The movie industry has a need to predict outcomes similar to the political campaign industry. Whereas in an election, the winner takes it all, the movie industry is built on a few blockbusters that create the main part of the profit. If one could predict movie success early on, before the film came to the theaters, one could:

- Channel marketing budgets toward the movies more likely to be successful
- Change parts of the movie's story line, depending on viewers' expectations
- Alter the rollout of a movie to different countries to maximize box-office revenues

Once the movie is released, there are enough prediction models to forecast the success based on a weekend of box-office sales. However, by that time, it is already too late, as the movie production and marketing investments are done.

Could you use the hype that is building up for a movie to effectively predict the box-office outcome? Do the number of discussions and the amount of communication in those discussions about the movie, its sentiment, or the spread of information about it contain information that could be used to predict the box-office results? Compared to the situation of political campaigns, the movie industry has the advantage that the demographics of those who are active in social media and moviegoers overlap more.

Moreover, the selection bias might not be as strong because a comment on a movie can be taken as a serious opinion. The risk that people do not say what they think, which is strongly there in terms of political discussion, should be less pronounced within movie discussions. So could we use social media to predict box office outcomes?

INSIGHTS WITH CAUTION

There has been ample research, and it seems to say social media can be used, but with the warning that the results are not always clear-cut or certain. In early 2010, Bernardo A. Huberman (@bhuberman) and Sitaram Asur (@sitaramasur) from HP published a paper predicting box-office outcomes.[7] Their hypothesis was that movies that are talked about will become box-office successes. They used close to

7. Sitaram Asur and Bernardo A. Huberman, "Predicting the Future With Social Media," Proceedings of the ACM Conference on Web Intelligence, 2010, *http://bit.ly/1hdSGse*.

three million Tweets to build a model predicting box-office revenues (see Figure 7-4). Their model had an adjusted R^2 value of 0.80 (further reading on the coefficient of determination value), indicating that a good part of box-office revenues was explained by the predicted revenue. This led them to conclude that social media can be an effective indicator of real-world performance. Moreover, using a sentiment algorithm, their predictions were better than those produced by the Hollywood Stock Exchange and other information markets.

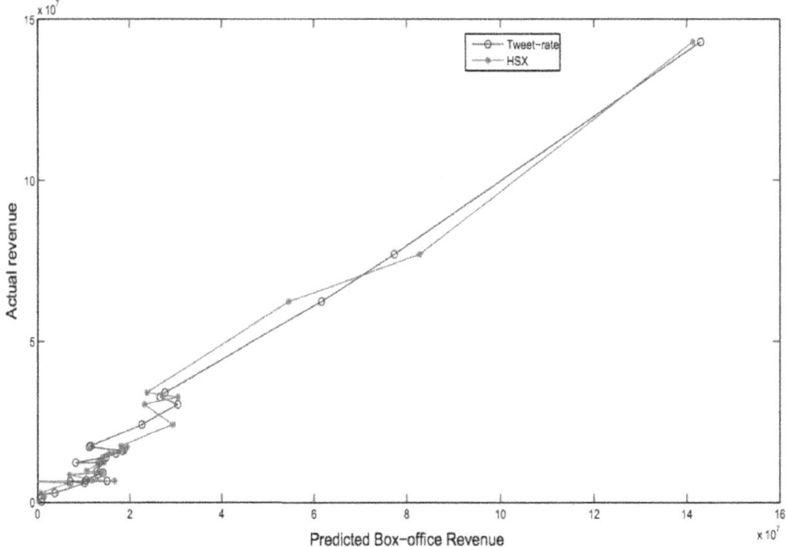

Figure 7-4. Twitter can predict box office results (Courtesy of HP.[8])

A similar movie study two years later by Felix Ming Fai Wong from Princeton University[9] found evidence that the number of tweets carried insights about the box-office results, but concluded that those results can only be indicative. This means that even if there are a lot of tweets, you cannot be sure of a box-office success. Ming Fai Wong detailed the actual metrics by looking at what he calls "hype approval." This looks at the number of tweets before and after launch to find out

8. *http://bit.ly/1hdSGse*

9. Felix Ming Fai Wong et al.," Why Watching Movie Tweets Won't Tell the Whole Story?" Mar 2012, *http://arxiv.org/pdf/1203.4642v1.pdf.*

whether hype within social media is sustained or not. While this metric seems to work for the sample of movies he investigated, it was not a bulletproof metric.

Overall this shows that social media can provide insight that is worthwhile to use. However, you have to be careful not to completely rely on the social media results, but combine them with other data. In the aforementioned study, Ming Fai Wong used structured data from IMDb. The combination of IMDb, together with his Twitter metrics, generated a sufficient predictor.

Facebook used a similar approach in September 2011.[10] It selected a "statistically relevant" sample of Facebook users and looked at how many of them stated that they wanted to go to the movie. This approach was similar to a classic polling mechanism where one would select a statistically representative user group. Such a selection process would not be possible based on the usage of Twitter users, as tweets do not contain as massive an amount of information as Facebook comments. Twitter data as a whole is often unstructured, while Facebook demands a certain degree of structure (where you live, what you study, etc.). In a way, this approach showed the power of Facebook to do polling without users even realizing that they were being polled.

The result of this sampling was yielding a similar high R^2, which the leader of this study Jacobson mentioned during the interview with Lucas Shaw. Facebook had only used 1,500 data points and was able to predict the opening box office performance a week before launch of the movie with an R^2value of 0.89.

CONCLUSION

The answer to the question of whether we can predict movie financial performance is so far an unsatisfactory "sometimes." Yes, the movie industry hinges on emotion, and yes, our social media discussions reveal those emotions to a certain extent. However, as we saw in Chapter 1, we love the surprise of the unexpected, and emotions are extremely hard to predict. Back then we quoted Arthur S. De Vany, and since his quote is so powerful, we want to repeat it here:

10. Lucas Shaw, "Facebook's Jacobson to Studios: Use Us to Track, Promote Movies," The Wrap, Sep 2011, *http://bit.ly/1k7Y8zd*.

> *There is no formula. Outcomes cannot be predicted. There is no reason for management to get in the way of the creative process. Character, creativity and good storytelling trump everything else.*
>
> **—ARTHUR S. DE VANY IN "EXTREME UNCERTAINTY SHAPES THE FILM INDUSTRY"**

Nevertheless, sometimes if the norm is the expectation, we will be able to make a prediction. Out of those situations we will be able to create products either as B2B applications that that show where and when to apply marketing spending on movies or as B2C products that suggest what kind of movie to recommend next, as Netflix did.

Privacy and Big Data

> *As the* Guardian's *Charles Arthur has argued, Google+ is not really a social network at all; it's more like The Matrix.* [11]

We are now 30 years past the year 1984, and George Orwell was not far off. Today we are living in a world where in many of the major cities we are starting to see a CCTV camera on each corner, our actions get monitored while we are online, and our private lives are more known to the public than ever.

In a very real sense, we live in a post-privacy society, and this has implications for big data as well. Orwell foresaw a world where a totalitarian government known as Big Brother knew and recorded everything about its citizens. We argued in Chapter 5 that we should save all data in legal boundaries, despite not yet knowing how we would use it. Edward Snowden revealed to us that secret services around the world are doing exactly this: they save billions of interceptions of messages from our private lives, and all they need now is the right question. Then the loop is closed and we can get to the work of analytics. WikiLeaks founder Julian Assange formulated

11. *Natasha Lomas*, "Facebook's Creepy Data-Grabbing Ways Make It The Borg Of The Digital World," *Tech Crunch*, June 2013, *http://tcrn.ch/Jyz7Q4*.

this slightly differently: all that we need to create totalitarianism nowadays is for someone to "turn the key."[12]

We as citizens are often all too willing to give up this privacy. Often when we click a link, our data is being sent to a number of companies, from large players like Google to smaller ad-serving networks. Many of us are even looking to get our hands on Google Glasses eyewear, which will literally put the world's biggest marketeer between you and reality.

Can you ever get your privacy back? The short answer is no. In essence, it is close to impossible to hide out there, unless you live like a hermit with no digital services, no credit or loyalty cards, and no mobile phone. Even former snowboarder Xavier Rosset, who emulated Robinson Crusoe by retreating to an island for 300 days, still maintained a voice blog to contact the outside world. And when 28-year-old Paul Miller returned from a year off from the Internet, he noted that it involved a severe loss of connectivity to others.[13]

If you do not want to go to these extremes, here are a few tips to preserve your online privacy, and become less a part of big data yourself:

- Change the security settings of your browser (check this guideline).
- Hide your name by using constantly changing pseudonyms online.
- If you use social media, use privacy settings carefully to control who you share information with.
- Avoid apps that transmit your personal data.
- Use a VPN, a private point-to-point network, to transmit data.

You think this is all too much hassle? You are not alone. Some 13 million users have so far not ever touched their privacy settings in Facebook, according to Mashable.

Privacy is an issue, and it is here to stay. In time, legislation may catch up with the growing relationship between data and our privacy. In the

12. DOT Media, "The Brian of Human Civilization: keynotes from Julian Assange interview," Dec 2012, *http://bit.ly/1fgKExt*.

13. Paul Miller, "I'm Still Here: Back Online After a Year Without the Internet," *http://bit.ly/1gBuYsk*.

meantime, this is a trend we will need to deal with it, and it will be hard to ever turn back the clock. [14]

Predicting the Stock Market

After looking into examples of predictive analytics in learning, politics, and movies, let's turn to financial markets. Unlike the movie industry, there are massive amounts of structured financial data available. And the financial industry is probably more advanced than any other industry in predictive analytics. For decades it has used historical behavior to predict future moves. This level of technical analytics is already a standard for many firms. Within the financial industry, we can best see that the data is not the main asset for predictions. Historical courses of data are available to everyone who is willing to pay. The main assets are the insights into how to create metrics and how fast you can put together a calculation to predict the next few seconds on the stock market.

The onset of social media promised to be another data pool for things like hedge funds that you could tap into to improve even today's accuracy. These hopes seemed to be promising. Google's search API, for example, was recently reported to help predict global stock trends.[15] A group of researchers using historical data from 2004 to 2010 found that changes in the search volume of specific terms such as debt, stocks, or portfolio correlated with up or down movements of the market, and a specific strategy of long or short selling in response netted hypothetical investment gains of over 300% versus the control strategy.[16]

But are those trends enough? Not really because most likely we have here an issue where we are mixing cause and relation. The more important question is can you actually decide on a buy or no-buy decision for each and every individual stock by itself upfront? Can social media be used to make this sort of decision accurately?

In Chapter 9, we discussed the BP case and showed that public opinion is not necessarily a driver for the stock market but most likely a lagging factor. Does this mean that we cannot use social media to predict how a stock will trade? You will find companies claiming that their algorithms can be used to predict stock price

14. Bob Al-Green, "13 Million Facebook Users Haven't Touched Their Privacy Settings," *Mashable.com*, April 2013. *http://on.mash.to/18uRm3P*.

15. Jason Palmer, "Google searches predict market moves," BBC, April 2013, *http://bbc.in/1cwvOzK*.

16. Tobias Preis et al., "Quantifying Trading Behavior in Financial Markets Using Google Trends," Scientific Reports 3, April 2013, *http://bit.ly/1dG8Bgt*.

movements. Companies in this space include StockTwits, Chart.ly, WallStreet Scanner, and Covestor.

But how good are they? In essence a company that would be able to predict the stockprice well would rather keep this knowledge to itself to start its own hedge fund just like Derwent Capital, a London-based hedge fund. Derwent Capital started with the promise of investing based on Twitter analysis, and it undoubtedly did not publish its formula widely. However, similar to the movie or election discussions, there is a good portion of skepticism to be applied in using social media data to predict stock curves:

- As in the other examples, you would need to create an algorithm to detect, from the unstructured data, whether a certain person is thinking of selling or buying a specific stock. Those algorithms would have a high error level. But Wall Street already has enormous amounts of structured data. Those data points are, by definition, better suited for computers to analyze and probably produce a more accurate signal. Or as Paul Rowady, senior analyst with consultancy Tabb Group, told Mashable, "The signal-to-noise ratio for that dataset is simply way too low."[17] It would be useful to look at unstructured data only if all other structured data had been effectively analyzed, so you hope to gain the competitive edge from the unstructured data.
- Secondly, time has always been a critical factor on Wall Street. Some funds, such as Renaissance Technologies, became renowned for moving offices to be closer to the stock exchange. Today the fight for speed is bigger then ever before. Social media, however, is slower than most other stock market trading indicators. You have to wait for information to be written, published, aggregated, and analyzed. Such a time delay might cause too much of a downside for this measurement to be useful.
- The last point that would make us worry about such a prediction algorithm is that it might be easily influenced by fake social media attempts, as shown in Chapter 6.

Maybe it is due to those shortcomings that Derwent Capital is no longer active as a self-standing fund, instead becoming a platform for offering insight to others.

17. Andrew Graham, "Why Wall Street Is Betting Big on Your Social Media Data," Mashable, April 2011, *http://on.mash.to/1bakjwK*.

All in all, these promises have not come true to the extent many had hoped. The best approach we have seen so far is probably focusing and reducing the scope (see Chapter 9). Instead of looking at all social media data, analyze only highly focused data. In respect to stock predictions, Michael Liebmann explained, "When drawing inferences from stock news, it is a question of cause and effect. Most tweeps simply reuse content and discuss older news. This creates another layer of complication, where the researcher needs to first identify which topic is entirely new and indeed introducing novel facts."

He and his team focused exactly on only such *novel facts*. They restricted their unstructured media data analytics to the use of company announcements. For them, company announcements could reveal an information asymmetry, meaning that the PR person in the company wrote an announcement knowing things that the market did not know.

This asymmetry can be revealed by the pure wording of press releases. This approach moves away from social media. However, it is close to social media analytics in that it relies on unstructured content. Michael's approach has two main advantages:

- It reduces the amount of data to be analyzed. Looking at all the tweets and blogs of the world might be too distracting. As often discussed in this book, more data only means more pain but not necessarily more insights.
- Language is relatively uniform, since press releases are written in a certain style. You will not find slang or smear words here, and emotions are kept out. There will be no cynicism, there will be no irony, and even the words used are from a restricted vocabulary. As we learned in Chapter 4, the more focused the vocabulary is, the easier analytics will be.

Using machine learning, Michael and his team have created an algorithm suggesting whether a share price will rise or not. The curve in Figure 7-5 is based on testing using past data, and it suggests that stocks selected based on their formula have a potential 2% higher return.[18]

18. Michael Hagenau, Michael Liebmann, Dirk Neumann, "Automated news reading: Stock price prediction based on financial news using context-capturing features," Decision Support Systems 55, 2013, *http://bit.ly/1k80VZg*.

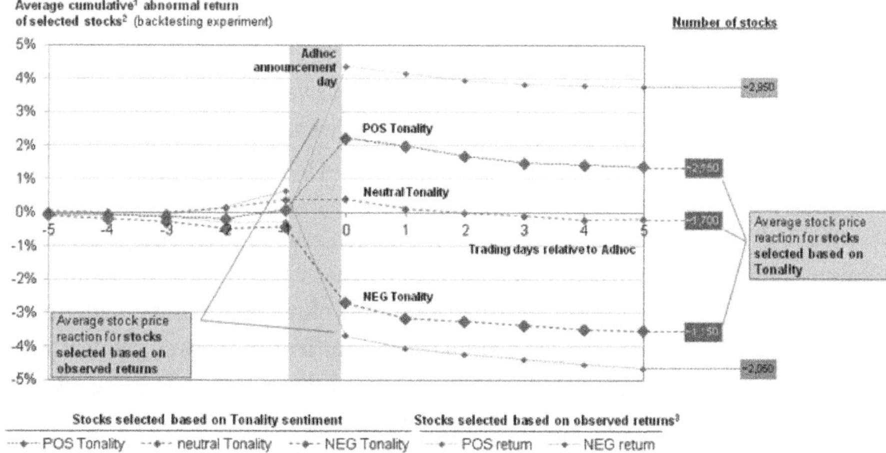

Figure 7-5. Stock correlation with unstructured data from press releases (Courtesy of Michael Hagenau, Michael Liebmann, and Dirk Neumann.)[19]

Closing Predictions

Let's finish this chapter with some closing predictions about big data. We have the technology fundamentals, and we have started to save everything about our human behavior: the way we move (mobile phones), the way we discuss (social networks), the way we learn (MOOCs), the way we shop (online shopping), the way we talk (Apple's Siri and others), and even the way we breathe (new ways of measuring ourselves).

Not all data is easy to mine, and often our hopes are much higher then the yield from the actual results. The three main issues here are the following:

- Lack of the actual business-relevant question
- The difficulty (because of noise) of working with unstructured data
- Our own sensitivity about personal data

19. 1) Base: 20 trading days prior to announcement. 2) Experiment based on 12,200 ad hoc announcements, ~5,000 validation events (back testing) in graph. 3) Observed returns on event day, based on close-to-close adjusted prices. Note that stock price effect is measured by abnormal returns very similar to day-to-day observed returns. Events between 1996-2010.

Because of this gap between hope and reality, we will see this industry follow the typical hype curves (see Figure 7-6) as many other industries before. We will start high and expect that data will give us all the answers. We then will realize in disappointment that many of those answers are answers to questions we never had and that do not even interest us. But despite this upcoming disappointment, essentially we will get to the plateau of productivity.

It is only a question of when this will happen. Do you remember the hype around online translations? It took longer then expected, and for years we needed to cope with terrible translations. Brute force and many data points made those translations more useful. We see a similar development in the way we deal with unstructured data. Just recently Google announced the bundling of voice and semantic search. As we have seen, it is hard to measure semantic context. At the moment Google is far from perfect, but over time, with more and more training samples, this approach should also start to work.

The same development will be seen in measuring and interpreting unstructured data. Moreover, as with the second issue of missing correlation, we will see more and more data points popping up as we start to measure more and more. Even when things such as creativity or fashion are still impossible to predict in the long run, we will become better and better at predicting those emotional and creative-based products successfully in the short run.

But whenever this happens, whenever a product or a service will prove useful, questions about security will come up. The data companies use are generated by their customers; therefore, there will be an upcoming discussion about who owns this data and who is allowed to use it. The public outrage and discussions that we saw around the data saved for access by the National Security Agency will only be the beginning.

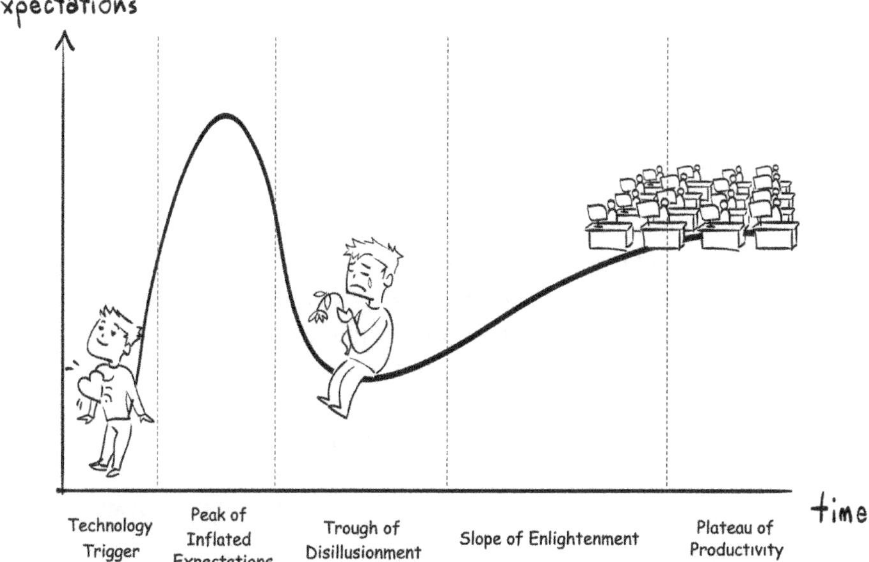

Figure 7-6. Stock correlation

Big data, social media, and data analytics are part of your life now and will become an even bigger part in the future. So what will this look like for you—more hype than reality, or an important strategic part of your business? The race is on, and the winners and losers of this next epoch of data analytics will be determined by how well and how fast each company can cross the gap from hype to strategy.

This first part of the book has given you important guidelines for being successful in the brave new era of data:

Find the right question.
: A question that is SMART: specific, measurable, actionable, realistic, and timebound.

Find the right data.
: Not all data is equally suited for your question.

Be predictive.
: The way of kinds is to predict and to create a product out of data.

Avoid the traps.
: Be mindful of attempts to skew your system by bots or other tricks.

Start small.

Start feature by feature to build your model.

Mind the sensitivities such as privacy.

Even if we can measure today almost everything, we should be mindful of the needs for privacy.

Whether you're a winner or a loser will depend on how much your organization will start to live and breathe data. How effectively can it use data? And above all, how much is it able to unearth the fourth "V" of data, value? We close this chapter by bringing up the quote from the beginning of the book, from the great W. Edwards Deming:

> *In God we trust. All others must bring data.*
>
> **—W. EDWARDS DEMING**

Workbook Questions

Think about the following with your colleagues:

- Where could your organization improve most? In framing the question (*ask*)? In measuring the data (*measure*)? In putting all the insights to work (*learn*)? What should you do to drive this change?
- For many people, the biggest *value* from data analytics lies in predicting the future. What kinds of predictions would most improve the future of your company? Does social media and/or other sources of big data hold the potential to make these predictions?
- What kinds of *data* would have the most impact on your business? And are you currently making the best use of the data you have? Do you leverage this data to improve your products and services?
- What would your clients and consumers think if you start using *their* behavior or *their* data to predict the future of your business? How should you deal with this? Is openness the best way?
- Are there improvements you could make to your services or products using crowdsourcing? What would those look like?

Up until now, we have always asked you to share your thoughts with us publicly. While respecting confidential areas such as product strategy, you might have many ideas on what could be good data products, and how data can help to make this world a better place. Please share with us—and the world—your ideas on future products for data and/or predictions. Reach out to us in Twitter, @askmeasurelearn, or write on our LinkedIn or Facebook page.

From here, for those of you who want to drink a little deeper from the methodology of working with social media and big data analytics, the next and closing section of this book will take you on a tour of how to construct your own "ask, measure, and learn" system. We will explore in detail how to construct the right questions, use the right data, and create the right metrics to gain insights from data, particularly when this data is populated by the digital footprints of people. These sections will help you learn to think like a professional data analyst, and ultimately learn to frame this process as a teachable set of skills and expectations. From there, it will become much easier to crack open the secrets of social data, and use it to learn the things that will make us successful.

PART II

Build Your Own Ask-Measure-Learn System

Ask the Right Question

Once, a leader was the person who could convince others to act in the absence of data. Today, the leader is the person who can ask the right questions.

—ALISTAIR CROLL (@ACROLL)

You have data and you have metrics based on this data. But neither will help you to get the value of data if you do not have the right question. Let's look at a typical example of a metric: "views on YouTube." What do millions of views on one YouTube video mean?

- It could mean a hit music song at the top of the charts. For example, Justin Bieber's "Baby" was the most-watched video on YouTube as of late 2012, with over 800 million views, and was a triple-platinum hit, selling over 3 million digital downloads.
- It could mean a successful product. After Utah dentist Dr. Bob Wagstaff tried and failed to market his Orabrush tongue brush through traditional advertising, a series of quirky YouTube videos about how it cured bad breath helped it launch as a successful online product and later gain national distribution in chain stores. Today Orabrush has sold over two and a half million units, and its videos have been watched more than 50 million times.[1]
- But it could also mean very little. The music video "United Breaks Guitars," a song detailing Canadian musician Dave Carroll's failed attempts to get compensation from United Airlines when baggage handlers damaged his expensive

1. Lane Shackleton, "The Orabrush story: How a Utah man used YouTube to build a multimillion dollar business," Google Official Blog, Nov. 2011, *http://bit.ly/1gBx6R1*.

guitar, was a runaway viral hit with over 10 million views and a major public relations disaster for United, which we discussed in more detail in Chapter 4. However, neither the song itself nor a subsequent book by the same name reached bestseller status.

In each of these cases, the question, "How many views did we get on YouTube?" would not necessarily have been the *right* question to ask. Views on YouTube is a metric that might lead to invalid conclusions if you are trying to understand the underlying business question. What do you want to achieve? Justin Bieber wanted to create awareness during the launch of his new album. Thus the viewership data reflected a broader launch strategy to promote his music. The created awareness could be harvested by the channel strategy of his music label. OraBrush, on the other hand, needed more than just awareness. Dr. Bob Wagstaff needed to first educate his potential customers about the reasons bad breath exists. Thus the purpose of the video was educational and not just for it to go viral.[2] He kept the same approach through all different media channels.[3] And Carroll's video, while it certainly boosted both his music and speaking career, serves as evidence that social media popularity does not automatically equate to commercial success.

This underscores the most important task in any analysis: you need to be clear about the question to ask. Often a measurement such as the number of views on YouTube is a number that will not mean anything if there is not a relevant underlying business need or business question associated with it.

During the 2010 World Economic Forum in Davos, Switzerland, the director Adrian Monck (@AMonck) looked over some daily reporting and said, "1,300 tweets in one day? So what? What does this mean for me?" A single number did not make any sense to Monck and it surely failed the "so-what" test; social media exposure or being talked about is not an end in itself. Too often we have seen that technology is leading a data investigation. New technology seems to generate new insights, with people analyzing something just because it's possible. However, it should be the way around, that the *question* determines the *measurement*.

2. The word "viral" is actually misleading. We rather like to use the term "contagious," as we explained in "Virality versus Contagiousness" on page 98.

3. Grant Crowell, "Screw Viral Videos! The Orabrush YouTube Marketing Strategy," ReelSEO blog, 2012, *http://bit.ly/1k84Q8g*.

In "The Right Question" on page 227, we will discuss what makes a question the *right* question. In short, there are two types of questions: benchmarks (how did we do compared to...) or predictions (what will happen...).

Thus for Adrian Monck from the World Economic Forum, it would be more useful to put this number of 1,300 tweets in the context of benchmark. Has a given idea, topic, or argument discussed during a World Economic Forum been placed sufficiently within the media? And if not, why not? To begin to answer this benchmark question, you would need to compare those 1,300 tweets with the number of tweets on another subject or with the number the same subject received last year and so on. Only then would you get an insightful answer.

To formulate the *objective, aim*, or *question*, as we will call it from now on, is the most fundamental challenge for any data-mining project. That also makes it the subject of the first chapter in this book. We will begin to explore that challenge by examining a case study.

Case Study: Major Telecom Company

In May 2010, the CEO's office of a major company in Europe approached us. They wanted to measure social media. Short of a real question of what they wanted to measure, we gave them just numbers like how the CEO got 450 mentions within the last two weeks. But that was surely not helpful. The fact that he got 450 mentions would have failed any "so-what" test. Potential questions could be:

Benchmark

Is the CEO a laggard in social media compared to other CEOs? The answer to this question would have been "no." You can see in Figure 8-1 the comparison of the top 50 CEOs as defined by *Harvard Business Review*[4] and their presence in news and social media.[5] The more the CEOs are publicly discussed overall, the higher their social media split is. Steve Jobs, for example, was at that time the most discussed person, with about 90,000 articles during the two weeks surrounding HBR's 2010 study. The majority of those articles were within social media. The average split between user-generated content and news was about 51% for all top CEOs. The CEO in question had a social media profile that fit right in with 50%, so he was likely not lagging.

4. Morten T. Hansen et al., *Harvard Business Review*, Jan 2010, *http://bit.ly/19NhKkv*.

5. Two weeks in May 2010.

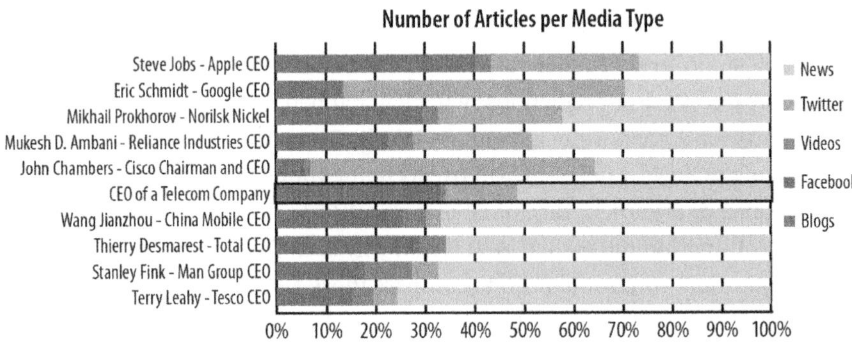

Figure 8-1. Is our CEO lagging in social media (courtesy of Fisheye Analytics)?

Predictive

Is there a PR issue in the making? This is a question about the future and, as we saw in Chapter 7, those predictions are very hard to make. We can, however, try to analyze the amount of negative sentiment. Most of the sentiment algorithms in the market are not worth their money and are often misleading, as we observed in Chapter 4. For our CEO, we used a standard algorithm to get a first indication whether there was enough negative sentiment in the discussion that we could conclude that there was an issue. The answer to this question seemed to be "no," as one can see in Figure 8-2.[6]

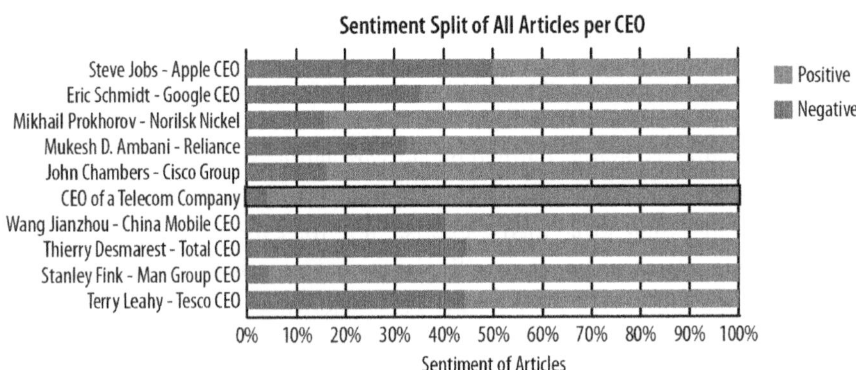

Figure 8-2. Is there a PR issue (courtesy of Fisheye Analytics)?

6. Same two week time-window applied.

Without any substantial analytical findings, the data analysts started to read social media content. Reading and judging human-created content does not seem scalable, nor does it seem objective and so it would be surely a bad measurement, but it supplies ideas about some things that might be interesting to look at.

There were a few nasty social media actions taken against this CEO. There were very negative fake Facebook identities and Twitter parodies. The number of messages, as well as the reach of those messages, was small in the overall reach of the CEO's brand, but the messages themselves were highly aggressive.

BACKGROUND KNOWLEDGE

What had happened? All the negative commentary had started to gain traction in February. The CEO had just given a talk at a business school, where he had supported the idea to charge more for some kind of traffic:

> *Internet search engines use our networks without paying us anything (...) This can not continue (...) This will change (...).*
>
> **—CEO**

Over the subsequent quarters, the CEO had seen that the stock price of his telecom company was outperformed by Google and other Internet giants, using the capabilities of the infrastructure they and other network operator had built. There was an imminent risk for any network operators to just become the commodity bit pipe. The aim of the CEO was therefore to change the tariff system to participate in the value of the data channeled through networks. This approach is not without controversy. It has become known as the discussion about net neutrality.

A change in price structure can't be done without support in the market from other competitors. Thus he tried to reach out to potential allies in his quest to regain a better position in the value chain. During his university speech, he started to call out for change. Similar statements on other occasions such as the Mobile World Congress followed.

The opponents of his idea saw freedom of speech as being in danger. Many started to rally against his idea, prompted either by professional opinion or personal conviction. The fake Facebook identities and Twitter parodies were a consequence of his initial talk and the rally against his ideas.

Only now and with this background knowledge in mind could we start to ask useful questions such as the following:

- Was his message to change the tariff structure heard and supported? Who picked it up? Who supported it? Who opposed it?
- Are the negative comments he is getting from his opponents a threat to his quest?

WAS HE HEARD?

Let's focus on the first question. To analyze this situation further, you need to make it measurable beyond anecdotal evidence. You either have to redefine the data (as we discuss in Chapter 9) or redefine the sentiment measure (as we discuss in Chapter 10). Looking at the origin of the negative comments and the satirical parodies, we decided to change our data set to only look at discussions evolving around net neutrality.

We created a subsection within the data on our CEO and reduced it to only those discussions. By doing so, it became quite clear that there was a highly negative debate going on. Did this mean that his attempt to end net neutrality failed? Not necessarily. Let's introduce a metric classifying the source. We will talk more about the role of measurement in Chapter 10. The classification analyzes what the sources say, tweet, or write when they do not talk about the CEO. The source comments clearly revealed two types of sources: one group was financially focused, and the other group was tech-focused.

You can probably already guess without looking at Figure 8-3 that the financial sources were mostly positively disposed toward his idea because a change in tariff structure would mean an improved share price and share outlook for the telecom company. We can thus conclude that the CEO had made a good impression with the business media. If we reduced the sources even further and only looked at top news sources that would most likely get read by other CEOs, we would see an overwhelming number of positive to neutral reactions. Also, many in the business news media had recognized his approach, and thus we can assume as well that the people he wanted to reach heard his call to challenge the status quo of net neutrality.

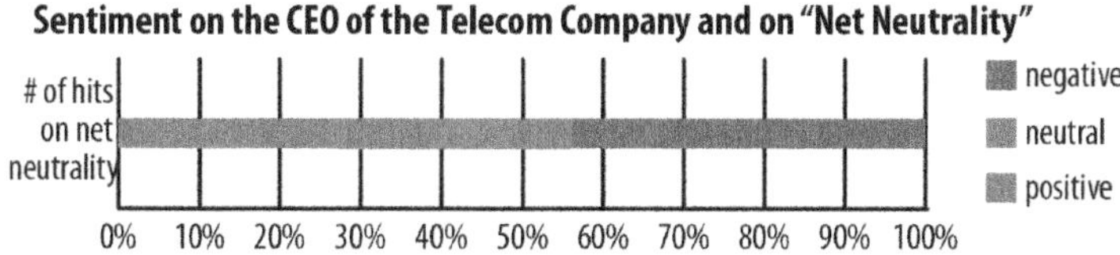

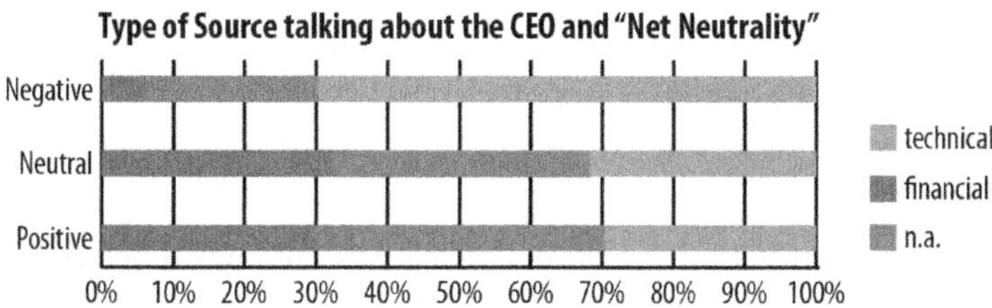

Figure 8-3. Comparing negative versus positive comments (courtesy of Fisheye Analytics)

And indeed, many other CEOs from telecom companies followed his example and took a position against net neutrality. For example, Vittorio Colao, at that time the president of Vodafone, called publicly for all "to revise the value chain" of the Internet. Politicians also got involved. Spain's minister of industry, Miguel Sebastian, prepared a statement for the European Commission. He explained that content providers such as Google's YouTube should contribute some of the investment in network infrastructure. Those statements got support not only from Jacques Toubon, former French culture minister, but also from French president Nicolas Sarkozy, who called for a "Google rate."

In sum, we could say that the CEO's outreach on net neutrality had reached its target. The negative reaction had been a kind of "collateral" to this discussion. A second *benchmarking question* could be how bad this collateral was. We discussed how to measure this in Chapter 3. In this case, however, volume and intensity were within expected norms.

Formulate the Question

As could be seen in the case of this telecom company, it is not always easy to formulate a question, but without a question, an answer will almost never be useful. Even worse, we can be lulled into thinking that social media metrics themselves form the answer, in much the same way that in Douglas Adams' bestselling book, *The Hitchhiker's Guide to the Galaxy*, the computer *Deep Thought* calculated the answer to the ultimate question to "life, the universe and everything" as being 42.

> *That is not a question. Only when you know the question will you know what the answer means.*
>
> **—DEEP THOUGHT**

So how to formulate the question? There are two major approaches to finding the question. Either you look at the data and try to find something interesting, using a process known as creative discovery, or you formulate the question using your business sense, also often called domain expertise.

CREATIVE DISCOVERY

Creative discovery is an effort to find something which was not known before. In a simple way, reading through selected tweets and Facebook posts to find something interesting, as we did in the preceding example, counts as creative discovery.

This process, however, is often done in a more structured way, as described by statistics. The aim of statistics is to describe data with a few numbers such as the mean or median. As we saw in the example with our telecom company, the simple metrics such as average number of articles per period or number of negative articles per period did not tell us much. One of the more complex ways to describe data is to describe the different features, or variables, of a given data set.[7] These variables are then examined in relationship to one another to see whether there is a dependency. However, these metrics do not necessarily reveal any insights, as shown by the statistician F.J. Anscombe. He demonstrated that data as diverse as that in Figure 8-4 can still share the same statistical properties; therefore, it can have the same mean, variance, correlation, and regression line.

7. Statisticians and physicists will call them variables. In machine learning and within the new discipline of data science, they are called features. However, both mean the same: if we measure something, features or variables are the columns in our table with data.

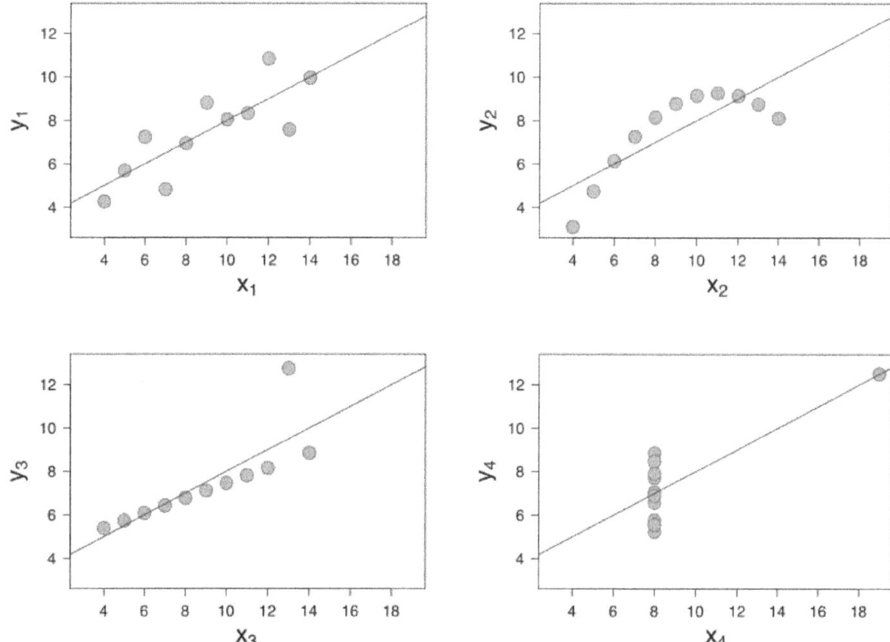

Figure 8-4. Data with the same usual statistical properties—mean, variance, correlation, and regression line (Courtesy of Wikipedia.)

If statistical measures and metrics do not reveal anything of interest, the process of *creative discovery* can turn to charting data. The human eye is often more helpful in discovering dependencies than elaborate data-modeling techniques. Thus data scientists use visualization tools to display the data in two- or three-dimensional spaces. By now there are many ways of doing such a visualization: you can use simple tools like the data-mining user interface for Rattle from R or good full-blown visualization tools like Tableau Software.

Creative discovery seems to carry a very strong and powerful promise: that by working with data, you will find something new and interesting. The way you will approach it is by taking your data and cutting and slicing it into different segments. Within each segment, you will compare and group different data points.

One of our clients actually planned to give the data team a target of three interesting findings every month. This is wishful thinking and probably as useless as to expect Christopher Columbus to find one America every decade. As the word "discovery" implies, not every search will result in something interesting. Very often the outcome is just a lot of hairballs, which is the term you use for a totally uninspiring image of dots and lines.

Our client thought that three findings a month might be feasible due to the widely publicized *success stories* on creative discovery. One of these newer stories was the newly created model from a leading camera manufacturer. The company introduced a waterproof pocket video camera. The idea for this product came as the company's marketing teams studied the social media conversations around their brand. They found that people were often not daring to take the expensive models on sports trips. Thus the idea to create a waterproof pocket camera was born.

Please do not become lulled into thinking that you simply click a button on a black box and a new product idea emerges. From this story alone, you can tell that there were no metrics or statistical formulas involved. The process required reading all of those tweets, and it was a very manual process. This camera brand most likely was discussed hundreds if not thousands of times. You can use technology to group and sort those discussions, but to find the few discussions of people stating publicly that they would love to take the more expensive camera on a sports trip but did not dare to do so is like finding a needle in a haystack. It takes luck and many hours.

Especially in the area of social media content, new services and startups have surfaced that have promised to automate this, so far, manual process of creative discovery. The promise of their software is to automate the finding of *unknown* areas of customer needs or concerns and thus to spot new ideas easily.

We believe that those promises will fall short because the complexity of human language renders this approach very difficult, if not impossible, most of the time. It might work if the area of discussion is highly predictable and specialized and there are not too many different ways to talk about it. In the case of the usage of a camera, creative discovery, as we discussed earlier, cannot be automated, at least not with today's technology and resources.

A good metaphor for creative discovery, particularly with online social media, is the analysis of computer network behavior. Creative discovery would be to spot network communication that can't be considered normal or standard. And research agrees that the best way to spot an intruder into a computer system would be to look for the *not normal* behavior. However, as Robin Sommer from the Berkeley Lab described, this approach has remained theoretical and is seldom used in real-life applications. Unfortunately, network transactions are so complex and individual that it is very difficult to differentiate between legitimate or criminal use. In much the same way, the dream of automated creative discovery from social media data often faces a difficult reality in the real world.

DOMAIN KNOWLEDGE

Domain knowledge is a second means of formulating the right question. Overall, it helps to have the right background knowledge. The CEO's office from our telecom company could have formulated the question at stake more easily than Fisheye Analytics could due to specific domain knowledge about the industry, the company's goals, and the CEO's history of intentions and actions.

The value of domain knowledge might best be described by the following example of email marketing. Within email marketing, the marketeer's aim is to reach as many people as possible and create the highest buying conversion. A simple question to ask would be "What kind of content and what kind of mail addresses will create the highest opening rates?" While the question in this case is valid, the actual way of measuring the question might prove way more complex, as one might think. A domain expert will know that the measurement of *opening* is skewed by the actual email client. Different email clients will open an email at different points in time. Outlook™ will call an email open if it was loaded into a small preview window for a certain time, while for Gmail™ the user needs to actively click the email to open it.

Setting *opening* as an outcome metric and optimizing the system for the greatest number of *openings* would clearly create an incorrect result because it would most likely optimize the email to appeal to Outlook™ users.

While such an example clearly shows the advantage of domain knowledge, use of that knowledge is as difficult as it is with creative discovery. The massive data of unstructured social media content has created new opportunities for businesses. It has changed the way we do marketing (Chapter 1), the way we find new sales prospects (Chapter 2), and the way we communicate with our customers (Chapter 3). In such a new environment, past experience might not always be as helpful. It might even be distracting. You might overlook what has become possible, and you might not be ready to challenge the status quo.

There has been quite a lot of discussion about which is more helpful, creative discovery or domain knowledge. Those discussions often center around, "Who should I hire for my analytics?" There is no right or wrong answer; we believe the right mix will always contain both elements.

THE RIGHT QUESTION

No matter whether you use creative discovery or your own domain knowledge, at the end, there should be a question which satisfies the following requirements:

- A good question needs to be *measurable.*
- A good question yields answers or outcomes that are *actionable.*

Thus the questions (or aims or objectives) formulated for data sets should be in no way different to goals and objectives formulated for humans or projects. For such situations, George T. Doran coined the mnemonic device S.M.A.R.T when setting objectives.[8] Thus the *right* question asked about data is a question that is *specific, measurable, actionable, relevant,* and *time bound.*

As discussed in the beginning of this chapter, those S.M.A.R.T. questions typically fall into two categories: benchmarking questions, "how did we do compared to..." and predictive questions, "what will happen..." And prediction questions are the ones more important for business success. A recent study by the Economist Intelligence Unit asked which types of data insights were considered *critical* by C-level executives. A total of 70% of the respondents indicated that the predictive insights were *critical,* while only 43% thought that *trends* (or benchmarks) were *critical* for them.[9]

But we all know from our daily work at companies that benchmarking questions are the main ones we use. We often look at historical trends or compare ourselves to the competitor. Those metrics are not *ambiguous* or *soft,* but *specific.* That essentially means you can describe the answer to the question through a set of numbers. Transported into the world of social media data, benchmarking questions could mean, for example:

Reach versus reach
: Which of two tweeps (people tweeting) has more reach?

Reach over time
: How far-reaching was a given event versus the last one?

Reach absolute
: Will the reach of this campaign be over two million eyeballs as per our internal reach metric?

8. G.T. Doran, "There's a S.M.A.R.T. way to write management's goals and objectives," *Management Review,* 1981.
9. "In search of insight and foresight: Getting more out of data," Economist Intelligence Unit, 2013, *http://bit.ly/1e5hFQA.*

Predictive questions are used way less in our day-to-day work, even when C-level executives see them as more important. We discussed prediction algorithms more in Chapters 2 and 7. After formulating the right question, the next biggest difficulty is often having the *appropriate* data to make a prediction. To create a prediction, the question should not only contain a "hard measurement," but also define what a positive *answer* or *outcome* would look like. Let's look at a few more examples, and as you read each one, decide whether those questions contain a clearly defined successful outcome:

1. A positive outcome is when the user clicks the product displayed.
2. A positive outcome is if we distribute our message to 10,000 people or more using our internal reach metric.
3. A positive outcome is when there is no negative public relations issue happening.
4. A positive outcome is when our product is well received by the general public.
5. A positive outcome is when we get more fans on our Facebook page.

All of them are correct except 4. That is not specific enough because one does not know what "well received" means in numbers. The outcome criterion would need some rewriting like: "Success is when 60% of the public reviews are neutral to positive, as indicated by our internal sentiment algorithm."

Example 5 is generally correct, but sloppy in the way that it was written. Success would occur in this case even if only *one* new fan was gained. As this was probably not the initial intention, it would be better to state an exact number that defines the level that qualifies as "more."

Item 3 is correctly formulated; however, we will see later that this question will not result in any insights, as we will have difficulties defining *contributing variables*.

Once a hard measurement is defined, the "so-what" question from the beginning can be asked. If the outcome is negative, what would we do? Would this trigger any change? A question is useful only if it leads to action.

An Industry in Search of a Question

Perhaps an appropriate final case study of the importance of forming the right question is the nascent social media industry itself. The social media revolution brought on the launch of many companies devoted to the measurement of social media data. They collected all kind of data, measuring quantities ranging from the number of articles to consumer sentiment. However, many of these companies soon vanished from the landscape, often because they had one of the following two issues:

Sales costs were too high.
: These companies needed to do too much free consulting until they could sell their measurements.

Retention of clients was an issue.
: Clients could easily sign up for these tools online; however, they would rarely use these tools for the long run.

Both of these issues could be seen as a case of not being able to formulate the right questions for customers. If it is not clear what kind of question the client wants answered, and if it is not clear what kind of *action* the client wants to take, the measurement company will not be able to answer anything of substance. Thus many companies employed the marketing slogan "Listen to the conversation," indicating that the client should use them as a tool for a kind of creative discovery.

The survivors in this industry often built up consulting support to first define the *question* and the potential *actions* behind it, to inform the creation of relevant answers. To do this, you have to understand business needs as well as the available data influencing these needs. Nevertheless, many of those companies sold out or vanished.

Summary

The hardest and most complex part in any data work is the formulation of the *right* question. The right questions regarding data follow the same principle as a well formulated business goal or aim. They are S.M.A.R.T.

The complexity in the correct formulation of questions can be seen in the issues faced with social media metrics. Those metrics are often presented as the answer to a question. However, it is often a question you have never asked: if you attract enough fans on Facebook, or if enough people follow or mention you on Twitter, or if your view count is high enough on YouTube, then you are perceived to be successful. In reality, however, successful use of social media data requires understanding your strategic objectives at the front end of the process. The right questions revolve around business goals first, which then inform your use of this data. Social media data itself can be only loosely related to business needs, or even orthogonal to them, without careful planning and analysis.

To formulate the right question, you can either use the data itself and conduct the process of *creative discovery* or use your *expert knowledge* about the business. The more the data industry matures, the more we will see that the latter is used.

A good example here is again the use of social media. As it continues to mature, we are seeing more *specific* and *actionable* questions being asked and more targeted metrics created. This situation is very similar to the earlier growth of the World Wide Web in the 1990s. In the heady early days of the Web, simply having a website or implementing ecommerce was thought to be a competitive advantage for early adopters. Today, these tools are routine and commoditized for nearly everyone, and only the ones with a clear business goal in mind will profit from them. In much the same way, social media data is now maturing to the point where it is no longer sufficient to simply "join the conversation"; you must now ask good questions based on business outcomes, and then form a data measurement strategy around these objectives.

WORKBOOK QUESTIONS

Each and every business is different. Thus each business will have different questions. Continue the discussion with us and your peers:

- What are the objectives of your business?
- Based on those objectives, what are your key questions? Write them down and revisit them throughout the book.

Are those questions good questions? Be tough on yourself. Are those questions really S.M.A.R.T.? Focus especially on the *S* (*specific*) and the *A* (*actionable*). Since we will use a lot of social media examples throughout the book to create the "fourth *V*" of the data, let's look at this area specifically: is your company using social media? What kind of question would you like to ask about social media data on your brand, your customers, and your company?

Again, focus on being S.M.A.R.T. Questions are asked easily. The art is in being S.M.A.R.T. Short of questions? You might get a better angle if you try the preceding steps with someone who does not have the same domain knowledge as you do. Do you want to know more? Reach out to us in Twitter, @askmeasurelearn, or write on our LinkedIn or Facebook page.

Use the Right Data

It's not about "good" or "bad" data, it's about "right" data.[1]

—THOMAS ANDERSON (@TOMHCANDERSON)

Tom Anderson, the CEO of OdinText, sounds almost philosophical in his statement on "good" and "bad," but his quote summarizes nicely what many have tried to say: Only with the "right" data will you be able to draw conclusions and act on them. But what is "right"? Once you have defined a good question—that is, once you define the *ask*—the next challenge is to determine what data can help answer this question. The best question might be unanswered because we are using or measuring the wrong data. There are two important factors in this discussion:

- What kind of data (sometimes also called features or variables[2]) should we use? Often companies have premade measurements available, such as click rates of users, their ages, or financial KPIs. The more of them you use, the harder it is to find relationships and not get overwhelmed by noise. With too few variables and features, however, you might not find what has the biggest effect in a given situation.

  Take as an example the work of a behavioral-targeting company. It has many variables about a visitor, such as the pages she has clicked before, the time she clicked the advertisement, and her network ID. It might even store the stock market situation and the weather at the time of the click. Not all of these data elements are equally helpful. For example, it turns out that the information about the browser is one of the best features to select for a campaign selling online games, since not every game runs in every browser window.

1. Thomas H.C. Anderson, "The Social Media Analytics Expectations Gap," *http://bit.ly/1kOYiJi*.
2. In this book, "features" and "variables" have the same meaning.

Feature selection is thus the balance between utility and volume of data. It is a crucial step in getting to the right data.

- How much data should we use? Social media has created massive data amounts, and there is always the temptation to use it *all*. Fisheye Analytics stores 25 terabytes of data, or more than 300,000 CDs, every month. Ideally you want to use all data at once, but this poses engineering challenges and often might not improve the result. How much data would you need to describe a line? Correct, two data points. Would it improve your model if you were to have a million data points? No! The question about how much data to use is often a question about how to sample your data to be statistically relevant.

  Even worse, using all available data might disguise the actual issue, as we saw in the example in Chapter 8. In that case, the issues surrounding social media comments about a corporate CEO only became apparent after the data was reduced to discussions on net neutrality.

> Note
>
> The world of data science and the world of statistics are very similar. Nevertheless, both domains have developed out of different areas. Therefore, often their language might be slightly different. Within data science, you will find more engineers. They call a "feature" what a scientist or statistician would call a "variable." Both terms have similar meanings: if you were to put your data into a spreadsheet, the "variables" or "features" would typically be described by the column headings of the spreadsheet.

Which Data Is Important?

It is an early, sunny afternoon, and we are in one of New York's best independent coffee shops. The coffee is excellent and the discussion is exciting. The entrepreneurs around the table are discussing matchmaking algorithms. How can a computer best match two people to create the greatest likelihood of a marriage? For sure, there is a market out there for those kinds of applications, and there are hundreds of sites already trying exactly this. This group of entrepreneurs have many ideas on the table:

- Use each person's social graph.
- Use the social graphs of all of that person's friends.

- Ask the person to rate pictures, articles, movies, and so on to see what he likes.
- Measure how long it takes him to fill out the initial application form.
- Check how many spelling mistakes he makes.
- Check what type of language the person uses (slang, easy and conversational, or stiff and formal).

The list became longer and longer as more data points were added. "We should even use DNA information to match the best couples," suggested one youngster. Then there was silence. Was this too unrealistic? Not really: GenePartner even offers this as a service, based on research[3] that found that partners are more attracted to each other if a specific antigen is highly different. Thus DNA, taste, friends, language—if all of this seems reasonable, what stops us from making the perfect matchmaking machine? Get *all* the data from Facebook, Twitter, questionnaires, preferred books, preferred movies, and even from DNA analysis and load it up into a big dark "black box" called machine learning and just let a big computer do the job? In this case there would be no need for *experience*, and all our conclusions could be drawn by statistical algorithms.

Is it that simple? No—at least not today! The more variables there are, the more difficult the task will be. Also, computers have the same issues as humans, that we can't see the forest for the trees.

In sum, it is not wise to use *all* data, but it is necessary to carefully select the data sets that have a high causal impact. This process is also commonly referred to as feature selection or regularization. To guide this selection process, you can use one of the following ways to look at features, as illustrated in Figure 9-1.

Causation
: Is this variable in a causal relationship with the outcome to the question?

Error
: How easily and cleanly can you measure this variable?

Cost
: How available is the data?

3. Giovanni Frazzetto, "The science of online dating," EMBO reports Nov 2010, *http://bit.ly/IPHKVQ*.

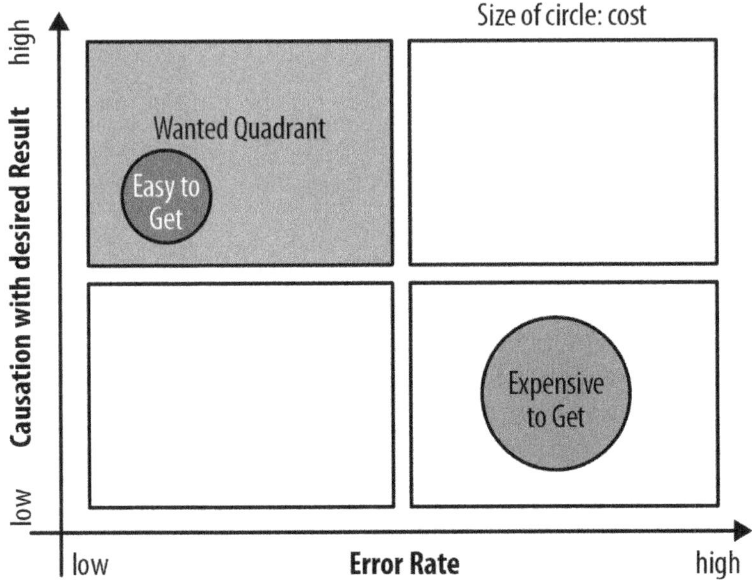

Figure 9-1. Causation versus error versus cost

CAUSATION

You should select features that have the biggest effect in terms of answering the question. However, it is not always easy, if even possible, to distinguish between causation and correlation. Let's look at the case from British Petroleum: in 2010, the BP platform Deepwater Horizon spilled 4.9 million barrels (780,000 m^3) of crude oil and created a disaster along the US gulf coastline.

The reaction was a public outcry in the United States as politicians, journalists, celebrities, and the general public all reacted negatively to the disaster. Their outrage was visible in the media. Fisheye Analytics collected all media data (blogs, Twitter, Facebook, news forums) on this oil spill and created a Net-Sentiment-Score using its own proprietary sentiment algorithm. The Net-Sentiment-Score is a ratio based on the difference between the amount of negative sentiment and positive sentiment in all articles, tweets, and blog posts.

During the same time this public outcry occurred, the share price from BP collapsed. Was there a causal relationship? The graph prepared by the Fisheye Analytics team shown in Figure 9-2 might suggest a weak correlation. The graph shows in the upper part the Net-Sentiment-Score and in the lower part the share price.

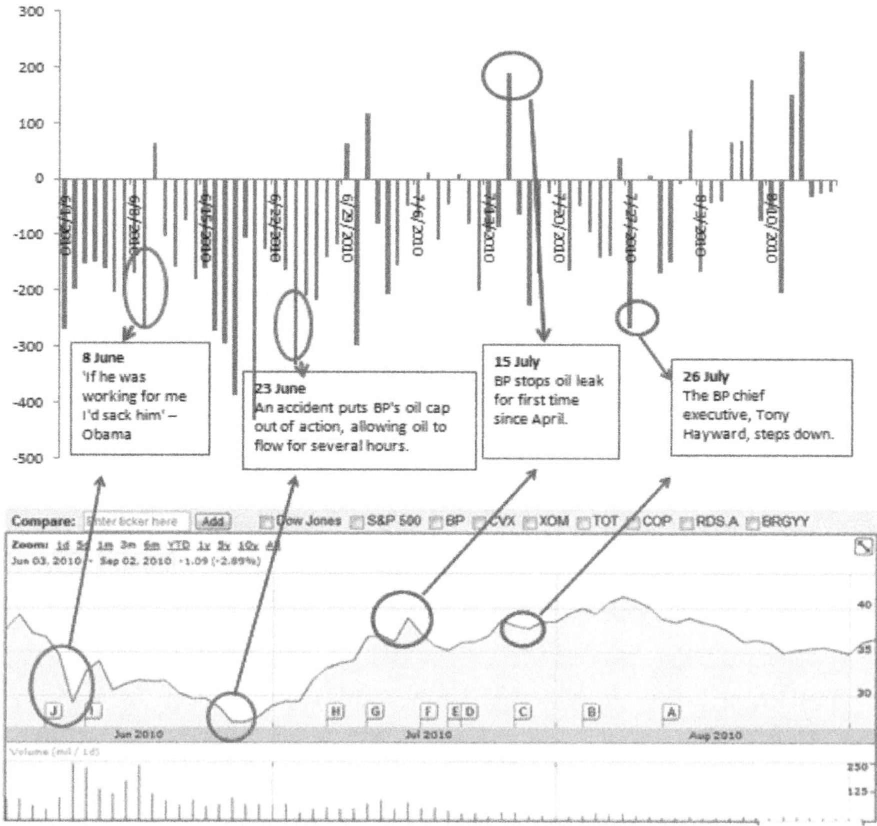

Figure 9-2. BP share price versus Net Promoter Score (Courtesy of Fisheye Analytics.)

Correlation versus causation

As you can see, there is some form of correlation between the stock market movements and the Net-Sentiment-Score of the public discussions. In other words, there is some form of *dependency* relationship between these two data sets. Correlation enables us to link Net-Sentiment-Score and the share price with a mathematical formula: for each reduction in the Net-Sentiment-Score, the share price will reduce by a certain amount in USD.

However, can you conclude that negative tweets are causing a lower share price? No, not solely on the basis of statistical correlation. To do so would be wrong.

While correlation is easily established through statistical analysis, causation is not easily concluded. Even worse, we will see in this section that is never possible to absolutely prove a causal relationship. However, the combination of statistical evidence and logical reasoning can help to suggest a certain likelihood of a causal relationship.

To establish whether the number of negative articles caused the share price to drop or vice versa, we can look to so-called Structural Causal Models (SCM), as introduced in 2009 by UCLA professor Judea Pearl.[4]

SCMs represent the different measurements or data sets diagrammatically, indicating causal relations via arrows.

Direct effect. The oil spill disaster caused an outcry from the public in all types of media. This outcry caused stockholders to sell their shares because they worried that the company's brand name would be damaged, which might impact future revenue. Thus the SCM will look like the one depicted in Figure 9-3.

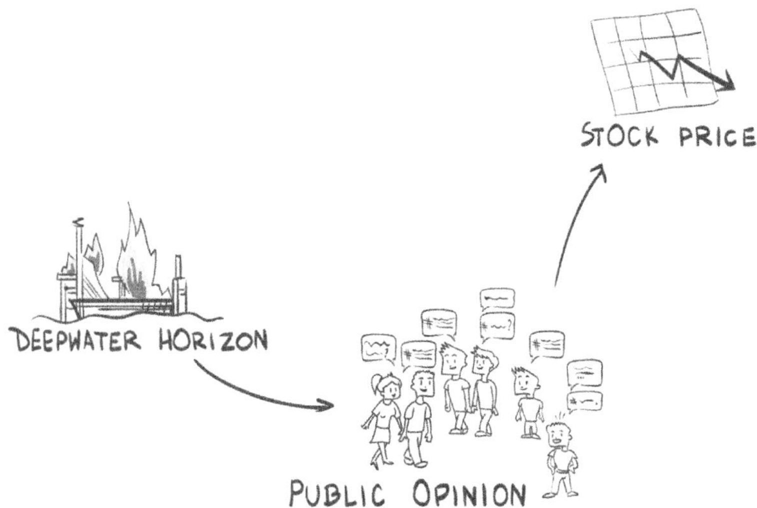

Figure 9-3. Direct correlation

Reverse effect. The reverse order might also be possible. The stock price dropped due to the oil disaster, as shareholders assumed bleak times to come. The drop caused the general public to talk about it. In this case, cause and effect were reversed, and the Net-Sentiment-Score would have no effect on the share price. In

4. Judea Pearl, *"Causality: Models, Reasoning, and Inference,"* Statistics Surveys, 2009, doi:10.1214/09-SS057.

this case, the SCM would show the public opinion only after the stock-price drop, as depicted in Figure 9-4.

One way to test which of those two scenarios was true is to use a timestamp. If the share-price drop was before the public reaction in the media, one could at least reject the other hypothesis that the public reaction in the media caused the share-price drop. In the case of BP, however, both reactions are overlapped in time and thus no conclusion can be drawn.

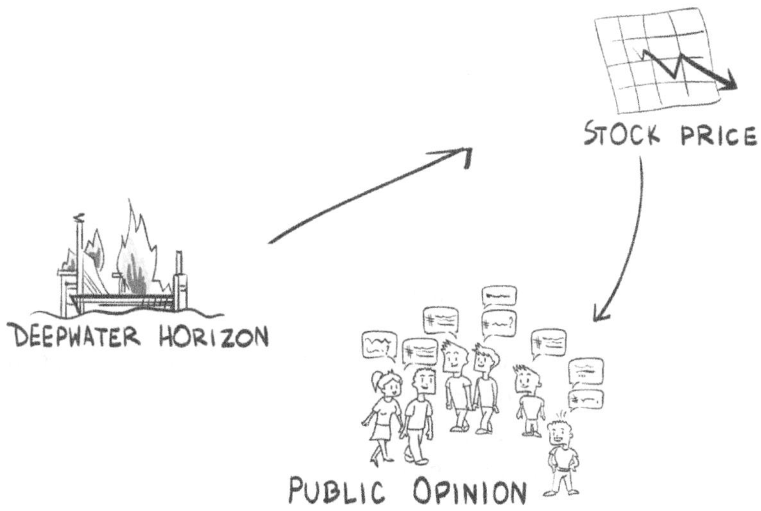

Figure 9-4. Inverse correlation

The unknown third. So far, the SCM only included two variables: stock price and Net-Sentiment-Score. It might happen, however, that there are important variables that we have not yet identified. Those variables are called lurking, moderating, intervening, or confounding variables. In our example with BP, it could be the role of the government. How was it reacting? To include the government, we need to include a new entity into our SCM, as done in Figure 9-5. If the government was very demanding in terms of remedies for the environmental damages, that would in turn create a future liability for BP and thus let the share price drop. The negative Net-Sentiment-Score might only mirror the reactions from the government, but not cause the actual drop in the share price.

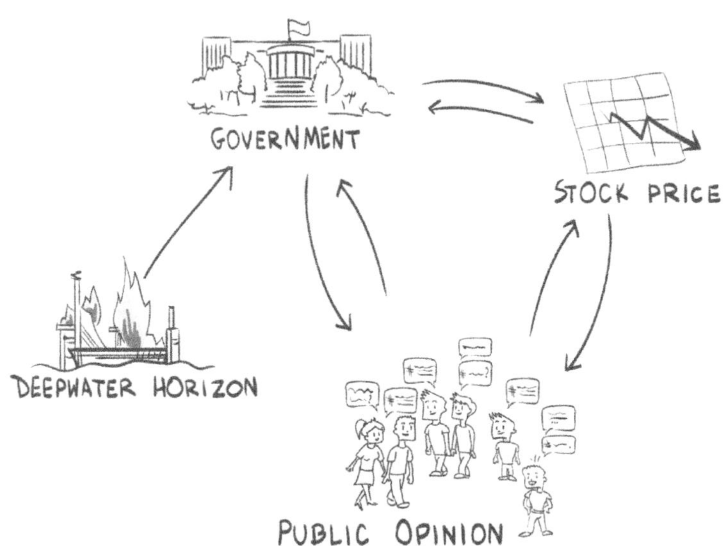

Figure 9-5. Government is the confounding variable

Another explanation could be that initially there was no reaction by the politicians. But forced by a loud public outcry over this spill, politicians started to react and to demand compensatory payments, which in turn created future liabilities for BP, causing the share price to drop. In such a case, the Net-Sentiment-Score actually caused the share price drop.

All of the above. There are way more combinations possible than previously shown, and which is the real one is hard to figure out. It is not easy to know what is cause and what is correlation. However, we can all probably agree that all of the preceding effects played some role. Thus the SCM can be displayed as in Figure 9-6. But even if we were to know the causal relationships, we still would not know how strong those relationships are.

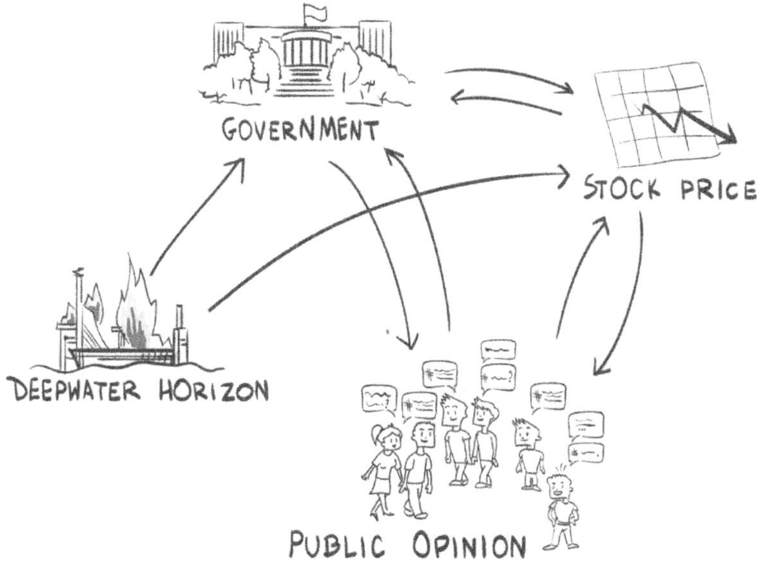

Figure 9-6. In social media cause and effect are often highly mixed

TESTING FOR CORRELATION

In theory, it would be easy to find the weights for those *causations*. You just have to repeat the event exactly the same way and only change the variable you would like to investigate. For our example, this would mean we need to turn time back and have the same oil spill again, but either reduce the tweets or silence the government. Afterward, we look at the reaction of the share price. In practice, such time warp experiments are not possible, which leads us to the fundamental problem of causal inference. Paul W. Holland explains in an excellent paper on statistics and causal inference[5] that there will never be certainty when establishing a causal relationship. This is good news for any manager who gets questioned over and over again whether one can determine cause and effect. However, even if it is theoretically impossible to establish causal relationships with certainty, you can compute statistical analyses to test for causal relationships at a certain level of probability:

5. Paul W. Holland, "Statistics and Causal Inference," *Journal of American Statistical Association*, Dec 1986, *http://bit.ly/1gBGgge*.

> *It is also a mistake to conclude from the Fundamental Problem of Causal Interference that causal inference is impossible. What is impossible is causal inference without making untested assumptions. This does not render causal inference impossible, but it does give it an air of uncertainty.*
>
> **—PAUL W. HOLLAND**

Those tests would try to keep all circumstances constant and change only one parameter at a time. The gold standard for this can be found in medicine. Clinical trials are set up as randomized controlled trials to best estimate the causal effect of a drug. The key here is that patients are split randomly into two groups. One is taking the medication, and the other one is only taking a placebo. In some situations, even the doctors conducting the test do not know which group is which (double-blind trial). One of the biggest worries in those tests is that we have overlooked a lurking variable and that the sample split is not really randomized. In the online world, randomized controlled trials are best known as A/B tests. In an A/B test, we try to limit the risk of lurking variables by just increasing the testing sample. In medicine, we cannot put all available patients into a health-related test. However, in online retail, we can.

No matter whether it is a medical or an online test, we control the surroundings. In an A/B test, we make sure that someone selected for website design A will never see the website B. We are able to do this because we have almost full control of our environment. For example, we can identify visitors by cookie or IP address and only show them a certain website. Those systems are never perfect because some visitors might use several devices and therefore are exposed to both versions. Other visitors might decide to delete cookies and therefore see different versions of the website. Here, Holland's conclusion that we can't be sure about causal effect is true. However, to the best of our abilities we have reduced potential lurking variables.

In social media analyses, controlled trials are often not possible. BP, for example, cannot just create another oil spill to create a test of another media strategy. Even if it could or would create another oil spill (obviously it would not), a second oil spill would be judged by the same worldwide audience that saw the first one, and this prior experience would affect their reactions, so we would have even less control of outside variables. The Deepwater Horizon oil spill was, unfortunately, not the only one in history, and you could attempt to use those past events to try to separate cause and effect. But those comparisons pose significant challenges. A spill of similar size damaging the United States would be the Lakeview Gusher spill about 100 years ago. In 1910, social media didn't exist, and the ways people express their opinions have changed quite radically since that time.

A more recent one would be the Prudhoe Bay oil spill, which happened in 2006. Social media already existed at that time, and you might be able to measure the public reaction to it. But this spill was only 1% the size of the Deepwater catastrophy in terms of spilled oil. It also was in Alaska and thus did not impact as many people. Both differences make any comparison quite complicated.

Past media response might give an indication of a basis for comparison, but it will not be the hard measurement we are looking for.

It is true that BP is an extreme example, but as a general rule, it is difficult to understand correlation within social media, since no two events are identical. Take for example an online retailer that communicates rebates to potential customers via social media. Similar to BP, it can't easily control who sees the vouchers and who does not. The open nature of social media makes it impossible to control. Without a control group, the retailer will never be sure about what made people react to the offered discounts.

ERROR, OR WHY STRUCTURED DATA IS SUPERIOR

The second area to watch out for in feature selection is the error. It might seem strange at first to consider error in our data. However, almost any data type comes with error. No machine and no process is 100% accurate and thus any data will have errors. In the online world, we are used to the fact that this error is small. A click is a click. Some clicks might be reported and others might not, due to different measurements or different systems that process those clicks afterward.

The situation gets even worse if we look at social media. In order to automatically understand the written text by humans, social media uses additional metrics that are calculated using fuzzy logic. Take the measurement of sentiment or influence as an example. Those metrics are measured more like probability. A "negative" sentiment means in reality: "There is a good chance that there is a negative sentiment." We have seen algorithms on sentiment where the amount of error was so great that they were yielding measurements that were only slightly better than guessing. So you should think twice before using those features in any measurement setup.

As we see in this book over and over again, structured data has a lower error rate and therefore is often preferred over unstructured data.

Structured

Structured data is exactly what it says it is. It is data that has a predefined order so that a computer can easily read and work with it. The data is in records that a computer is able to store, fetch, and process. A simple example would be Table 9-1. Any computer can read this and use the variables it represents.

Table 9-1. Example of structured data

Item	Price	Currency	Quantity	Unit
Apple	1.99	USD	1	Pounds (lb)
Oranges	0.99	USD	1	Pounds (lb)
Strawberries	2.99	USD	250	Grams (g)

The previous example is a simple list, but data structure can be more complex as well, taking forms such as arrays, trees, graphs, or hash tables.

Unstructured

The opposite of *structured* data is *unstructured* data. Unstructured data is information that is not easily analyzed by a computer. This could be text (like a tweet), pictures, voice, or other data.

Figure 9-7. Example of unstructured data

The information kept in Figure 9-7 might be the same as in Table 9-1, but it is not as easily retrieved by a computer. Another example might be the following tweet: “I am craving apples—$1.99—I thought they were kidding.” This tweet contains some information, which is as well stored in Table 9-1, mainly the price of apples. However, some information is missing:

- *You can assume* that $1.99 should be a price.
- *You know the author of the tweet* and that he lives in New York, thus the price is in USD and not in Singaporean dollars. Additionally, this means that the price is for one pound of apples.
- *You can assume* that "kidding" indicates some kind of emotional reaction such as being upset or surprised.

A computer, on the other hand, will have a hard time understanding the underlying content of those types of tweets. Even when trained to understand this kind of unstructured data, an algorithm will most likely have a higher error rate than it would with structured data. Therefore, if you are deciding which feature to select, you will most likely drop features that exhibit *error*. Structured data is often more powerful than unstructured data because it has fewer errors.

This insight explains why social media is often not as powerful as we might have hoped it would be. Social media largely produces unstructured data, and it often comes with a relatively larger degree of error as compared to structured sources. However, despite this shortcoming, it is often the case that unstructured data is the only data available. Take for example efforts to improve marketing (see Chapter 1) or customer care (see Chapter 4). Success is dependent on user-generated comments, and any successful project will rely on unstructured data.

Another reason unstructured data is getting used more and more despite its shortcomings is that you have already used all available structured data for analysis and prediction and now you are looking for the next competitive edge. An example can be found in the financial industry, as noted in "Predicting the Stock Market" on page 206. Hedge funds have already used most of the existing data signals to predict market behavior, and thus unstructured data is left as largely unexplored ground. While the relationship of the unstructured data to financial metrics might not be as strong as the relationship of structured data such as revenue, the hope is that you can gain additional insights that you did not have before.

COST AND INSIDER KNOWLEDGE

There is a cost associated with data retrieval and data storage. Despite massive data volume, most of the time, you will not simply get the needed data. You might need to buy it externally, or you may need to create a new IT infrastructure to get it. Again, take as an example the concept of sentiment. If an automated algorithm is not sufficient, then you can always use manual readers to determine the sentiment. Looking at 25 TB of text data, it does not seem very feasible. Why? Because of cost. In any feature selection process you might use, the cost to acquire or retrieve the data will play a role.

Next to cost, there is the power of insider knowledge. Data exclusively owned by you can, if relevant, create more of a competitive advantage than any public data. Public data can be used by everyone else, which in turn will mean no sustainable competitive advantage.

Take the example in Chapter 7 of *Moneyball*, a great book by Michael Lewis and a fascinating movie. Billy Beane, general manager of the Oakland Athletics, used publicly available in-game activity statistics to spot underevaluated players. By using this technique, he could create a winning team despite having a smaller budget than many of his competitors.

It is an exciting story. But did this create a long-lasting competitive advantage? No! Once the competition understood that data usage can help to predict performance, they caught up quickly, and today all major baseball teams use sabermetrics to monitor players' performance.

A similar example can be found in financial service companies. They rely on public data. Their competitive advantage is their algorithm, meaning the way they synthesize data. This kind of advantage is hard to keep. Thus it is no wonder that quantum hedge funds are one of the most secretive organizations we have seen. We have been asked for a nondisclosure agreement just so that we could have a look at a company brochure. Asked why the company thought it was necessary, since no information about their algorithms was displayed, the response was, "But our performance charts are in it, so you might be able to reverse-engineer our formula."

We use the idea of competitiveness coming from inside often within this book. This might be one of the main reasons Twitter is not as valuable as Facebook. Facebook has much better control over its data, while Twitter has sold its data to companies like Dataswift and Gnip. Because of this idea, we argue in Chapter 4 not to use public customer care platforms but to own them.

CASE: A MATCHMAKING ENGINE

Back to the New York coffee bar full of entrepreneurs discussing matchmaking algorithms, which we had described in "Which Data Is Important?" on page 234:

they understood that they needed to cut down on their variables. But which variables should they use, and which should they ignore? The best guide here is to use the framework displayed in Figure 9-1. Let's as an example consider the suggested variable of the social graphs. This means that the team plans to analyze all Facebook and Twitter connections of the user. Should this variable be used for the matchmaking algorithm?

Error
: Is it technically feasible to analyze the social graphs of someone in regards to social networks such as Facebook and Twitter? And if so, what would the error rate be?

Causation
: Is the measurement of someone's interest graph a true representation of his real interests? How likely is it that this measured interest graph is a good influencer for the partner selection?

Cost
: How expensive is it to retrieve the data? Are you the only one with this data, and is it a potential competitive advantage?

However, the social graph might not be our first pick to do couple matchmaking. Why?

Error
: Measuring the number of connections and to whom is easy. Either it is publicly available information as in Twitter or it is easily accessible once you access the user's Facebook profile. What is less easy to measure is the strength of a connection. Methods could include analyzing retweets and messaging behavior. However, such measurement will most likely include significant errors since:

  - Not all communication might be mapped. For example, the user might have only high school contacts on Facebook because he didn't want to lose contact with them. However, his important daily activity might not be happening on Facebook.
  - There are privacy settings. More and more guides help the users to keep parts or all of their content private and thus not easily accessible. Maybe this person is even keeping multiple identities online in order to protect his privacy?

Causation

Long ago, Goethe knew that there should be a causal relationship between your identity and your friends: "Tell me with whom you associate, and I will tell you who you are." But how strong is this causation? Especially in a time where we have 500+ friends in Facebook and where social heritage does not define who we are allowed to meet. Yes, the causational effects are probably low, as we saw in Chapter 1, where we discussed whether social networks have sufficient information in order to place advertisements.

Cost

The cost of getting to the public part of this information is low. Services like Twitter offer a publicly available access (API) so that everyone can tap into this data. However, if everyone can tap into this information, creating a competitive advantage will be difficult. Private data is not easily available and often has to be bought.

Thus the social graph might not be our first pick. One might argue that the way people use a social network will change over time and all communication will be mapped out. If that is the case and if that information is accessible, then we would need to revisit this discussion.

Are there other variables that might be a better fit for a matchmaking algorithm? Following the idea of *structured data is superior*, the team soon turned to a questionnaire. The structured data obtainable through a questionniare provides a couple of advantages:

Error

Measurement is generally more accurate. For example, let's say you ask in a questionnaire how old someone is or how much education someone has achieved. We can be fairly confident that most people will provide an accurate response to this question, and so the error rate will be low.

Causation

The causation depends on the question. For example, consider the amount of educational achievement. There is ample research showing that similar educational background is important for a good personal match. And you should be able to ask several questions covering all kinds of areas of a relationship, such as trust and habits.

Cost

The cost is higher because you have the burden of creating a survey and finding respondents. However, afterward that information is yours and could, if relevant, be a competitive advantage.

We don't know whether the young startup OkCupid (@okcupid) followed the concepts outlined in this chapter. Chris Coyne and Sam Yagan did in fact meet in New York, and they certainly adopted the right methods. They only use a questionnaire in which for each question (for example, "How messy are you?") they ask you to:

1. Answer for yourself.
2. Answer how you would like your partner to answer.
3. Indicate how important this question is to you.

(Read more about their approach on their website.) The system seems to work, and users say it is beating most matchmaking engines. The Boston Globe calls them the "Google of online dating." [6] OkCupid was acquired in 2011 by Match.com.

Privacy Concerns

The question of what data you use has another dimension: privacy. It has been always an issue. But the recent revelations by the former CIA agent Edward Snowden have made everyone painfully aware of the fact that we are monitored.

Not everything we can measure should be measured. Not every new invention based on data will meet public approval. The use of data to create insights about your life is seen more and more as critical.

One Russian developer found this out the hard way after releasing the iPhone application Girls Around Me. This app combined location data from Foursquare with social media profiles to show you women who had checked into nearby locations, together with personal information such as their age, preferences, and family situation.

6. Hiawatha Bray, "Online dating: The economics of love," The *Boston Globe*, February 2007, *http://bo.st/1eiAfVv*.

Following an article about this app, there was an outcry about having personal information used this way, with some claiming that it made it easier for sexual predators to stalk women. Soon Foursquare withdrew permission for Girls Around Me to use its data, rendering it useless, and it was withdrawn from the market shortly afterward.

Thus, there are clearly social considerations on top of the challenges of getting the question right and getting the data right. In "The Creepy Factor" on page 21, we look at the issue of privacy. One of the big hurdles in using social media data is the creepiness factor or how consumers react to it. [7]

Data Selection

In the last section, we discussed *features* or *variables* and how to reduce them. But even if all features are selected, it is sometimes worthwhile to reduce the amount of data used. This might seem strange at a time when big data is being discussed by everyone. Today you have all the technology in place to handle large amounts of data, so why should you reduce it? If data is value, shouldn't more data equal more value?

> *Data without a sound approach is just noise.*
>
> **—XAVIER AMATRIAN (@XAMAT)**

The answer is no. More data might simply be noise if not used correctly, as Xavier Amatrian has pointed out. In other situations, more data might only create more of a burden. How many data points do you need to describe a line? Two! Even if you use two million points, it will not change your accuracy. There are two ways to reduce data:

Sampling
: Are two points enough, or will I need more? And if I need more, how many? Those questions will be answered by sampling.

7. Paul, Ian, "Girls Around Me App Voluntarily Pulled After Privacy Backlash," *PC World*, April 2, 2012, *http://bit.ly/1fh1V9K*.

Subsets

Sometimes, as we saw in "Case Study: Major Telecom Company" on page 219, a subset can actually reveal insights that we would not have seen otherwise due to the noise.

SAMPLING

Sampling is the process of only using a small statistically relevant sample of all potential data to gain some knowledge of a statistical population. In the case of a line, two data points would be sufficient. However, how many points do we need to train a recommendation system? Figure 9-8 shows the number of trees used in a random forest.[8] The model is already optimally set up after a little over 100 trees. At least in this case, the algorithm does not need to create all potential branches of a decision tree model.

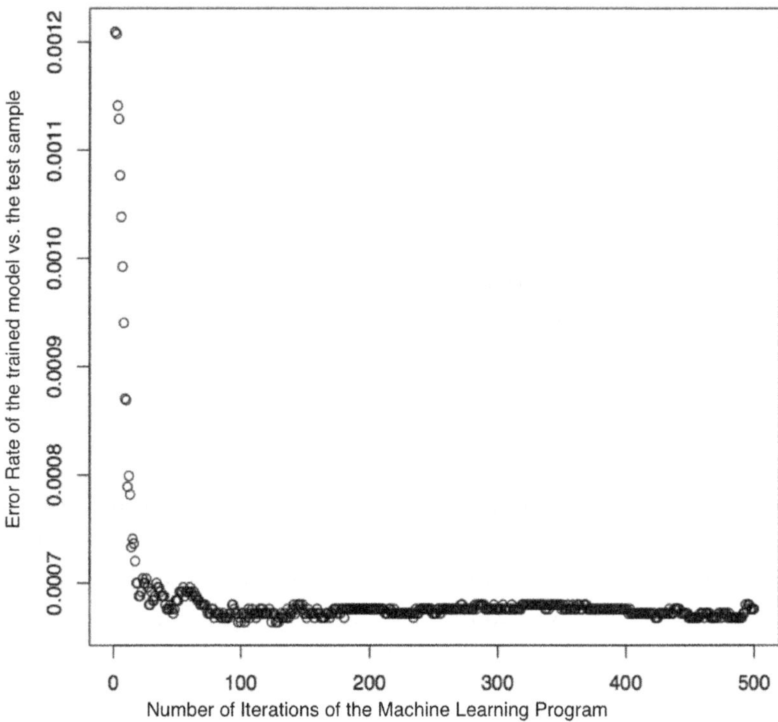

Figure 9-8. Random forest model

8. Random forest is a machine-learning technique that helps to do classification and regression models.

Xavier reported something similar. He analyzed the needed sample size to train the suggestion engine from Netflix sufficiently. As one can see in Figure 9-9, more data does not improve the algorithm.

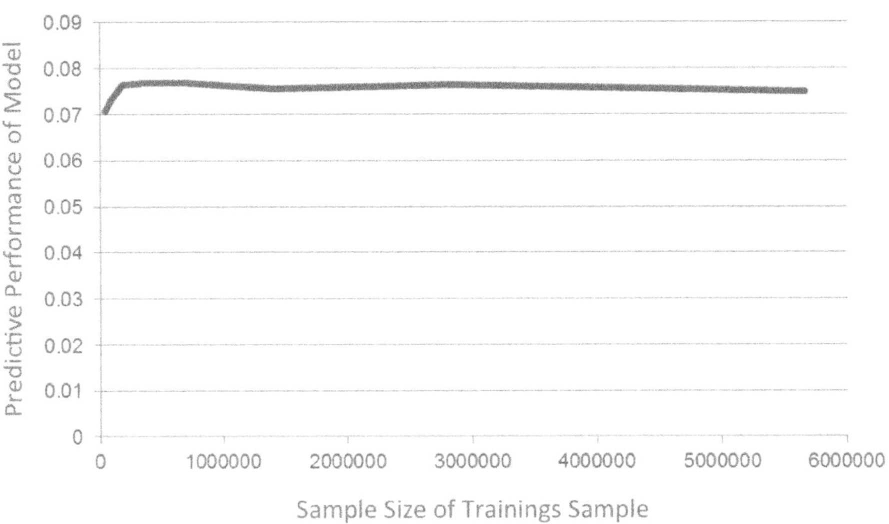

Figure 9-9. Model performance vs. sample size (Courtesy of Xavier Amatrian.)

SUBSETS

A subset of the data can be used if we purposely limit one or more of the variables. This way we might reduce the variation or noise and see certain relationships within the data better.

We have spoken so far about the benefits of working with structured versus unstructured data. To deal with unstructured data, we introduce measurements in order to make that data semi-structured. In the context of social media such a measurement is the *keyword*. A keyword is a word or phrase that must be contained in our unstructured text. Keywords represent an effective way to cut part of your unstructured data out for further analytics or benchmarking.

However, a keyword also creates an effective subset within your data set. Let's say you want to analyze how social media conversations affect sales. You could take all the billions of tweets ever written and try to correlate them with your sales figures. This kind of work is not only very resource intensive (since this is truly big data), it is also totally useless. You will not get anything useful out of it because it will not generate any insights. The noise level will be beyond the actual signal you wanted to measure.

Thus we use a keyword, and you will only analyze the correlation between the tweets that mention your brand and your sales revenue. While this seems a sensible approach, there is no single truth in how to set up a keyword. Human language is multifaceted, and there are many ways to express even one brand. As a result, any subset we create using keywords is a new source of error.

As depicted in Figure 9-10, the use of keywords can filter specific articles out of billions of social media articles. The filter used in the picture filters out all of the ones containing a "RED box." In real life, this could be all articles containing a certain brand term. Everything without a RED box will be filtered out. Based on this selection, further algorithms can be applied such as sentiment, place, and language. In Figure 9-10, only the amount of RED boxes and the source, such as Facebook, or Twitter, are calculated. In real life, these results could then be correlated with other internal figures such as the sales revenues. However as discussed earlier, correlation does not mean causation. Just because the RED box has a high correlation with high sales revenues does not mean that the RED box actually caused this high revenue.

Figure 9-10. Keyword setup

"I know keywords"

You might now nod and say that you know the concept of *keywords*. At the end, every one of us has already used Google, Bing, or another search engine. Therefore we think we understand what keywords are. But be ready for a surprise. Keyword setup in Google and keyword setup for big-data analysis are vastly different. A good keyword design can take weeks or even months and is not a trivial problem.

Why? Have you ever had a problem with Google search such that the first entry was not what you were looking for but the second or third on the list displayed? Like for most of us, it probably happens often. Google search is a two-step process. In the first step, we type in a keyword and Google displays some results. In the second step, we manually screen those results and choose the one we like best from the top 25 results.

With social media monitoring, there can't be a second manual step because it needs to be an automated process. A keyword for a brand might generate hundreds or even thousands of articles a day. Consequently, there is no opportunity or capability to do a manual screening process such as the one we do with Google search.

The expectations for a keyword for a social media–monitoring company are way higher than those for a Google search.

No truth

A keyword supporting the marketing team in analyzing the value of a brand will look different than the keyword that will warn the PR department about viral discussions of the brand. Unfortunately, there is no simple golden rule in keyword design. Each and every keyword has its own shortcomings. It's either set too broadly or too narrowly. See the sidebar for more on keyword setup.

If a keyword is set up too broadly, it will allow too many irrelevant articles, posts, tweets, etc. to be included into your data set. This will distort the analytics. If the filter is too narrow, it may only allow correct content but might miss relevant articles. This will distort the analytics as well. There will never be a 100% correct keyword. You need to be aware of this fact before you use keywords to make decisions. Let's look, for example, at all articles published about a car brand. The volume of articles is depicted in the Venn diagram Figure 9-11. Here you can see how difficult it can be to find the right balance for the actual brand term.

The data set comprises all articles mentioning the brand term. For the sake of our discussion, let's say the brand term is "Renault." The data analytics is done for the marketing team and should tell them how the public discussion on "Renault" correlates to their positioning efforts. That would mean that secondhand sales or any local news about an accident involving a Renault is not interesting. They most likely have no relationship to the marketing positioning effort and thus can be treated as noise. We thus need to make a subsample out of the data. But how? By introducing another word filter. For example, we could exclude all the articles mentioning the word "accident" or "sales." The result is depicted in the Venn diagram in Figure 9-11. Each exclusion will unfortunately cut out wanted articles as well. We would no longer see a news article that talks about the fact that "car sales from Renault" went up. Nor would we see the "recall to prevent further accidents" information. Both are, however, highly relevant for our positioning efforts.

Figure 9-11. Example filter setup

The Issues with the Right Keyword

Keywords are a way to navigate a data set. Similar to an index in this book, one will create an index within unstructured data. Keywords are helping to quickly find the appropriate part within the text. However, no matter whether you use the latest technology such as Lucene, which includes a fast and easy "full-text-search," the issues to define a clear-cut subset of data remains the same. Each and every person would set up keywords differently. There is no right and no wrong. Thus keyword setup is often only *best effort*.

In order to define a subset of data, we should use simple keywords and no full text search. Simple keywords follow a set structure: each keyword has a base term that then gets narrowed down by additional filters and exceptions. Base-word, filters, and exceptions are text strings:

```
(Base-word) AND (Filter) NOT (Exceptions)
```

Because of the complexity of the keyword design, the setup should never be done without extensive testing. Someone needs to judge whether the found articles fit the question or not. This is a manual step like the screening we do in a Google search. For each base-word, you need to do a separate iteration process to check whether the filters are appropriate. Once all base-words are defined, they are combined into one data set for further processing.

The step-by-step guidance is:

1. Research.
   a. Research main base-term.
   b. Find exclusions to base-term.
   c. Research abbreviations.
   d. Find exclusions to abbreviations.
   e. Research ways to mention the term within social media (such as a hashtag or via a Twitter handle).
2. Test the results of the search, and return to step 1 as long as the test is not sufficient.
3. Repeat step 1 with other ways of referring to the keyword.
4. Translate the base-word, abbreviations, and exclusions into other languages of interest.
5. Test the results of those translations.

Step 3 can often be simplified. Often the brand name is the best and only way to describe what you are looking for. However, to encounter all data, you will need to take spelling mistakes into account. If the main keyword is a common topic that can be described in many ways (e.g., soccer), you will need support from ontological models.

Step 4 also can often be simplified. Many index and search algorithms, like elastic search, offer multilanguage support. While convenient, one should use those with a lot of care. Those translations might sometimes be highly misleading.

Let's go through one complete example, using the car manufacturer "Renault." The task should be to store all articles about Renault so that it can be used for further research later, including all discussions on accidents and secondhand sales.

Research will reveal that Renault is also a brand of Cognac, thus we will need to refine our keyword as:

`“Renault” NOT “Winery” NOT “Cognac”`

Does Renault have an abbreviation? Yes, the stock market symbol "RNO." It might be worthwhile to include this term into the search; however, that will mean that we need to exclude certain other "RNO" terms, as they can mean something else besides the stock. Also you might want to include hashtags or Twitter handles about Renault. This research would result in the following search expression:

1. `("Renault” NOT “Winery” NOT “Cognac”)`
2. `("RNO" NOT “Nuclear” NOT “NITRID”)`
3. `("Renault-Nissan")`
4. `("#Renault")`
5. `("#RNO" NOT “Nuclear” NOT “NITRID”)`
6. `("#Renault-Nissan")`
7. `("@Renault_Live")`
8. `("@NissanMotorCo")`

One would now need to go on to research all brands from Renault, as people might refer to Renault by just stating "Clio" or "Twingo," etc. After that work is done, all those terms need to be checked individually, per media type and per language. Let's take only those eight terms and restrict ourselves to only online news, Facebook, and Twitter. Even with the limiting, there are still 3 × 8 = 24 different checks. Let's further assume you want to analyze six languages. At the end, you would need to have 6 × 8 = 48 different keyword strings.

CASE: HAITI

On Tuesday, January, 12, 2010, an earthquake of 7.0 Mw shook the earth in Haiti. This disaster and its 52 aftershocks killed more than 316,000 and left many injured and homeless. The World Economic Forum appealed to the international community of business leaders to help. Former U.S. President Bill Clinton and the World Economic Forum's chairman Klaus Schwab together led this initiative. Media data for such an event should be overwhelmingly positive, right?

Sure, if you look only at the subset of data regarding the initiative. However, automated analytics would result in a misleading conclusion due to two issues. First, documents about the earthquake tragedy would overshadow the fundraising story. Also, automated sentiment algorithms are not very well equipped to understand a positive reaction to such a fundraising effort. We discussed the limitations of sentiment in "Automation and Business Intelligence" on page 123. But as a summary, one can say that human sentiment is probably one of the most difficult things to compute using a statistical algorithm:

- An algorithm cannot differentiate between the *message* and the *messenger*. The message was that something terrible had happened in Haiti, but the messengers Clinton and Schwab were trying to bring hope.
- The computer does not know the question you are trying to answer. Is this analysis about the reaction to a tragic accident in Haiti or the impact of the noble actions taken by Clinton and Schwab on their respective brands? An algorithm would need to be clearly trained to answer one or the other of those questions.
- The computer will not be able to understand when something is ironic or satirical.

The only way to deal with those two issues is to reduce the data and to fine-tune the sentiment algorithm exactly toward this setup:

- Reduce the number of media used. For example, use only one media type, such as news articles or blog posts, so that the way people express themselves is similar.

- Reduce the amount of data used to what is relevant for the sample. For example, only use articles that talk about Schwab's session to raise funds, versus all articles on the World Economic Forum and Haiti.
- Reduce the use-case for the algorithm and fine-tune the algorithm to just answer one and only one question: what is the public perception of those fundraising activities?

Only through a subset can you make visible that the world respected and applauded Clinton and Schwab for their efforts to help Haiti.

Summary

When it comes to data and the task of finding some common structure within data, the paradox is that less is often more. Unfiltered, massive datasets can hide both trends and valuable artifacts within the dataset. Therefore, finding appropriate features or variables and doing good data reduction are among the key aspects of finding the fourth "V" of the data. Only a focused approach will realize the underlying value beneath the data. Including all data and trying to find common clues will lead to failure.

Sampling, data selection, and keywords all play roles in turning masses of social information into workable data sets. The latter two skills in particular represent an art as much as a science, given the subjective nature of interpreting data, as this chapter's case studies and anecdotes have revealed. They underscore the human dimension of big-data analysis, even as we seek to increasingly automate the process over time. By linking our knowledge with effective use of these tools, we can turn this process into a manageable goal that supports our desired outcomes.

WORKBOOK

We often find that many people underestimate the amount of data they have within their own company. Let's first ask about what data you have in-house:

- List data sources you have in-house. Don't worry if these information sources are not saved so far. At least there is one point in time that your company knew. Be creative and think outside of the box. Images of surveillance cameras. Yes, write it down. User behavior, sales figures, log files...you will be surprised how much data you have.

- Now let's look back at the question you formulated in Chapter 8. Take the data sources you have listed and score them according to these three dimensions: correlation with your question; noisiness of the data (or how strong you expect the signal to be); and cost of acquiring and storing this data.

Questions? Don't hesitate to ask us on Twitter, @askmeasurelearn, or write your question on our LinkedIn or Facebook page.

Define the Right Measurement

Every company has many existing measurements that lead to data. In the last chapter, we discussed which data and how much of it we should use. But not all of this data might help to answer the question we defined in Chapter 8. Therefore, we need new metrics to bundle and aggregate different data sets to form new insights. This is the fundamental task of any metric.

New measurements or new metrics have become important in a world that now generates more and more unstructured data. As explained in "Unstructured" on page 244, unstructured data is hard to correlate and difficult to implement into mathematical models, except when a metric or measurement aggregates this data down to a few data points. In this chapter, we will look at the common pitfalls in creating metrics and measurements. As Figure 10-1 depicts, it is easy to create metrics, but that does not mean they make sense.

Figure 10-1. Discussion at a funeral parlor: inventing new metrics

Lets start first with a shining example of a good measurement meeting the right business question. Google was far from being the first search engine. In fact, at the time of its 1998 launch, it had many competitors, and the boom in Internet search usage was well underway. So what single factor helped propel this company, started by two Stanford students in a garage, to become a company with a marketcap of close to $350 billion?

A measurement.

What differentiated Google from its competition was its PageRank metric. This measurement was new, despite the fact that it was built on data everyone had. It analyzed the importance of a page based on how many other pages linked to it, and the importance of those pages. It was a watershed measure compared to other search-ranking approaches; it determined your position within Google search results and was hugely successful. But it was not just the measurement that made Google successful, but the right measurement for the right question.

Google was successful because it designed a measurement for a question that everyone, including competing search-engine vendors, was asking. Google focused on, "What is a search user looking for?" There was no metric yet for this question. Competing search engines used to pride themselves on having the most indexed pages. Thus Google defined a metric that measured how relevant a page was to a specified set of search keywords. Google knew that for many users, it is not important to see all the web pages on the World Wide Web, as long as Google found the *one* page they were looking for. Google's value is the bridge between billions of indexed pages of unstructured content and the relevant answer to the user's question. Moreover, the data this metric created had all the advantages of being "right," as described in Chapter 9:

Causation or correlation
: The new way of ranking was superior because it really correlated to more *relevant* results than the competition.

Error
: The new metric was a "hard" metric and did not use probability. It did not rely on unstructured content to classify web page but instead used the structured data of links. Thus the measured outcome had a small error.

Cost
: The metric was a newly created metric which only Google owned and knew. It relied on public available data, but since the competition did not store the data in an easy accessible format, the metric was in itself a good example of competitive advantage.

The creation of metrics has become especially important within the realm of unstructured data. Again, let's take social media as an example. What do all those conversations mean? How can we learn something meaningful from them?

What do Facebook posts or tweets tell you about your customer satisfaction levels, your brand image, or your potential market share? At best, individual posts will yield anecdotal evidence. It only becomes useful if you combine the information from many posts or tweets into a metric such as a keyword analysis, sentiment, statistics, or network topography. More general in any set of unstructured data. Metrics are key, as they create a single number from a large data set that, in turn, can be used as a benchmark for comparison to other metrics or within data models.

But it is hard to create the right metric. Much the same as when other search engines did not at first find the right metric to display relevance page rankings, it will equal parts skill and luck to define the right social media metric. This quest becomes even harder as social media analytics companies are not short of creative thinking when it comes to the development of new indexes or metrics without a given question. They correlate, filter, average, and then present a new index just to claim the *bleeding edge* in their marketing material. This can lead to an inflation of metrics. But more metrics will not necessarily mean that we have found the *right* metrics. It will be similar to the sentiment expressed a century ago by Lord William Lever of Lever Brothers: "I know half my advertising (replace with metrics) isn't working, I just don't know which half."

In this chapter, we will show in various examples why it is difficult to define the right metrics. Moreover, we will see that even correctly defined metrics carry the risk of being misused. This means that finding the right metrics, while forming a crucial link between data and outcomes, represents a process that must be nurtured and maintained rather than serve as an end goal or destination. Let's begin by looking at some of the considerations in creating these metrics.

Examples of Social Media Metrics

A well-defined metric provides an answer to a question, and it makes it clear what to do with this answer. In the case of Google PageRank, the answers to "how popular is a web page" makes it clear that you should show the most popular pages first.

It is relatively easy to form metrics from social media data itself, such as the number of retweets or the depth of one's social graph. Relating these to real questions and having a clear idea of what the business outcomes should be is often much more challenging. Here we will look at three examples of the issues surrounding effective social media metrics: influence, consumer preference, and return on investment (ROI).

INFLUENCE

To show the complexity involved in designing the right metric, let's look at the measure of influence. Today, influence is a hot topic, as judged by the numbers of startups trying to measure this quantity or the number of books published in this field.

However, it is not a new topic. Research investigating what an influencer is and how he or she relates to our decision-taking process has been going on since the 1940s. Harvey Mackay described one example in his book *Dig Your Well Before You're Thirsty* (Harvey Mackay), where the daughter of a friend got a summer job as a waitress because, during her interview, she showed a Rolodex containing all her friends and claimed that she would invite them all to come and eat at the restaurant. The underlying assumption that the restaurant owner made was that this young girl would have the influence to get all her friends to eat at his place.

This book was published in 1999. Today the same pitch of this young lady might have sounded completely different: "Check out my friends on Facebook, Twitter, and LinkedIn. If you hire me, I will invite them all to come." How could the restaurant owner have validated this claim? How could he decide whom to hire if there were two applicants who were both offering to invite all their friends?

If we were to assume that this were the primary hiring criterion, in theory all this restaurant owner would need is a social media metric measuring influence by which he could rank his applicants. Is it that easy? Unfortunately not. The biggest issue is that any commercially available metric would simply be a measurement of something which, in some form, would possibly correlate with what can be called "influence."[1]

The term *influence*, however, might mean different things to different people. While the restaurant owner wants a metric to predict how many new clients will come to his business, the measured influence metric might focus on people who can "shape a discussion on Italian cuisine." The term is deceiving as long as it is not clearly defined. Thus any metric needs to fulfill the criteria as defined in Chapter 9:

1. In Chapter 1, we see that the power of *influencer* in most cases is overstated. Influence exists, but it is very hard to measure, if measurable at all, in a social network context.

Causation
: In this case, a high influence score should result in many new guests at the restaurant.

Error
: In this case, the influence metric should be reliable over time.

Cost
: In this case, the cost for the social media measurement company should not exceed the gain from the additional guests.

What could potentially be relevant social network metrics that somehow describe influence? The following metrics spring to mind:

Network size
: How many connections a person has in his social network. The more connected he is, the more influential he is.

Network centrality
: The degree of "betweenness," i.e., the level at which one connects others within a network. If she is very central to her network, then any information needs to be passed by her. She is influential because she can control the content flow within the network.

Network proximity
: How close someone is in terms of location, interests, or other criteria. The closer someone is to someone else, the higher the likelihood that they influence each other.

Location
: How physically close this person—and her network—is to a given location. The closer the person is to, let's say, the restaurant, the more likely that she will be visiting.

Engagement
: The degree to which a person and her network are communicating with each other. Likewise, in the real world, a discourse shows a higher level of influence as people react to the ideas.

Authority
: How much this person is quoted or retweeted by others. If many repeat the ideas, then this person should be an authority in this field.

You probably nodded as you read this list of metrics. Yes, they all seem to somehow describe influence. However, the list could easily go on. For example, demographic factors such as age distribution could be important for specific restaurants: the operator of a fast-food chain would weigh the importance of the over-30 age group differently than the owner of a high-end dining place. While our personal experience seems to tell us that all of those metrics somehow have an effect on influence, it is by no means clear how strong this effect is. As we discussed in Chapter 1, the traditional view on influencers does not hold ground. Influence does exist, but we too often assume that someone *influences* someone else, while in reality it is more *homophily* or *reach*, and not influence.

Today we know that influence depends on metrics like readiness to be influenced, topic, and reach. The metrics described might especially link to the latter two.

It's likely factors other than social media will play a more prominent role in the restaurant owner's decision on whom to hire.

CONSUMER PREFERENCE

While it is not easy to create an influence metric to support hiring decisions at a restaurant, it is easier to assess consumer preferences using social media. We are looking for a metric that can predict consumer preferences of the buying public. Such a metric could benefit consumers, who could base their buying decisions on it by answering the question, "Should I go to this or to that service or shop?" It can also benefit the businesses because it will act as a kind of competitive intelligence.

Here, we will look at two real-world examples: the hospitality industry and physicians.

For the first of these, consumers and businesses alike have long searched for ways to evaluate hotels and restaurants. Is there a good way to tell whether the food and the service is good or not? This is exactly what the company NewBrandAnalytics tries to do. Launched in 2008 by Ashish Gambhir, the company uses proprietary algorithms to turn unstructured customer feedback on the Web into specific metrics for hospitality businesses.[2]

Its metric has exactly one need of the client in mind—the question, "What is a good consumer experience?" To answer the question, the service uses only one input source, the unstructured data from social media text. The algorithms from

2. Irene Kim, "What's that Buzz?" Cornell University, *http://bit.ly/1bKxEfd*.

NewBrandAnalytics are looking for insights into criteria such as food presentation, food quality, and service.

The company takes the Net Promoter Score (NPS) metric initially developed by Fred Reichheld and Bain & Company to a new level. The NPS is based on customer survey data, while NewBrandAnalytics uses only unstructured data from social media comments. Its measures reflect the power of aggregating unsolicited opinions.

At the time of writing, it was not yet clear whether this approach would be sufficient. NewBrandAnalytics primarily uses unstructured data. As we have seen, structured data normally generate insights more easily and accurately, so it could be that services like Qype, which queries customers directly to give feedback in a school-like grading system, will be better suited to judge consumer preferences.

You see a similar situation when you turn your attention to the quest for good doctors. How do you locate a good physician for you and your family? People generally do one of two things: they ask the opinions of family and friends, or they simply choose one based on criteria such as location. Today, social media often also enables consumers to see what other members of the public think of these doctors. Thus, similar to the approach from NewBrandAnalytics or Qype, you could create a metric mining this commentary about the doctors. However, such a metric might not be as reliable as in the case of restaurants. While each of us is totally able to judge a given meal or a service received, we are less able to judge whether a treatment was correct or whether an examination by a physician was done well.

But what if you could see what doctors themselves think of other doctors, particularly the patterns of referral from one doctor to another? Thanks to publicly available data, we may see more of this in the future. Health data activist Fred Trotter (@fredtrotter) recently crowdsourced funding for a product called DocGraph, based on US Medicare referral data he obtained via a Freedom of Information Act (FOIA) request,[3] while startup firm HealthTap is combining this data with its own physician database to provide customers with a view of these referral networks.[4] In the future, it might be that the process of choosing a physician will become increasingly informed by referral data in the same way that link data has helped Google to rank web pages.

3. Fred Trotter, "DocGraph: Open social doctor data," Strata O'Reilly, Nov 2012, *http://bit.ly/1helGQA*.

4. Ki Mae Heussner, "Who are the doctors most trusted by doctors? Big data can tell you," GigaOm, Nov 2012, *http://bit.ly/JshosT*.

Again, the success of this metric will surely depend on how it performs in terms of:

Causation
: Are doctors who are referred by others actually better physicians?

Error
: Is this metric stable and helpful more of the time and more helpful than asking family and friends?

Cost
: In this case, the data is publicly available.

In both of these cases, restaurants and doctors, the key point is to what extent are metrics such as these related to the question. This relationship often does not exist despite seeming to based on our human logic. As we saw in Chapter 8, the number of views or comments on a YouTube music video are not necessarily the best predictor for music sales. The percentage of negative tweets about a politician sometimes relates to and sometimes does not relate to whether this person is ultimately elected. The creation of such a metric demands more than pure wishful thinking. The degree of causation, error, and cost of the resulting data needs to be validated by in-depth research for each situation where the metric is applied.

THE QUEST FOR ROI

One special metric is the return on investment (ROI). Few metrics are more controversial than the ROI in social media. Many believe that there should be a ROI, since a link between marketing or communication spent and a financial return seems logical. However, it is not enough to simply believe in the link. Since ROI is a measurement, you need to be able to actually measure it.

Some have compared the use of social media with the use of business cards. Like business cards, social media is a must, or a kind of "hygiene factor,"[5] something that will effect you negatively if you do not have it. Arguably business cards are cheaper then an engagement within social media. However, in both cases, it is hard to correlate directly with ROI. Even if the use of social media is beneficial, it does not mean that a ROI exists.

5. The term hygiene factor was first used Fredrick Herzberg. It refers to factors that affect an outcome negatively if they are not there (*http://bit.ly/18RdbZz*).

In order to calculate ROI, you need to be able to quantify the "R", i.e., the return on a given investment. However, you can only quantify the return in the following cases:

- If there is a direct relationship between the investment with financial return. Only then ROI values can be calculated. However, all too often, other factors may have an impact on the return, and thus a return on this very investment can't be calculated.
- If there is no direct link, you can test to see if there is a correlation between the measurements and a financial return. This, however, is only possible if the measurements can be taken independently.

The easiest situation is the one in which there is a direct correlation. However, in most cases, a direct link can't be easily established. For example, in 2005 a computer manufacturer, which sold much of its offerings online, invested in radio advertisements. The manufacturer assumed that there was a good correlation between the investment in a radio advertisement and the number of systems sold. Thus the company took the sum of all margin dollars earned on this computer bundle and subtracted the investment. The result was highly negative. Dividing it by the number of computers sold, our client lost $650 for each computer sold via this advertisement.

Would it appear to be a no-brainer to stop such a waste of expenditure? Not necessarily, as customers might have heard of the offer but decided to buy another bundle.

Situations such as these are very common for social media or broadcasting media like TV and radio. The main problem is that a decision to purchase something might be caused by many things, most of which are not easy to measure. In Chapter 1, we discussed how brand awareness and intention are linked. Before a client buys something, he might have had other interactions with the brand. Each of those interactions might have had an impact on his purchase decision. For example, he might have first visited the Facebook fan page, then seen an article in the news, and then exchanged some tweets with others before buying the product. All of those interactions might have played a role in triggering the purchase. Many analytics tools today try to map out this kind of customer journey. This works only if the customer can be tracked, not easy within a broadcasting medium like radio. One way to track a radio advertisement is to establish a link through a dedicated landing page or through a dedicated phone number to better track what those clients have done. Another way is to use multiple regression analytics to see whether each time the radio advertisement was played there was an impact on other marketing channels.

More often than not there is *no* ROI. This is either because the direct link to a financial number is missing or because a multivariance analysis might confirm that it is not easily possible. The analysis issue is that each test needs to be *independent* from others. That is, unfortunately, not the case for a lot of social media activity, similar to the situation from BP as discussed in Chapter 9. Take, for example, the impact of an active Twitter account. Unlike a promoted tweet, this cannot easily be turned on and off. Even if you were to switch the Twitter account off, the test would not be independent because the users who always listened to and engaged with the Twitter account would also see it switched off. Thus in those situations where testing is not possible, you *cannot* calculate a ROI.

The Risks of Metrics

Let's assume we have created an accurate metric, one that addresses an appropriate question. Thus, the metric allows us to get the fourth "V" from the data. Or in more technical terms, following our three dimensions in Chapter 9, a metric that correlates with the desired question has low error and is overall not too costly. Can you simply rest easy and start using this metric? Not quite. Any given metric will trigger attempts to either influence the metric or to over-optimize the system to look good for this metric.

As one example, we will once again return to Google's PageRank metric, which we praised so many times. It was brilliantly designed to reflect the actual popularity of a web page. However, if you do a Google search on the phrase "rank first on Google," you will find over a quarter of a billion pages containing advice on how to change this rank. This is the art of search engine optimization (SEO) services. This means that the top page ranking sometimes may not go to the most popular site, but to the craftiest web developer. The risk that a metric is influenced or gamed applies to every metric. We call it the "measurement paradoxon." The more successful a measurement is, the more effort is undertaken to influence it.

INFLUENCING THE METRIC

Even the best of metrics, with the best of intentions, create a risk of people focusing on improving the number instead of improving the desired outcome. This is particularly true when there is a financial incentive for doing so.

In general, you can say that as soon as a measurement becomes a defining factor for the measured, there are attempts to improve or influence this score. Take Klout as an example. The San Francisco-based startup claims to be the standard for influence. It looks at different patterns on Facebook or Twitter to assess one's personal influence.

There are many who claim that the Klout score is an important criteria for being hired by someone. If this is true, what would those looking for a job do? They would try to influence it. The measurement paradoxon demands that if this claim is actually true and Klout is really an important metric, then there should be many attempts to influence the score or to game the system. For sure, there are already hundreds of sites that claim they can help you to improve your Klout score. Paradoxically, if those attempts are successful, it will reduce power of the metric, since it would be gamed and not correlate sufficiently with the desired question.

Let's test how easily the Klout score can be influenced. We set up a Twitter robot using very simple tools.[6] This robot, called @spotthebot, admits that he is a bot. He only repeats common news sources. We bought a couple of followers to influence any metric about him. The result? Without lots of work, he managed to get to a high Klout score. This small experiment is supported by ample research showing that social media influence scores can be influenced easily. @spotthebot used fake users to build up his metric; however, with a little bit more diligence, one can actually influence those scores by using real users. One of the first to show this was the Web Ecology Project. In a competition, social robots grew their Twitter networks with real users. The bot JamesMTitus managed to get 107 followers in just three weeks just by automated means.[7] Since then, many have followed suit and shown how easily you can increase online interaction[8] not only in Twitter but also in Facebook.[9] Friends, followers, and interactions can be manipulated, but all those metrics are important for measurements such as the Klout score. We saw more of those examples in Chapter 6.

What does this mean? On one hand, the Klout score or any other similar score showing importance is very much the right metric to look at. The market demands it; otherwise, there would not be so much attention in trying to game such a metric.

6. Michael Wetzel, "Remote-Controlled Spin," Sep 2013, Deutsche Well TV, *http://youtu.be/TwOdxnkVP7Y*.

7. @aerofade, "Robots, Trolling & 3D Printing," Feb 2011, *http://aerofade.rk.net.nz/?p=152*.

8. Max Nanis et al., "PacSocial: Field Test Report."

9. Yazan Boshmaf et al., "The Socialbot Network: When Bots Socialize for Fame and Money," ACSAC, Dec. 2011, *http://bit.ly/Jzllar*.

On the other hand, the measurement paradoxon tells us that Klout is most likely not the right metric, as it is too easy to game and thus will not have sufficient correlation with the question asked.

WRONG BEHAVIOR

A good metric is one where many try to influence it but where those attempts fail. Right? Yes! However, this is not the only description of a good metric. Unfortunately, a metric—even when it is hard to be influenced—can create wrong behavior. Take financial metrics as an example. Accounting figures are hard to fake, except if you commit a crime. Also, most financial metrics have a good correlation to your question, in this case, the future enterprise value of the measured business.

Does this all sound like a clear win in terms of how to get to the fourth "V"? As we learned in the 2008 financial crisis, financial metrics are far from perfect and within each metric there is an inherent risk of creating a wrong conclusion or wrong behavior. This was unfortunately quite clear during the subprime mortage crisis. The performance metrics for many financial institutions would incentivise the upside of the risk and not the potential downside. Thus the financial institutions ended up taking too much risk.

Thus creating wrong behavior is an imminent risk for any given metric, and you may well find examples of this in your own company. One of our customers was a large online retailer that praised itself for having the lowest CPO (cost per order) in the industry. CPO is a metric in the online advertisement world. Though not impossible, it is hard to influence. Moreover, it seems to link quite well with the overall question of increasing revenue. The cost of an advertisement is only accounted for when, and only when, the consumer clicks and buys after the advertisement is shown. This metric seems to be a great one. No orders, no accounted cost within this metrics.[10] So do we just have to focus on reducing the CPO?

This is exactly what the company did, and it created wrong behavior. Working with agencies, the company launched campaign after campaign and optimized each campaign for a low CPO, until it realized that its active customer base had become smaller and smaller. What happened? The agencies or the algorithms at the agencies had learned how to identify a low CPO. The agencies showed the online advertisement *only* to existing customers. Those former customers knew and trusted

10. We use the term "accounted" here because there might be real costs. Companies might buy large placements and pay whether there was a resulting order or not. But the CPO metric is an overlaid metric, describing only the cost associated with the ones who bought.

the brand, thus they had a higher likelihood to buy again compared to users who never had been in contact with the brand. Taken to an extreme, the company only addressed current users and did not win any new customers.

CHANGES OVER TIME AND SPACE

In addition to the impact of people, there is the impact of the changing environment. This is especially true in high-growth fields such as social media. If the underlying content changes dramatically, the outcome of the metric will change as well, which will mean that the metrics are not easilty benchmarked or compared, unless you account for those changes.

For example, the massive growth of Twitter usage (as seen in Figure 10-2) means that tweet statistics from one year may be completely meaningless relative to the following year. Tweet volumes that were once on the order of thousands of tweets per day are now on the order of half a billion per day as of late 2012, simultaneously increasing your audience while often making it harder for your message to be heard. This can make backward comparisons in time almost impossible, unless you know how this metric evolved. Similarly, click-through rates for online advertising dropped precipitously from the 1990s to the second decade of the 2000s, as usage of the Internet became ubiquitous and banner ad exposure became saturated.

Not only is the absolute usage an issue, but regional differences are important as well. Within social media, it can be hard to compare metrics across regions. Currently, the adoption of Twitter is quite different in English-speaking regions compared to the rest of the world. Not only do you need to account for regional adoption rates before you can compare across countries, but the relative rates can change quickly.

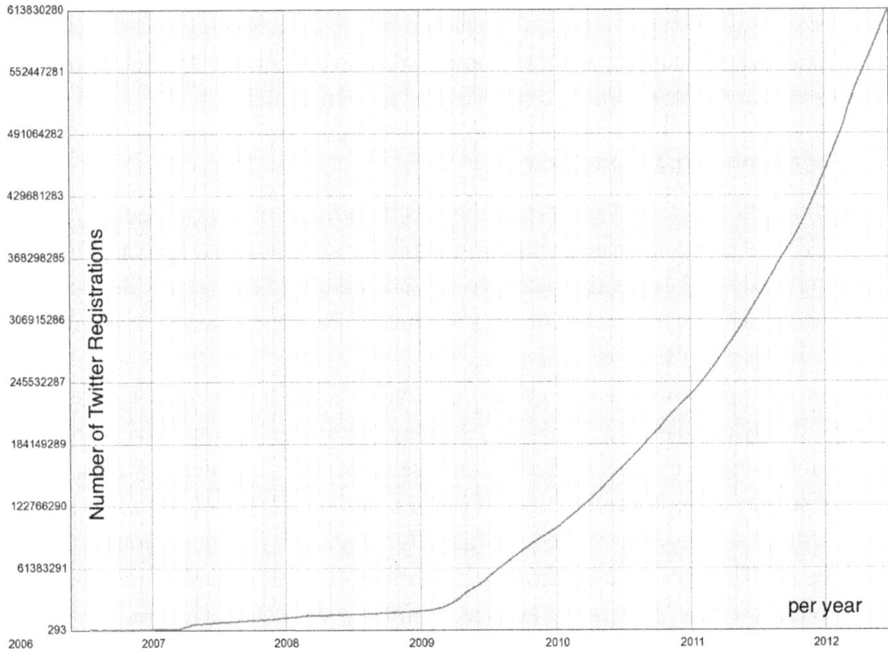

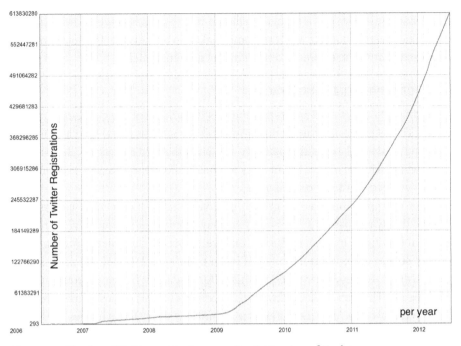

Figure 10-2. Number of Twitter registrations over time[11] *(Courtesy of Raak.)*

Take Twitter again as an example. From November 2010 until mid 2012, most tweets (27%) originated in the United States, followed by Brazil (23%) and then Indonesia (11%). The Netherlands, with 3%, is actually in fourth place, despite its population size, which is less than 3/10 of a percent of the world's population.[12] However, those figures are still changing as the adoption of social media progresses, making it very difficult to compare metrics across time and space.

Despite the difficulty of comparing any metric over time or space, whether it is a Google PageRank, the volume of retweeting, or a more complex metric tied in with business outcomes, it must be benchmarked against time, space, or other similar data to reveal relevant information. In much the same way that personal income values are substantially different in most countries than they were in the 1950s due to forces such as inflation and growth, both the value and the context of these metrics will continue to evolve.

11. This graph is accurate only up until mid-July 2012, when Twitter changed the way it allocates user IDs.

12. Britney Fitzgerald, "Where Tweets Are Born: The Top Countries On Twitter (MAP)," *The Huffington Post*, July 2012, *http://huff.to/19tgEy1*.

OVERCOMING THE ISSUES

We saw that the measurement paradox, wrong behavior, and changes over time all create issues in setting up a good metric. There are no bulletproof ways around those issues, except being aware. Anyone setting up a metric should ask whether or not it's on risk. If it is, there are ways to reduce this risk by altering the way the metric is set up:

Closed metrics
: Companies will develop individualized metrics for a specific situation or defined groups, making it difficult for the metrics to be influenced. For example, we see that TripAdvisor now uses Facebook's Open Graph to create a closed measurement group of "recommended" hotels. Since I know (or should know) all my friends, influencing this score is more difficult.

Secret metrics
: Google is the best example. It doesn't publish its PageRank algorithm because that would easily open the doors for any search engine optimization company to directly influence the ranking at Google. Any new measurement company, however, can't keep its metric secret so easily. As argued earlier in this chapter, you should not trust an approach that is like a *black box*. To create trust, you need to be open about the metric.

Change metrics
: Changing the metrics has two positive side effects. On one hand, people trying to influence the metrics can't follow them so easily. On the other hand, the metrics company itself can react to the underlying changing environment. Again, Google is a good role model. As Stephan Spencer (@sspencer) showed at the PubCon, Google updates its relevance algorithm more then 40 times in a given month (Figure 10-3). However, changing the metric will create the additional difficulty in comparing present-day data to past.

Rate of Google's Algorithmic Changes

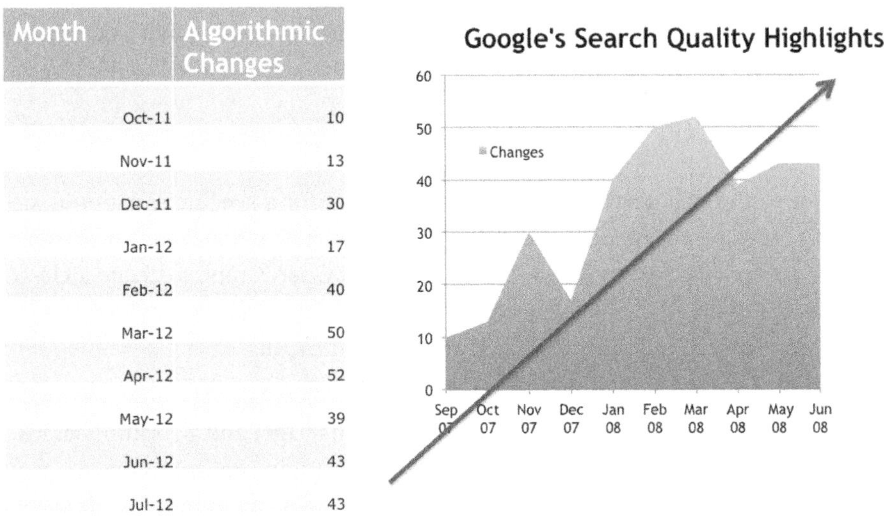

Month	Algorithmic Changes
Oct-11	10
Nov-11	13
Dec-11	30
Jan-12	17
Feb-12	40
Mar-12	50
Apr-12	52
May-12	39
Jun-12	43
Jul-12	43

Figure 10-3. Google updates its algorithm very often (Courtesy of Stephan Spencer [@sspencer].)

Summary

Metrics ultimately provide structure to the interpretation of data. Moreover, they are a necessary component of the process that links unstructured data of social media to outcomes such as customer satisfaction, brand recognition, and market share, topics we explored in more detail in previous chapters. At the same time, the definition of appropriate metrics remains a task that has both qualitative and quantitative aspects: your experience and your data both play an important role in creating the right measurements. The *right* metric to yield the fourth "V" will correlate the question with data and satisfy the three criteria discussed in Chapter 9: causation or correlation, error, and cost.

By using examples from restaurants to doctors, we showed that defining a metrics is both an art and a science that is hard to perfect, and at times hard to predict. We saw that social media presents a unique opportunity to quantify the relationships we have with customers and other stakeholders. We also saw that social media might not always be sufficient, as in the example of doctors and the hiring process.

Second, metrics have inherent risks that must be managed over time. They carry the potential for misuse and misinterpretation. You can overcome this paradox of measurement by using metrics in *closed groups*, keeping the metric *secret* and *changing* it often. Thus, metrics are not static entities, but rather dynamic measures that evolve in response to both change and human intervention. Any metric will need constant checking and reiteration and will continue to evolve.

WORKBOOK

Each business is different, therefore each business will need its own metric. There are very few "one-size-fits-all" metrics. So let's get you started on your own metrics. But be aware that getting to the metric that creates value is partially trial and error (some call this hard work) and partially just pure luck.

Let's look at the data sources you listed during the last exercise. What could be good metrics to form out of those? Lets start with descriptive metrics. Try to do different ratios to get your thinking started. How about the time customer care needs to solve a ticket versus the length of the ticket? Or how about the numbers of followers someone has versus the number of tweets he writes? Found something interesting that can be shared? Tweet at @askmeasurelearn or write your question on our LinkedIn or Facebook page.

Any metric is exposed to the *measurement paradoxon*. To detect it is super important because a wrong metric could easily risk the future of your company. Ask yourself, ask your friends, and ask your clients if any metric you use is misleading. A good indication could be any sentence that starts with "this is stupid" or "this is just not true."

PART III
Appendix

All Names

Endorsement

Alex (Sandy) Pentland
  Professor, MIT

Annet Aris
  Adjunct Professor of Strategy, INSEAD

Ben Verwaayen
  Acatel-Lucent

Bjoern Herrmann
  CEO, Compass.co (@bjoernlasse)

Björn Ognibeni
  CEO, BuzzRank (@ognibeni)

J. Frank Brown
  General Manager, General Atlantic Partners

Loic le Meur
  CEO, LeWeb conference (@loic)

Narayana Murthy
  Cofounder, InfoSys

Stephan Roppel
  Director of Ecommerce, Tchibo

Tim Weber
  SVP Edelman, former business & technology editor, BBC News interactive (@tim_weber)

Uwe Weiss
  CEO, BlueYonder

Introduction

Adam Lashinsky
Senior editor at large, *Fortune Magazine* (@adamlashinsky)

Chris Anderson
CEO, 3D Robotics; former editor in chief, *Wired* (@chrisa)

David Brooks
Commentator, the *New York Times* (@nytdavidbrooks)

Diya Soubra
CPU product manager, ARM (@DSoubra)

Erica Goode
Reporter, the *New York Times* (@eGoode)

Gregory Piatetsky-Shapiro
Analytics and data-mining expert; editor, KDnuggets (@kdnuggets)

Jeff Weiner
CEO, LinkedIn (@jeffweiner)

Kalev Leetaru
Yahoo! Fellow, Georgetown University

Steve Lohr
Reporter, the *New York Times* (@SteveLohr)

Chapter 1, Marketing

Andrew Lewis
Software consultant (@andlewis)

Arthur S. De Vany
Author; professor of economics (@ArtDeVany)

Avinash Kaushik
Author, blogger, and digital marketing evangelist (@avinash)

Carolyn Heller Baird
Communications strategy leader, IBM North America

Dan Piraro
Author

Danny Brown
Cofounder and CEO, Bonsai Interactive Marketing (@DannyBrown)

Elihu Katz
Professor, University of Pennsylvania's School for Communication

Eytan Bakshy
Data scientist, Facebook

Gautam Parasnis
Partner, IBM

Giuseppe D'Antonio
CEO, CircleMe; Internet entrepreneur, investor, and advisor (@giudantonio)

Henry Blodget
CEO and editor, *Business Insider* (@hblodget)

Kasper Skou
Cofounder and CEO, Semasio

Kevin Lewis
Assistant Professor, University at UC San Diego

Kun Liu
Staff software engineer and applied researcher, LinkedIn

Marcel Salathe
Assistant professor of biology, Penn State University (@marcelsalathe)

Paul Felix Lazarsfeld
Sociologist

Paul M. Rand
Chief digital officer, Ketchum; president and CEO, Zocalo Group (@paulm-rand)

Robert Merton
Sociologist

Rushi Bhatt
Machine-learning scientist, Amazon

Stuart Kemp
Journalist, Gallus Owl Enterprises

Chapter 2, Sales

Andrew Ng
Cofounder, Coursera (@AndrewYNg)

Arjun Mukherjee
PhD candidate, University of Illinois at Chicago's Department of Computer Science

Arthur Samuel
Computer gaming and artificial intelligence researcher

Björn Lasse Herrmann
Founder, Compass (@bjoernlasse)

Carol Roth
Author (@caroljsroth)

Catharine Smith
Editor, the Huffington Post (@catattack91686)

Jure Leskovec
Assistant professor, Stanford University (@jure)

Lasse Clausen
Founder and CEO, FOUNDD (@lalleclausen)

Robert Cialdini
Professor Emeritus of psychology and marketing, Arizona State University

Tim O'Reilly
Founder, O'Reilly Media (@timoreilly)

Xavier Amatriain
Director of research and engineering, Netflix (@xamat)

Chapter 3, Public Relations

Aja Dior M
(@AjaDiorNavy)

Brian Abelson
OpenNews Fellow (@brianabelson)

Edward Snowden
Former CIA employee; whistleblower; computer specialist

Eytan Bakshy
Data scientist, Facebook

Fon Mathuros
Head of media relations, World Economic Forum (@mathuros)

Fon Mathuros Chantanayingyong
Senior director and head of media, World Economic Forum (@mathuros)

Gilad Lotan
Chief data scientist, betaworks (@gilgul)

James E Gruning
Public relations theorist

Jimmy Kimmel
Billionaire; talk show host (@jimmykimmel)

Joseph E. Phelps
Professor and chairman, University of Alabama's Department of Advertising and Public Relations

Ken Sweet
Copy editor and reporter, Dow Jones (@kensweet)

Kevin Alloca
YouTube trends manager, Google

Linton C. Freeman
Research professor, University of California's Department of Sociology and Institute for Mathematical Behavioral Sciences

Manal al-Sharif
Political activist (@manal_alsharif)

Mark Granovetter
Sociologist

Mark Zuckerberg
Founder and CEO, Facebook

Michael Buck
Executive consultant and senior business advisor (@mikegbuck)

Robert Cialdini
Professor of psychology and marketing, Arizona State University

Samantha Murphy
Tech reporter, Mashable (@HeySamantha)

Yann Zopf
Associate director, World Economic Forum (@yannzo)

Chapter 4, Customer Care

Ashish Gambhir
Founder and CEO, newBrandAnalytics

Björn Ognibeni
Cofounder and managing director, BuzzRank GmbH (@ognibeni)

Casey Hibbard
Author (@casey_hibbard)

Dave Carroll
Musician; cofounder, Gripevine (@DavidCarroll)

Dylan Stableford
Media editor, The Wrap (@stableford)

Frank Eliason
Director of global science media, Citi (@FrankEliason)

Jeff Jarvis
Blogger, Buzz Machine; media pontificator (@jeffjarvis)

Jeffrey Breen
Academy practice manager, Think Big Analytics (@JeffreyBreen)

Jens Riewa
TV presenter and broadcast news analyst

Katie Delahaye Paine
PR expert (@kdpaine)

Lindsey Vonn
Skier, United States Ski Team (@lindseyvonn)

Luke Brynley-Jones
Blogger, Our Social Times (@lbrynleyjones)

Michael Liebmann
Project leader, Bain & Company

Ravi Sawhney
President and CEO, RKS (@rksravisawhney)

Rebecca Reisner
Senior editor and writer, Online Media

Stuart Shulman
Vice President for text analytics, Vision Critical

Chapter 5, Social CRM: Market Research

Anthony Patino
Assistant professor in marketing, Loyola Marymount Towson University

Cade Metz
Senior editor, *Wired Magazine* (@CadeMetz)

Hank Nothhaft
Cofounder and chief product officer, Trapit (@henryhank)

Jacqueline Thong
Cofounder, Ubiqi

Jamie Heywood
Cofounder, PatientsLikeMe (@jamie_heywood)

Johanna Blakley
Managing director and director of research, USC Annenberg's Norman Lear Center (@Mojojohanna)

John Rose
Senior partner, BCG

Lee Michaels
Musician

Mark Zuckerberg
Founder and CEO, Facebook

Martin Giles
US technology correspondent, *The Economist* (@martingiles)

Mike Vernal
Director of development, Facebook's Open Graph (@mvernal)

Nicolas Checa
Managing director, McLarty Associates

Peter Crayfourd
Managing partner, qifasolutions

Robert Moran
Partnet, the Brunswich Group (@robertpmoran)

Tim Berners-Lee
Founder, World Wide Web

Tim Macer
Market research analyst and writer (@timmacer)

Xavier Amatriain
Director of research and engineering, Netflix (@xamat)

Chapter 6, Gaming the System

Alexis C. Madrigal
Senior Editor, The Atlantic, (@alexismadrigal)

Ashwin Reddy
Cofounder, Fisheye Analytics (@ashwingayam)

Carlos Castillo
Social computing scientist (@ChaToX)

Dan Rowinski
Reporter, ReadWriteWeb (@Dan_Rowinski)

David Bandurski
Researcher, Hong Kong University

E. Bakshy
Data scientist, Facebook

Erica Ho
Reporter, *Time Magazine (@ericamho)*

Filippo Menczer
Professor of informatics and computer science, Indiana University Bloomington

Gerry Shih
Tech reporter, Reuters (@gerryshih)

J Ratkiewicz
Software engineer, Google

Jim Edwards
Deputy editor, *Business Insider (@Jim_Edwards)*

Lutz Finger
Author (@lutzfinger)

Michael Graham Richard
Editor and writer (@michael_GR)

Michael Hussey
CEO, PeekAnalytics (@HusseyMichael)

Michael Wetzel
Journalist, *Deutsche Welle*

Nigel Leck
Environmentalist, programmer, and founder of bot AI_AGW (@NigelLeck)

Sam Gustin
Reporter, *Time Magazine* (@samgustin)

Shea Bennett
Writer, blogger, and social media marketer (@Sheamus)

Stephen C. Webster
Web editor, the *Progressive Magazine*; online media consultant, the Climate Reality Project (@StephenCWebster)

Vikas Bajaj
Editorial board member, the *New York Times (@vikasbajaj)*

Yazan Boshmaf
Intern, Telefónica (@boshmaf)

Chapter 7, Predictions

Andrew Ng
Cofounder, Coursera (@AndrewYNg)

Arthur S. De Vany
Author; Emeritus of Economics, UC Irvine (@ArtDeVany)

Bernardo A. Huberman
Director, Hewlett Packard's Social Computing Lab

Chris Good
Political reporter, ABC News (@C_good)

Edward Snowden
Former CIA employee; whistleblower; computer specialist

Felix Ming Fai Wong
Researcher, Cornell University

Jason Palmer
Knight Science Journalism Fellow, MIT

Julian Assange
Founder, WikiLeaks (@wikileaks)

Lucas Shaw
Media reporter, The Wrap (@Lucas_Shaw)

Marc Parry
Reporter, *The Chronicle of Higher Education (@marcparry)*

Martin Harrysson
Associate partner, McKinsey & Company

Michael Lewis
Author and journalist

Natasha Lomas
Writer, AOL's TechCrunch (@riptari)

Nils Bohr
Physicist

Patrick Ruffini
President, Engage (@PatrickRuffini)

Paul Miller
Writer, speaker, and moderator (@PaulMiller)

Paul Rowady
Senior analyst, Tabb Group (@eprowady)

Rachel Van Dongen
Congressional editor, Politico (@RachelVanD)

Rayid Ghani
Chief scientist, Obama for America

Sebastian Thrun
CEO, Udacity (@SebastianThrun)

Sitaram Asur
Research scientist, Hewlett Packard Labs

Tobias Preis
Associate professor of behavioral science and finance (@t_preis)

Tom Webster
: Vice president, Edison Research (@webby2001)

Xavier Rosset
: Emulated Robinson Crusoe (@xavier_rosset)

Chapter 8, Ask the Right Question

Adrian Monck
: Managing director, World Economic Forum (@AMonck)

Alistair Croll
: Entrepreneur, Strata, Cloudconnect, Startupfest, YearOneLabs, Bitnorth, and Decibel (@ACroll)

Deep Thought
: Fictional computer in *The Hitchhiker's Guide to the Galaxy* by Douglas Adams

F.J. Anscombe
: Statistician

Grant Crowell
: YouTube manager, CDW (@grantcrowell)

Lane Shackleton
: Product manager, YouTube/Google (@lshackleton)

Robin Sommer
: Researcher, Berkeley's International Computer Science Institute (@rsmmr)

Chapter 9, Use the Right Data

Chris Coyne
: Cofounder, OkCupid and Sparknotes (@malgorithms)

Giovanni Frazzetto
: Senior manager, Eli Lilly

Goethe
: Writer, artist, and politician

Judea Pearl
: Former professor, UCLA

Michael Lewis
: Author and journalist

Paul W. Holland
Statistician

Sam Yagan
CEO, *Match.com*; cofounder, OkCupid

Thomas Anderson
CEO, OdinText (@tomHCanderson)

Xavier Amatrian
Research and engineering director, Netflix (@xamat)

Chapter 10, Define the Right Measurement

@aerofade

Ashish Gambhir
Founder and CEO, NewBrandAnalytics

Britney Fitzgerald
Web editor, *KIWI Magazine* (@bittyfitz)

Fred Trotter
Heathcare data journalist (@fredtrotter)

Fredrick Herzberg
Professor of occupational science under clinical psychology, University of Utah

Irene Kim
Communications, Cornell University

Ki Mae Heussner
Writer, GigaOM (@kheussner)

Max Nanis
Biologist, TSRI; developer, futurist (@xoxMaximus)

Michael Wetzel
Journalist, *Deutsche Welle TV*

Stephan Spencer
Author, SEO expert, and Internet marketeer (@sspencer)

Yazan Boshmaf
Intern, Telefónica

Index

A

A/B tests, 242
Adams, Douglas, 223
advertising
  Coca-Cola and, 11
  Google and, 19
  impersonation PR disasters and, 97
  measuring, 68
  social media is cheap myth, 7
  Super Bowl and, 75
  targeted, xi
  Virgin Atlantic Airways case, 14–18
Advertising Value Equivalent (AVE), 68
Air Force (US), 173
airline customer satisfaction, 124–126
Aldi (company), 70
Alloca, Kevin, 99
Amatriain, Xavier, 59, 250, 252
Amazon.com
  big data and, xvii
  product reviews, 9
  recommendation systems, 50, 51, 59
Amleshwaram, Amit A., 164
analytical CRM
  about, 141
  Facebook and Open Graph, 145–147
  issues with traditional way, 142–144
  turning CRM around, 144
anaphora algorithm, 127
Anderson, Chris, xii
Anderson, Tom, 233
Anscombe, F. J., 224
antitrust case (Microsoft), 175
AP News, 71–72
Apache Hadoop, xv
Apple Computer, 123
Arab Spring, 80, 96
Aris, Annet, 143
Arizona State University, 193
Arthur, Charles, 204
ask-measure-learn systems
  asking the right question, xvi, 190, 217–231
  defining the right measure, xvii, 190, 261–277
  using the right data, xvi, 190, 233–260
asking the right question (AML)
  about, 217–219
  analytic focus, xvi
  chapter summary, 230–231
  formulating the question, 223–229
  measurement companies and, 229
  predicting the future, 190
  telecom case study, 219–223
  workbook questions, 231
Assange, Julian, 204
astroturfing, 174–177, 181
Asur, Sitaram, 201
author, context of, 77
authority (influence principle), 80, 265
automation and customer care, 123–133
AVE (Advertising Value Equivalent), 68
awareness (brand)
  about, 5
  customer self-service and, 114
  reach and, 13, 44–45
  Virgin Atlantic Airways case, 14–18

We'd like to hear your suggestions for improving our indexes. Send email to index@oreilly.com.

B

Baird, Carolyn Heller, 17
Bakshy, Eytan, 34, 79, 179
Bandurski, David, 176
banking industry, 122
Beane, Billy, 246
behavioral targeting
  about, 20–24
  creepiness factor, 21
  limits of, 24
  machine learning and, 23
  social connections and, 31–34
Berners-Lee, Tim, 146
Best Buy retail chain, 121
Bhatt, Rushi, 32
bias
  bad PR, 197
  selection, 197
Bieber, Justin, 217
big data
  about, viii, xiv
  analytics focus of, xvi–xviii
  data focus of, xiii–xvi
  predictive policing and, x
  privacy and, 204
  promise of, x–xiii
  technology and, xv
  three Vs of, viii–x
  usage examples, xi
bin Laden, Osama, vii
Blakley, Johanna, 143
Blodget, Henry, 29
Blog Post Automator, 84
Bohr, Nils, 187
Boshmaf, Yazan, 158, 164
bots (robots)
  about, 155–158
  blurry lines, 183
  creating influence and intention, 170–174
  creating reach, 158–160
  prevalence of, 159
  setting up, 166
  smearing opponents, 167–170
  spotting, 160–166
  spreading paid opinions, 174–177
box offices, predicting, 200–204
branding
  brand awareness, 5, 13–18, 114
  Coca-Cola and, 11
  owned media and, 9
  ROI and, 15
  social media and, 11–18
Breen, Jeffrey, 124–126
Brenner, Jeffrey, xi
British Petroleum case, 236–240
Brooks, David, x
Brown, Danny, 7
Brown, Gordon, 91
Brynley-Jones, Luke, 121
Buck, Michael, 70
Bulova advertisement, 7
Burson Marstella (PR firm), 97, 183
business intelligence and customer care, 123–133

C

C-SAT score, 139
CAPTCHA codes, 165, 167
Carnegie, Dale, 80
Carroll, Dave, 111, 217
causal inference, 241
causal relationships, 16
causation
  data selection process and, 236–240, 247
  influence and, 265
centrality (metric)
  about, 35
  influence and, 265
  public relations and, 74
change metrics, 275
chatbots, 173
Checa, Nicolas, 144
Chinese 50-cent bloggers, 176
Cialdini, Robert, 62, 79
Circle Me (company), 27
Clausen, Lasse, 57
click-through rate (CTR), 13, 32
Clinton, Bill, 258
clipping articles, 81–85
closed metrics, 275
CLV (customer lifetime value), 16
co-creation concept, 142

Coca-Cola, 10–11
Cocozza, Frankie, 76
Colao, Vittorio, 223
cold-start problem (recommendation systems), 57
collaborative recommendations, 51, 57
Comcast service provider, 112
comments (see ratings and reviews)
commitment (influence principle), 80
communication, public relations and, 79–81
Compass.co, 45
Confirmit survey, 149
Consortium for Service Innovation, 113
consumer preferences, 266–268
contagiousness
  about, 177
  false information and, 180
  Kony2012 video, 177
  spotting attempts to create, 181
  viral by design, 178–180
content
  context of, 76
  grassroot movement success factor, 174
  Kony2012 video, 178
  measuring for customer care, 117
content-based recommendations, 53
context
  of author, 77
  of content, 76
  public relations and, 73, 75–78
  sentiment algorithm and, 128
controlled responding, 63
cookies, behavioral targeting with, 20
correlation
  causation versus, 237
  direct, 238
  testing for, 241–243
costs
  for data retrieval, 245, 247
  influence and, 265
Coyne, Chris, 249
Crayfourd, Peter, 138–141, 144
creating the right measure (see defining the right measure)
creative discovery, 224–226
creepiness factor, 21, 250
CRM (customer relationship management)
  analytical, 141–147
  dos and don'ts, 119–122
  journalism, 78
  social, 117, 119–122, 137–153
  social media channels and, 113
Croll, Alistair, 217
crowdsourcing
  confusion around, 188
  predicting elections, 195
  predicting learning, 191
CTR (click-through rate), 13, 32
customer care
  about, 109
  automation and, 123–133
  business intelligence and, 123–133
  chapter summary, 133
  cost cutting and, 109–112
  customer self-service and, 113–115
  Dell Computer cases, 110, 133
  Delta Airlines case, 112
  detecting dissatisfaction, 116
  dos and don'ts, 119–122
  engagement metric and, 117
  happier employees and, 115
  knowledge bases and, 113–115
  machine learning and, 132–133
  measuring content for, 117
  positive publicity, 117
  responding to clients publicly, 119
  ROI on, 114
  social CRM and, 117, 119–122
  social media channels and, 112–119
  Sony Ericsson case, 129–132
  staffing considerations, 121
  trolls and, 120
  United Airlines case, 111
  workbook questions, 134
customer lifetime value (CLV), 16
customer relationship management (see CRM)

D

data analytics
  challenges of, xvi–xviii
  data considerations, 148–151
  gaming the system, 155–185

marketing and, 3
sensitive data and, 149–151
social-sourced data, 148
data sparsity, 57
data-driven sales, 43
data-reduction process, 124
De Vany, Arthur S., 11, 203
defining the right measure (AML)
about, 261–263
analytic focus, xvii
chapter summary, 276
examples of social media metrics, 263–270
predicting the future, 190
risks of metrics, 270–275
workbook questions, 277
Dell Computer cases, 110, 133, 189
Delta Airlines case, 112
Deming, W. Edwards, 212
Derwent Capital hedge fund, 207
Deutsche Bahn, 120
Dig Your Well Before You're Thirsty (Mackay), 264
digital ethnography, 142
Digital Journalism Study, 157
digital Maoism, 53
Dior, Aja, 70
distributing information (public relations)
about, 67–68
aggregating articles, 83–85
by clipping articles, 81–83
engagement metric, 85–93
measuring, 81–95
measuring people, 70–81
reading lists, 85
resilient India case, 93–95
domain knowledge, 227
Doran, George T., 228
double-blind trials, 242
D'Antonio, Giuseppe, 27

E

earned media, 9, 13
eccomplished study, 48
edge stores, 147
elections predictions for, 195–199
Eliason, Frank, 113
ELIZA computer program, 173
employees
customer care considerations, 121
happier, 115
engagement (metric)
about, 13, 85–89
clicking, 87, 89
commenting, 87, 91
copying, 87, 91
customer care and, 117
influence and, 265
sharing, 87, 90
social targeting and, 20
tracking, 89
Virgin Atlantic Airways case, 14–18
entropy, defined, 21
Erlang C model, 121
error rates
influence and, 265
structured data and, 243–245, 247
European Union, 92
expectation gap in social media, 17

F

F-commerce, 42
Facebook
about, 5
bot detection and, 160, 164, 166
checking rate of escalation, 101
criticism of, 183
CRM and, 113
customer care and, 119
Delta Airlines case, 112
Deutsche Bahn and, 120
KLM airline and, 118
Open Graph and, 145–147
predicting box offces, 203
predicting elections and, 195
social commerce and, 42
social spam and, 156
social targeting and, 25
Virgin Atlantic Airways case, 14
Zuckerberg and, 67
filtering
keywords and, 256
recommendation systems and, 59
financial metrics, 69, 245, 272

Finger, Lutz, 77
Fisheye Analytics
  about, viii, 234
  on birthday party flash mob, 102
  on 50-cent bloggers, 176
  "mood of the nation" experiment, 76
  Net-Sentiment-Score, 236
  on share of voice within media lists, 85
  on sharing articles, 90, 99
flash mobs, 102
FOIA (Freedom of Information Act), 267
Ford Motor Company, 4, 30
FOUNDD, 57
Foursquare app, 249
Freedom of Information Act (FOIA), 267
Freeman, Linton C., 74
future, predicting the, 187–191

G

Gambhir, Ashish, 132, 266
gaming the system
  about, 155
  analyzing motivation behind, 170
  blurry lines, 183
  chapter summary, 183–185
  contagiousness and, 177–182
  creating influence and intention, 170–174
  creating reach, 158–160
  smearing opponents, 167–170
  spam and robots, 155
  spotting bots, 160–166
  spreading paid opinions, 174–177
  suppressing messages, 182
  workbook questions, 185
Gawker social media channel, 112
General Electric, 189
Gilles, Martin, 150
Gingrich, Newt, 169
Gladwell, Malcolm, 28, 30
Goethe, Johann Wolfgang von, 27, 248
Google
  customer self-service and, 114
  dominance of, xvii
  Facebook case and, 183
  grassroots movement, 175
  keyword setup, 254
  online advertising and, 19
  PageRank metric, 262, 270
  predicting voting behavior, 199
  predictions and, xi, 56
  recommendation systems, 52
  SEO algorithm and, 156
  social targeting and, 25
  spam blogs and, 84
Google Prediction API, 56, 197
Google Search API, 206
Gorkana Group, 78
GPS devices, xi
Granovetter, Mark, 98
grassroots movements, 174–177
Greenpeace environmental group, 97
Griffiths, José-Marie, xxv
Gruning, James E., 67, 95
Gutjahr, Richard, 92

H

Hadoop (Apache), xv
Haenlein, Michael, 10
Haiti case, 258
HealthGrades.com website, 46
Herrmann, Bjoern Lasse, 45
Heywood, Jamie, 149
The Hitchhiker's Guide to the Galaxy (Adams), 223
Holland, Paul W., 241
Hollywood Economics (De Vany), 11
homophily
  about, 30, 31
  influence versus, 30, 73, 266
Hotels.com website, 46
Houston, Whitney, 70
How to Win Friends and Influence People (Carnegie), 80
Huberman, Bernardo A., 201
Hussey, Michael, 160

I

IBM, xi
identity theft, 81
ifbyphone surveys, 69
ifttt.com service, 166
impersonation (PR disasters), 97

inappropriate selling (PR disaster), 96
Incapsula (company), 159
influence
  gaming the system, 170–174
  homophily versus, 30, 73, 266
  local scope of, 35
  measurements and, 270
  principles of, 79–81
  of ratings and reviews, 33, 49
  social media metric examples, 264–266
influencers
  about, 5
  brand message and, 5
  Ford Motor Company and, 4
  public relations and, 67
  purchase intent and, 34–35
  social targeting and, 27–30
information intake, behavioral targeting and, 20
insider knowledge, data retrieval and, 245
intent to purchase (see purchase intent)
IOC (International Olympic Committee), 117
IT Infrastructure Library (ITIL), 113
ITIL (IT Infrastructure Library), 113

J

Jacobson, Matt, 203
Jarvis, Jeff, 110

K

Kaplan, Andreas M., 10
Katz, Elihu, 28
Kauskik, Avinash, 24
KCS (Knowledge-Centered Support), 113–115
Kenneth Cole (manufacturer), 96
Kentucky Fried Chicken (KFC), 96
keywords, 252–255, 255
KFC (Kentucky Fried Chicken), 96
Kimmel, Jimmy, 99
KLM airline, 118
Klout (company), 271
knowledge as sales driver
  about, 41
  creating purchase intent, 45
  data-driven sales and, 43
Knowledge-Centered Support (KCS), 113–115
Knox, Steve, 80
Kony, Joseph, 178
Kony2012 video, 177
Krux Consumer Survey, 21

L

Lakeview Gusher spill, 242
Lanier, Jaron, xi, 53
Larson, Erik, xiv
Lazarsfeld, Paul Felix, 28
learning, prediction of, 191–195
Leck, Nigel, 171–173
Leetaru, Kalev, vii
Leskovec, Jure, 48
Lewis, Andrew, 21
Lewis, Kevin, 4, 30
Lewis, Michael, 190, 246
Library of Congress, xiv
Liebmann, Michael, 129, 208
liking (influence principle), 80
LinkedIn, 58
Liu, Kun, 31
LobbyPlag service, 92
Lohr, Steve, xiv
Lotan, Gilad, 71, 178

M

machine learning
  behavioral targeting and, 23
  dynamic approach to, 132–133
  supervised learning and, 55–57, 132
Mackay, Harvey, 264
market research
  about, 137
  analytical CRM and, 141
  chapter summary, 151
  customer lifecycle case study, 138–141
  linking data, 148–151
  workbook questions, 152
market research online communities (MROCs), 142
marketing
  about, 3

branding and, 5, 11–18
chapter summary, 37–39
crowdsourcing and, 189
purchase intent and, 5, 18–35
social media and, 4–6
social media myths, 6–11
workbook questions, 38
Marsteller, Burson, 28
massive open online courses (MOOCs), 192
master data management (MDM), 137
matchmaking engine case, 246–249
Mathuros, Fon, 93
McDonald's case, 104
McKinsey & Company, 4, 189
McServed website, 104
MDM (master data management), 137
measurement paradoxon, 270
measurements (metrics)
asking the right question and, 229
changes over time and space, 273–274
complaint importance, 116
defining the right measurement, xvii, 190, 261–277
differing platforms for, 12
gaming the system, 155–185
influencing, 270
measuring distributing information, 81–95
measuring people, 70–81
measuring ROI, 68–70
overcoming issues, 275
risks of, 270–275
sabermetrics, 246
social media examples, 263–270
social media myths and, 9–11
spotting bots, 160–166
wrong behavior, 272
YouTube views, 217
Meltwater, NLA v., 83
memes, 181
Menczer, Filippo, 181
Merton, Robert, 28
metadata, 147
Microsoft antitrust case, 175
Milgram, Stanley, 162
Milgrim experiments, 80
Miller, Paul, 205
Ming Fai Wong, Felix, 202
MIT Technology Review, 171
Monck, Adrian, 218
Moneyball (Lewis), 190, 246
MOOCs (massive open online courses), 192
"mood of the nation", 76
Moog (company), 69
Moran, Robert, 141
Morano, Nadine, 169
motivation behind fraudulent behavior, 170
movie industry, 200–204
MROCs (market research online communities), 142

N

National Center for Academic Transformation, xi
Net Promoter Score (NPS), 139, 267
Net-Sentiment-Score, 236, 239
Netflix
analytical CRM and, 144
personal relationships and, 62
recommendation systems, 50, 57, 59–61
newBrandAnalytics (company), 132, 266
Ng, Andrew, 56, 193
Niessing, Jörg, 139, 141
NLA v. Meltwater, 83
Nothhaft, Hank, 147
NPS (Net Promoter Score), 139, 267

O

Obama, Barack, 97, 168
Ognibeni, Björn, 116
online tracking, 21
Open Graph, Facebook and, 145–147
opponents, smearing, 167–170, 183
Osbourne, Ozzy, 143
owned media, 9
O'Reilly, Tim, 12

P

PageRank metric, 262, 270
paid media (see advertising)
paid opinions, spreading, 174–177
Paine, Katie Delahaye, 127

Parasnis, Gautam, 17
Pariser, Eli, 59
PatienceLikeMe patient community, 149
Patino, Anthony, 149
Paul, Ron, 195
Payless shoe retailer, 53
Pearl, Judea, 238
PeekYou (company), 160, 169
peer pressure, 47–49
peerindex (company), 77
personal relationships and sales, 62
Petraeus, David, 173
Phelps, Joseph E., 75
Piatetsky-Shapiro, Gregory, xviii
PIPA (Protect Intellectual Property Act), 175
politics
- predicting elections, 195–199
- smearing opponents, 168–170

positive reinforcement, 55
predictions
- about the future, 187–191
- for box offices, 200–204
- closing, 209–212
- for elections, 195–199
- Google and, xi, 56
- for learning, 191–195
- for stock market, 206–208
- voting behavior, 198–200
- workbook questions, 212

privacy
- AML systems and, 249
- big data and, 204
- matchmaking engine case, 247

Prophet consultancy, 139
Protect Intellectual Property Act (PIPA), 175
Provalis Research, 128
Prudhoe Bay oil spill, 243
public relations
- about, 67
- bad PR bias, 197
- chapter summary, 105–108
- communication and, 79–81
- context metric and, 73, 75–78
- crowdsourcing and, 189
- disaster examples, 95–98
- distributing information, 67–68, 70–95
- giving warning, 67–68, 95–105
- journalism CRM, 78
- McDonald's case, 104
- measuring people, 70–81
- measuring ROI, 68–70
- reach metric and, 73–81
- workbook questions, 107

purchase intent
- about, 5, 18
- behavioral targeting, 20–24
- finding, 19
- gaming the system, 170–174
- homophily versus influence, 30
- influencers and, 34–35
- peer pressure and, 47–49
- reach versus, 44–50, 171
- social confirmation and, 46
- social connections versus behavior, 31–34
- social targeting, 24–30
- user comments and, 46
- user ratings and, 46

R

Rand, Paul M., 30
randomized controlled trials, 242
RateMyProfessors.com website, 46
ratings and reviews
- creating trust, 46
- earned media and, 9
- influence of, 33, 49

Ratkiewicz, J., 180
reach (metric)
- awareness and, 44–45
- brand awareness and, 13
- creating, 158–160
- CTR and, 32
- grassroot movement success factor, 174
- O'Reilly measurement overview, 12
- public relations and, 73–75
- purchase intent versus, 44–50, 171

reading lists, 85
reason as sales component, 62
reciprocal altruism, 80
reciprocity (influence principle), 80
recommendation systems
- about, 44, 49–51
- building, 59–61
- cold-start problem, 57

collaborative, 51, 57
content-based, 53–55
data sparsity, 57
filtering information, 59
inaccuracy of, 52
personalization gap and, 147
popular choices and, 58
technology of, 55–61
Reddy, Ashwin, 176
regression analysis, 55–57
Reichheld, Fred, 267
Renaissance Technologies fund, 207
resilient India case, 93–95
return on investment (see ROI)
Riewa, Jens, 115, 118
risks of metrics, 270–275
robots (see bots)
Rogers, Carl, 173
ROI (return on investment)
about, 268–270
branding campaigns and, 15
on customer care, 114
linking effects from social media, 43
on public relations, 68–70
Virgin Atlantic Airways case, 15–18
Romney, Mitt, 168–169, 195
Rose, John, 150
Rosset, Xavier, 205
Roth, Carol, 52
Rowady, Paul, 207
Rowinski, Dan, 175

S

S.M.A.R.T. mnemonic device, 228
sabermetrics, 246
Salathe, Marcel, 35
sales
about, 41
chapter summary, 63–65
data-driven, 43
personal relationships and, 62
reach versus intention, 44–50
reason component in, 62
recommendation systems, 50–61
social, 41–43
trust component in, 41, 61
sampling data, 251
Samuel, Arthur, 55
Santorum, Rick, 195
scarcity (influence principle), 80
Schneider, Dave, 112
Schufa credit-rating company, 149–151
Schwab, Klaus, 258
SCM (Structural Causal Models), 238
search engine optimization (SEO), 157, 270
Sebastian, Miguel, 223
secret metrics, 275
selection bias, 197
self-censorship (PR disasters), 97
self-servicing customers, 113–115
semantic web, 146
Semasio (company), 23
sentiment analytics, 123, 126–129
SEO (search engine optimization), 157, 270
al-Sharif, Manal, 105
Shirky, Clay, 80
shortlink services, 90
Shulman, Stuart, 133
Sina Weibo, ix
Skou, Kasper, 23
Sky TV channel, 121
small world experiment, 162
smearing opponents, 167–170, 183
Smith, Catharine, 52
Snowden, Edward, 75, 204
social commerce, 41–43, 51
social confirmation
creating trust, 46
peer pressure and, 47–49
user comments, 46
user ratings, 46
social connections versus behavior, 31–34
social CRM
about, 122, 137
chapter summary, 151
customer lifecycle case study, 138–141
dos and don'ts, 119–122
linking data, 148–151
positive publicity, 117
workbook questions, 152
social media
expectation gap in, 17
myths about, 6–11
platform categories, 10

social media analytics
  about, ix
  marketing and, 3–39
  promise of, 4–6
social proof (influence principle), 80
social targeting, 24–30
socialflow (company), 76
Soghoian, Christopher, 183
Sommer, Robin, 226
Sony Ericsson case, 129–132
SOPA (Stop Online Piracy Act), 175
Sophos survey, 81
spam blogs, 84
spamming
  about, 155–158
  creating influence and intention, 170–174
  creating reach, 158–160
  smearing opponents, 167–170
  spreading paid opinions, 174–177
  suppressing messages, 182
  Twitter and, 164
Spencer, Stephan, 275
StackOverflow, xiii
StatusPeople (company), 160
stock market, predicting, 206–208
Stop Online Piracy Act (SOPA), 175
Structural Causal Models (SCM), 238
structured data, 243–245, 252
subprime mortage crisis, 272
subsets of data, 252–255
Sununu, John, 168
supervised learning, 55–57, 132
SupportIndustry.com portal site, 113
suppressing messages, 182
Sysomos (company), 126

T

T-commerce, 42
Tang, Lei, 31
targeted advertising, xi
tastemakers, 99
TBG Digital, 8
technology of recommendation systems
  about, 55–57
  building recommendation systems, 59–61
  cold-start problem, 57
  data sparsity, 57
  popular choices and, 58
telecommunication industry, 138–141, 219–223
testing
  for correlation, 241–243
  keyword setup, 256
Thong, Jacqueline, 149
Thrun, Sebastian, 193
The Tipping Point (Gladwell), 28
Toubon, Jacques, 223
touchpoints with customers, 144
tracking
  engagement metric, 89
  online, 21
Treehugger media outlet, 172
triggers to buying
  brand awareness as, 13
  social media as, 5
  social targeting and, 25–30
  Virgin Atlantic Airways case, 14
TripAdvisor.com website, 46
trolls, customer care and, 120
Trotter, Fred, 267
trust as sales driver
  about, 41, 61
  creating purchase intent, 45
  data-driven sales and, 43
  recommendation systems and, 57
  social confirmation and, 46
Turing Test (bot), 172
Turing, Alan, 172
Twitter
  about, xiii, 5, 8
  bot detection and, 160, 161, 166
  bot influence and, 171
  changes over time and space, 273
  checking rate of escalation, 101
  Comcast service channel on, 113
  customer care and, 121
  General Electric and, 189
  KLM airline and, 118
  O'Reilly measurement overview, 12
  smearing opponents and, 168
  social commerce and, 42
  social spam and, 156
  Sony Ericsson case, 129

spamming and, 164
trending topics, 104
virality by design, 179
Women2Drive campaign and, 105
Twitter API, 124
2Style4You, xi

U

unintended consequences, law of, 155
United Airlines case, 111, 217
unstructured data, 244, 252
uplift (metric), 32
US Air Force, 173
using the right data (AML)
about, 233
analytic focus, xvi
British Petroleum case and, 236–240
causation and, 236–240, 247
chapter summary, 259
costs for data retrieval, 245, 247
data selection, 250–259
error and, 243–245, 247
Haiti case, 258
identifying which data, 234–249
insider knowledge and, 245
matchmaking engine case, 246–249
predicting the future, 190
privacy considerations, 249
structured data, 243–245
testing for correlation, 241–243
workbook questions, 259

V

vaccinations, child, 35
value (Vs of big data)
about, viii
finding, xiii, xv
measuring ROI and, 68–70
Van Dongen, Rachel, 196
variety (Vs of big data), viii, xv
velocity (Vs of big data), viii, xiv
Verizon (company), 139
Vernal, Mike, 146
virality and viral outbreaks
about, 98
gaming the system and, 177–182
nondeterministic timing of, 98–99
rewording term, 11
social media speed myth and, 8
speed to disaster, 98–104
spreading customer dissatisfaction, 116
underestimating, 96
viral by design, 178–180
warning systems and, 98–104
Virgin Atlantic Airways case, 14–18
volume (Vs of big data), viii, xiv
Vonn, Lindsey, 117
voting behavior, predicting, 198–200

W

Wagstaff, Bob, 217
Warby Parker (manufacturer), 44
warning task (public relations)
about, 67–68, 95
early warning systems and, 98–104
McDonald's case, 104
organizational issues, 102
PR disaster examples, 95–98
technical requirements, 101
warning signals, 105
web scraping, 142
Weiner, Jeff, xiii
WikiLeaks, 204
Wikipedia, 3, 175
Wildfire Interactive, 15
Women2Drive campaign, 105
word clouds, 77
Wordstream study, 25
World Economic Forum, xvi, 81–84, 86, 93–95, 218

X

X Factor (TV show), 76

Y

Yagan, Sam, 249
Yahoo!, 42
Yes Men activist group, 97
York, Jillian, 182
YouTube
checking rate of escalation, 101
Deutsche Bahn and, 121

KLM airline and, 118
Kony2012 video, 177
measuring views, 217
United Airlines case, 111, 217
Women2Drive campaign and, 105

Z

Zafu, xi
Zopf, Yann, 81, 83
Zuckerberg, Mark, 67, 145

About the Authors

Lutz Finger (@lutzfinger) is a noted authority on social media and big data analytics who is director of Data Analytics at LinkedIn. Prior to this he was CEO and co-founder of Fisheye Analytics, a Singapore based firm that processes 70 TB of public media data monthly for numerous governments and NGOs that was successfully acquired by the WPP Group. Lutz is a highly regarded technology executive who built a 700-employee sales center for Dell Europe as well as an incubator for mobile applications at Ericsson. He serves as advisor and board member several data-centric corporations in Europe and the US.

A popular public speaker on data analytics issues, Finger also teaches regularly at top business schools such as the University of California at Berkeley, and other institutions. He has an MBA from INSEAD as well as an MS in quantum physics from TU Berlin (Germany).

Soumitra Dutta (@soumitradutta) is the dean of the Samuel Curtis Johnson Graduate School of Management at Cornell University. He previously served as the Roland Berger Chaired Professor of Business and Technology and founder and academic director of the eLab at INSEAD, a top-ranked graduate business school with campuses in Fontainebleau, France, Singapore, and Abu Dhabi. Dutta was the co-founder and Chairman of Fisheye Analytics. He is an authority on the impact of new technology on the business world, especially social media and social networking, and on strategies for driving growth and innovation by embracing the digital economy. He is the coeditor and author, respectively, of two influential reports in technology and innovation, the Global Information Technology Report (copublished with the World Economic Forum) and the Global Innovation Index (to be copublished with the World Intellectual Property Organization), which are used by several governments around the world in assessing and planning their technology and innovation policies. Soumitra received a B.Tech. in electrical engineering and computer science from the Indian Institute of Technology, New Delhi. He received an MS in business administration, an MS in computer science, and a PhD in computer science from the University of California at Berkeley.

Colophon

The cover and body font is Scala Pro Regular, the heading font is Benton Sans, and the code font is TheSansMono Condensed.

CPSIA information can be obtained at www.ICGtesting.com
Printed in the USA
BVOW11s1607260114

342905BV00006B/11/P

9 781449 336752